Security Administrator Street Smarts

A Real World Guide to CompTIA Security+™ Skills

David R. Miller

Michael Gregg

BICENTENNIAL
1807
WILEY
2007
BICENTENNIAL

Wiley Publishing, Inc.

Acquisitions and Development Editor: Jeff Kellum
Technical Editor: James Michael Stewart
Production Editor: Eric Charbonneau
Copy Editor: Liz Welch
Production Manager: Tim Tate
Vice President and Executive Group Publisher: Richard Swadley
Vice President and Executive Publisher: Joseph B. Wikert
Vice President and Publisher: Neil Edde
Book Designer: Judy Fung, Bill Gibson
Compositor: Laurie Stewart, Happenstance Type-O-Rama
Proofreader: Nancy Riddiough
Indexer: Ted Laux
Anniversary Logo Design: Richard Pacifico
Cover Designer: Ryan Sneed

Library of Congress Cataloging-in-Publication Data

Miller, David R., 1959 Nov. 5–

 Security administrator street smarts : a real world guide to CompTIA Security+ skills / David R. Miller,
Michael Gregg.

  p. cm.

 ISBN-13: 978-0-470-10258-9 (pbk.)
 ISBN-10: 0-470-10258-6 (pbk.)

 1. Electronic data processing personnel—Certification. 2. Computer security—Examinations—Study guides.
3. Computer networks--Security measures—Examinations—Study guides. I. Gregg, Michael (Michael C.)
II. Title.

QA76.3.M562 2007

005.8—dc22

                                        2006100831

I'd like to dedicate this book to my family, especially my children, Veronica and Ross, for keeping a subtle smile of pride and satisfaction warmly tucked away inside of me. It has helped to keep me going.
—David R. Miller

This book is dedicated to Christine, a loving wife and partner.
—Michael Gregg

Acknowledgments

I would like to thank Shon Harris, of CISSP fame, for her support, encouragement and undying friendship. I also give thanks to Michael J. Lester, one of the most certified (or is that certifiable?) guys I've ever known, for years of superb professional association, consultation, and loyalty. A better pair of friends could not be had.

Thanks also to the co-author, Michael Gregg, and to the excellent team at Sybex who have done a bang-up job to pull this book together. I hope we're able to help you, the reader, gain confidence and worthy skills to improve your careers and become the security professional you want and need to be.

—*David R. Miller*

I would like to thank my wife Christine for all her help and encouragement. I have been blessed that she has always encouraged me and helped in all my endeavors. Thank you for your love and support.

I would like to acknowledge Gen Cuellar, David R. Miller, Jeff Kellum, and the excellent team at Sybex.

To all those who read the book, keep learning and taking steps to move your career forward.

—*Michael Gregg*

About the Authors

David R. Miller, President of MicroLink Corporation, is a network engineer and IT security and project management consultant with more than two decades of experience. David has focused on writing and teaching for the last 10 years. He has written numerous books, curricula, presentations, and training videos for topics such as the entire MCSE track (eight courses), network security, wireless security, penetration testing, CISSP, A+, Network+, and Security+. David holds the following certifications: MCT, MCSE NT 4.0, MCSE: Security on Windows 2000 and Server 2003, CISSP, CNE, CCNA, CWNA, CEH, ECSA, LPT, A+, Network+, and Security+.

Michael Gregg (CISSP, CISA, MCSE, MCT, CTT+, A+, N+, Security+, CNA, CCNA, CIW Security Analyst, CCE, CEH, CHFI, DCNP, ES Dragon IDS, TICSA) is the founder and President of Superior Solutions, Inc., a Houston-based IT security consulting firm. Superior Solutions performs security assessments and penetration testing for Fortune 1000 firms. Michael is responsible for working with organizations to develop cost effective and innovative technology solutions to security issues and for evaluating emerging technologies. Michael has more than 20 years experience in the IT field and holds two associate's degrees, a bachelor's degree, and a master's degree. He has written or co-written seven other books including *Hack the Stack*, *Certified Ethical Hacker Exam Prep 2*, and *Inside Network Security Assessment*.

Contents at a Glance

Contents

Phase   7   Securing Internet Activity   265

Introduction

The Security+ certification was developed by the Computer Technology Industry Association (CompTIA) to provide an industrywide means of certifying the competency of computer and network administrators in the basics of securing their systems and networks. The security professional's job is to protect the confidentiality, integrity, and availability of the organization's valuable information assets.

According to CompTIA, the Security+ certification

> "validates knowledge of communication security, infrastructure security, cryptography, operational security, and general security concepts. It is an international, vendor-neutral certification that is taught at colleges, universities and commercial training centers around the world. Although not a prerequisite, it is recommended that CompTIA Security+ candidates have at least two years on-the-job networking experience, with an emphasis on security. The CompTIA Network+ certification is also recommended. Because human error is the number one cause for a network security breach, CompTIA Security+ is recognized by the technology community as a valuable credential that proves competency with information security. Major corporations such as Sun, IBM/Tivoli Software Group, Symantec, Motorola, Hitachi Electronics Services, and VeriSign value the CompTIA Security+ certification and recommend or require it of their IT employees."

Although most books that target certification candidates present material for you to memorize before the exam, this book is different. It guides you through procedures and tasks that solidify related concepts, thus allowing you to devote your memorization efforts to more abstract theories because you've mastered the practical topics through doing. Even if you do not aspire to become a security professional, this book might still be a valuable primer for your career.

What Is Security+ Certification?

The Security+ certification was created to offer an introductory step into the complex world of PC and laptop hardware and software support.

Security+ candidates must take the Security+ exam (Exam #SY0-101), which covers various security concepts.

NOTE A detailed list of the Security+ SY0-101 exam objectives is presented in this introduction; see the section "The Security+ Exam Objectives."

Obtaining the Security+ certification does not mean you can provide sufficient system and network security services to a company. In fact, this is just the first step toward true technical knowledge and experience. By obtaining Security+ certification, you will be able to obtain more computer and network security administration experience in order to pursue more complex and in-depth knowledge and certifications.

For the latest pricing on the exam and updates to the registration procedures, call either Thomson Prometric at (866) 776-6387 or (800) 776-4276, or Pearson VUE at (877) 551-7587. You can also go to either http://www.2test.com or http://www.prometric.com (for Thomson Prometric) or http://www.vue.com (for Pearson VUE) for additional information or to register online. If you have further questions about the scope of the exams or related CompTIA programs, refer to the CompTIA website at http://www.comptia.org.

Is This Book for You?

Security Administrator Street Smarts is designed to give you insight into the world of a typical system and network security technician by walking you through some of the daily tasks you can expect on the job. We recommend that you invest in certain equipment to get the full effect from this book. However, much value can be derived from simply reading through the tasks without performing the steps on live equipment. Organized classes and study groups are the ideal structures for obtaining and practicing with the recommended equipment.

 The *CompTIA Security+ Study Guide, Third Edition* (Sybex, 2006) is a recommended companion to this book in your studies for the CompTIA Security+ certification.

How This Book Is Organized

This book is organized into an initial system setup procedure, followed by 10 phases. Each phase is separated into individual tasks. The phases represent broad categories under which related responsibilities are grouped. The tasks within each phase lead you step by step through the processes required for successful completion. When performed in order, the tasks in this book approximate those required by a system security administrator over an extended period of time. The phases and their descriptions are as follows:

- *Administrative System Setup* walks you through the process of converting a system from a standard user's "warm and fuzzy" system into a highly refined administrative tool, where you have complete vision of and access to the system components, as well as easy access to a collection of powerful administrative tools.

- *Phase 1—The Grunt Work of Security* presents the initial, and essential, objectives that a security professional needs to have in place to understand, establish the basis for, implement, and enforce security within an organization.

- *Phase 2—Hardening Systems* shows you where the most common vulnerabilities exist within a system; the attack points; how to identify them, and how to minimize the attack surface of a system.

- *Phase 3—Protecting Against Malware* shows you how to implement filters, scanners, and other tools to defend the system against inbound threats, such as viruses, worms, spyware, and rootkits.

- *Phase 4—Secure Storage* provides real-world tools and techniques to ensure that data, while residing on a system, will remain secure. Discussed are the use of encryption, the assignment of permissions following the principle of least privilege, and the implementation of fault tolerance.

- *Phase 5—Managing User Accounts* presents procedures related to its user accounts that every computer network should have implemented. These procedures include implementing a strong password policy and securing default user accounts, such as the Administrator and the Guest accounts.

- *Phase 6—Network Security* shows you how to configure encryption for data while it's in transit on the corporate network, and between the telecommuter and the corporate headquarters (via VPNs). Further, it shows how to configure basic firewall rules, and how to configure a wireless network with acceptable security using 802.11i and WPA.

- *Phase 7—Securing Internet Activity* shows you how to secure your Microsoft Internet Explorer, e-mail, and IP settings, and how to use digital certificates in a Public Key Infrastructure (PKI) environment.

- *Phase 8—Security Testing* presents the use of security assessment tools to evaluate the general strength of a system, and penetration-testing tools to view your systems as an attacker would see them.

- *Phase 9—Investigating Incidents* shows you how to operate like a forensics investigator, and how to track down and uncover hidden details of some earlier security-related event. You will learn how to configure auditing and review audit logs, how to perform a memory dump to record the contents of physical RAM, how to recover deleted files and folders, and how to use and understand a sniffer on the network to view the network traffic.

- *Phase 10—Security Troubleshooting* examines multiple procedures to perform disaster recovery and focuses on Safe mode, Last Known Good Configuration, and System Recovery. It also looks at procedures and tools to sanitize media for secure destruction of confidential data to allow for reuse of magnetic media.

Each task in this book is organized into sections aimed at giving you what you need when you need it. The first section introduces you to the task and any key concepts that can assist you in understanding the underlying technology and the overall procedure. The following describes the remaining sections:

- *Scenario*—This section places you in the shoes of the PC support technician, describing a situation in which you will likely find yourself. The scenario is closely related to and often solved by the task at hand.

- *Scope of Task*—This section is all about preparing for the task. It gives you an idea of how much time is required to complete the task, what setup procedure is needed before beginning, and any concerns or issues to look out for.

- *Procedure*—This is the actual meat of the task itself. This section lists the equipment required to perform the task in a lab environment. It also gives you the ordered steps to complete the task.

- *Criteria for Completion*—This final section briefly explains the outcome you should expect after completing the task. Any deviation from the result described is an excellent reason to perform the task again and watch for sources of the variation.

How to Contact the Publisher

Sybex welcomes feedback on all of its titles. Visit the Sybex website at http://www.sybex.com for book updates and additional certification information. You'll also find forms you can use to submit comments or suggestions regarding this or any other Sybex title.

How to Contact the Authors

David R. Miller and Michael Gregg welcome your questions and comments. You can reach them by e-mail at DMiller@MicroLinkCorp.com and MikeG@thesolutionfirm.com, respectively.

The Security+ Exam Objectives

The Security+ exams are made up of the mandatory Security+ exam. The following presents the detailed exam objectives of each test.

At the end of each of the phases of this book, we've included the supported domains of the Security+ exam objectives. Exam objectives are subject to change at any time without prior notice and at CompTIA's sole discretion. Please visit the Security+ Certification page of CompTIA's website (`http://certification.comptia.org/security/`) for the most current listing of exam objectives.

Security+ 2006 Examination Objectives

The following table lists the domains measured by this examination and the extent to which they are represented on the exam.

Domain	Topic	Percentage of Examination
1.0	General Security Concepts	30%
2.0	Communication Security	20%
3.0	Infrastructure Security	20%
4.0	Basics of Cryptography	15%
5.0	Operational / Organizational Security	15%
	Total	100%

Domain 1.0: General Security Concepts

1.1 Recognize and be able to differentiate and explain the following access control models:

- MAC (Mandatory Access Control)
- DAC (Discretionary Access Control)
- RBAC (Role Based Access Control)

1.2 Recognize and be able to differentiate and explain the following methods of authentication:

- Kerberos
- CHAP (Challenge Handshake Authentication Protocol)
- Certificates

- Username / Password

- Tokens

- Multi-factor

- Mutual

- Biometrics

1.3 Identify non-essential services and protocols and know what actions to take to reduce the risks of those services and protocols.

1.4 Recognize the following attacks and specify the appropriate actions to take to mitigate vulnerability and risk:

- DOS / DDOS (Denial of Service / Distributed Denial of Service)

- Back Door

- Spoofing

- Man in the Middle

- Replay

- TCP/IP Hijacking

- Weak Keys

- Mathematical

- Social Engineering

- Birthday

- Password Guessing

  - Brute Force

  - Dictionary

- Software Exploitation

1.5 Recognize the following types of malicious code and specify the appropriate actions to take to mitigate vulnerability and risk:

- Viruses

- Trojan Horses

- Logic Bombs

- Worms

1.6 Understand the concept of and know how reduce the risks of social engineering.

1.7 Understand the concept and significance of auditing, logging, and system scanning.

Domain 2.0: Communication Security

2.1 Recognize and understand the administration of the following types of remote access technologies:

- 802.1x
- VPN (Virtual Private Network)
- RADIUS (Remote Authentication Dial-In User Service)
- TACACS (Terminal Access Controller Access Control System)
- L2TP / PPTP (Layer Two Tunneling Protocol / Point to Point Tunneling Protocol)
- SSH (Secure Shell)
- IPSEC (Internet Protocol Security)
- Vulnerabilities

  2.2 Recognize and understand the administration of the following e-mail security concepts:
- S/MIME (Secure Multipurpose Internet Mail Extensions)
- PGP (Pretty Good Privacy) like technologies
- Vulnerabilities
  - SPAM
  - Hoaxes

  2.3 Recognize and understand the administration of the following Internet security concepts:
- SSL / TLS (Secure Sockets Layer / Transport Layer Security)
- HTTP/S (Hypertext Transfer Protocol / Hypertext Transfer Protocol over Secure Sockets Layer)
- Instant Messaging
  - Vulnerabilities
  - Packet Sniffing
  - Privacy
- Vulnerabilities
  - Java Script
  - ActiveX
  - Buffer Overflows
  - Cookies

- Signed Applets
- CGI (Common Gateway Interface)
- SMTP (Simple Mail Transfer Protocol) Relay

2.4 Recognize and understand the administration of the following directory security concepts:

- SSL / TLS (Secure Sockets Layer / Transport Layer Security)
- LDAP (Lightweight Directory Access Protocol)

2.5 Recognize and understand the administration of the following file transfer protocols and concepts:

- S/FTP (File Transfer Protocol)
- Blind FTP (File Transfer Protocol) / Anonymous
- File Sharing
- Vulnerabilities
  - Packet Sniffing
  - 8.3 Naming Conventions

2.6 Recognize and understand the administration of the following wireless technologies and concepts:

- WTLS (Wireless Transport Layer Security)
- 802.11 and 802.11x
- WEP / WAP (Wired Equivalent Privacy / Wireless Application Protocol)
- Vulnerabilities
  - Site Surveys

Domain 3.0: Infrastructure Security

3.1 Understand security concerns and concepts of the following types of devices:

- Firewalls
- Routers
- Switches
- Wireless
- Modems
- RAS (Remote Access Server)
- Telecom / PBX (Private Branch Exchange)
- VPN (Virtual Private Network)

- IDS (Intrusion Detection System)
- Network Monitoring / Diagnostics
- Workstations
- Servers
- Mobile Devices

3.2 Understand the security concerns for the following types of media:

- Coaxial Cable
- UTP / STP (Unshielded Twisted Pair / Shielded Twisted Pair)
- Fiber Optic Cable
- Removable Media
  - Tape
  - CD-R (Recordable Compact Disks)
  - Hard Drives
  - Diskettes
  - Flashcards
  - Smartcards

3.3 Understand the concepts behind the following kinds of security topologies:

- Security Zones
  - DMZ (Demilitarized Zone)
  - Intranet
  - Extranet
- VLANs (Virtual Local Area Network)
- NAT (Network Address Translation)
- Tunneling

3.4 Differentiate the following types of intrusion detection, be able to explain the concepts of each type, and understand the implementation and configuration of each kind of intrusion detection system:

- Network Based
  - Active Detection
  - Passive Detection
- Host Based
  - Active Detection
  - Passive Detection

- Honey Pots
- Incident Response

3.5 Understand the following concepts of security baselines, be able to explain what a security baseline is, and understand the implementation and configuration of each kind of intrusion detection system:

- OS / NOS (Operating System / Network Operating System) Hardening
    - File System
    - Updates (Hotfixes, Service Packs, Patches)
- Network Hardening
    - Updates (Firmware)
    - Configuration (Enabling and Disabling Services and Protocols; Access Control Lists)
- Application Hardening
- Updates (Hotfixes, Service Packs, Patches)
- Web Servers
- E-mail Servers
- FTP (File Transfer Protocol) Servers
- DNS (Domain Name Service) Servers
- NNTP (Network News Transfer Protocol) Servers
- File / Print Servers
- DHCP (Dynamic Host Configuration Protocol) Servers
- Data Repositories
    - Directory Services
    - Databases

Domain 4.0: Basics of Cryptography

4.1 Be able to identify and explain the of the following different kinds of cryptographic algorithms:

- Hashing
- Symmetric
- Asymmetric

4.2 Understand how cryptography addresses the following security concepts:

- Confidentiality

- Integrity
  - Digital Signatures
- Authentication
- Non-repudiation
  - Digital Signatures
- Access Control

4.3 Understand and be able to explain the following concepts of PKI (Public Key Infrastructure):

- Certificates
  - Certificate Policies
  - Certificate Practice Statements
- Revocation
- Trust Models

4.4 Identify and be able to differentiate different cryptographic standards and protocols.

4.5 Understand and be able to explain the following concepts of Key Management and Certificate Lifecycles:

- Centralized vs. Decentralized
- Storage
  - Hardware vs. Software
  - Private Key Protection
- Escrow
- Expiration
- Revocation
  - Status Checking
- Suspension
  - Status Checking
- Recovery
  - M-of-N Control (of N appropriate individuals, M must be present to authorize recovery)
- Renewal
- Destruction
- Key Usage
  - Multiple Key Pairs (Single, Dual)

Domain 5.0: Operational/Organizational Security

5.1 Understand the application of the following concepts of physical security:

- Access Control
  - Physical Barriers
  - Biometrics
- Social Engineering
- Environment
  - Wireless Cells
  - Location
  - Shielding
  - Fire Suppression

5.2 Understand the security implications of the following topics of disaster recovery:

- Backups
  - Off Site Storage
- Secure Recovery
  - Alternate Sites
- Disaster Recovery Plan

5.3 Understand the security implications of the following topics of business continuity:

- Utilities
- High Availability / Fault Tolerance
- Backups

5.4 Understand the concepts and uses of the following types of policies and procedures:

- Security Policy
  - Acceptable Use
  - Care
  - Privacy
  - Separation of Duties
  - Need to Know
  - Password Management
  - SLAs (Service Level Agreements)
  - Disposal / Destruction
  - HR (Human Resources) Policy (Termination [adding and revoking passwords and privileges, etc.]; Hiring [adding and revoking passwords and privileges, etc.]; Code of Ethics)

- Incident Response Policy

5.5 Explain the following concepts of privilege management:

- User / Group / Role Management
- Single Sign-on
- Centralized vs. Decentralized
- Auditing (Privilege, Usage, Escalation)
- MAC / DAC / RBAC (Mandatory Access Control / Discretionary Access Control / Role Based Access Control)

5.6 Understand the concepts of the following topics of forensics:

- Chain of Custody
- Preservation of Evidence
- Collection of Evidence

5.7 Understand and be able to explain the following concepts of risk identification:

- Asset Identification
- Risk Assessment
- Identification
- Vulnerabilities

5.8 Understand the security relevance of the education and training of end users, executives, and human resources:

- Communication
- User Awareness
- Education
- On-line Resources

5.9 Understand and explain the following documentation concepts:

- Standards and Guidelines
- Systems Architecture
- Change Documentation
- Logs and Inventories
- Classification
  - Notification
- Retention / Storage
- Destruction

Phase

1

The Grunt Work
of Security

There is an old saying that success is doing what's right at the right time. While the individual who created this quote may not have been thinking of security in particular, security professionals can most certainly learn from this saying. Security is about doing the right thing at the right time. Before you can run a password-cracking tool, perform penetration tests, or fire up a vulnerability scanner, you must cover some basic groundwork. That grunt work is the subject of this first phase.

The groundwork of security requires that you know what is worth securing. Companies don't have unlimited funds, so a big part of the security process is finding what is most critical to the organization and focusing your security efforts on these assets. Finding what's critical is only the first step. You will next need to write a policy that matches up to your findings. Is that enough? No. Policies have no meaning if users don't know they exist. That's where user awareness comes in. Finally, you can have great ideas but unless they are written down they have little value. In other words, documentation is important in everything you do. These are the tasks that we will examine in this phase of the security process. Let's get started by performing a basic risk assessment.

The tasks in this phase map to Domain 5 objectives in the CompTIA Security+ exam (http://certification.comptia.org/security/default.aspx).

Task 1.1: Performing an Initial Risk Assessment

Risk assessment can be achieved by one of two methods: qualitative or quantitative. *Qualitative* assessment does not attempt to assign dollar values to components of the risk analysis. It ranks the seriousness of threats and sensitivity of assets into grades or classes, such as low, medium, or high.

Quantitative assessment deals with numbers and dollar amounts. It attempts to assign a cost (monetary value) to the elements of risk assessment and to the assets and threats of a risk analysis. The quantitative assessment process involves these three steps:

1. Estimate potential losses—Single Loss Expectance = Asset Value × Exposure Factor.

2. Conduct a threat analysis—The goal here is to estimate the Annual Rate of Occurrence (ARO). This numeric value represents how many times the event is expected to happen in one year.

3. Determine Annual Loss Expectancy (ALE)—This formula is calculated as follows: ALE = Single Loss Expectancy (SLE) × Annualized Rate of Occurrence (ARO).

    The goal of this task is to conduct these three steps of the quantitative risk assessment process.

Scenario

You have been asked to perform a quantitative risk assessment for a small startup web graphics firm.

Scope of Task

Duration

This task should take about 30 minutes.

Setup

For this task you need access to a pen and paper. In real life, assessments require knowledge of assets, an analysis of threats and team of people to help in understanding what is truly important to the organization. These people should be from key departments of the company to get more rounded view. I think in this case, to make this differ from the Equipment Used section below, we need to also discuss some of the personal info that you would use. That is, do you need to interview anybody? Do you need other information—company assets, etc.— to make an informed risk assessment plan?

Caveat

In real life, risk assessment is a complex process that is usually done with the aid of software tools that perform all the calculations.

Procedure

In this task, you will learn how to perform a quantitative risk assessment.

Equipment Used

For this task you must have:

- Paper
- Pen or pencil

Details

This task will introduce you to the risk assessment process. This is a critical step in the security process since an organization must determine what is most critical and apply cost-effective countermeasures to protect those assets. A quantitative risk assessment attempts to put dollar amounts on those risks, which makes it a valuable tool when working with management to justify the purchase of countermeasures.

Estimating Potential Loss

Your first step in the risk assessment process is to estimate potential loss. This is performed by multiplying the asset value times the exposure factor. The asset value is what the asset is worth. The exposure factor is the cost of the asset lost or damaged in one single attack. For example, if the threat was a computer virus and the asset was a server valued at $32,000 with an exposure factor of .25, the formula would be as follows: Single Loss Expectance = Asset Value × Exposure Factor, or $32,000 × .25 = $8,000. The SLE, which represents what one computer virus attack would cost, is $8,000.

Now that you have a better idea of how the process works, take a look at Table 1.1.1, which shows a variety of threats and their corresponding exposure factors.

With a list of exposure values, you are now ready to calculate the SLE for some common systems. These are shown in Table 1.1.2. Complete the table using the information provided by Table 1.1.1.

 NOTE   Answers to SLE values in Table 1.1.2 can be found in Table 1.1.4

TABLE 1.1   Threat Level and Exposure Factor (EF)

Threat Level or Vulnerability	Exposure Value
5=STOLEN or COMPROMISED DATA	.90
4=HARDWARE FAILURE	.25
3=VIRUS or MALWARE	.50
2=DoS ATTACK	.25
1=SHORT-TERM OUTAGE	.05

TABLE 1.2   Calculating Single Loss Expectancies (SLE)

IT Asset Name	Asset Value	Threat	EV	SLE Value
Symantec's Enterprise Firewall	$25,000	2	.25	
WAN Circuits (3 remote call centers)	$25,000	4	.25	
Cisco 6500 Switch/Router	$160,000	4	.25	
LAN Connectivity	$100,000	4	.25	
LAN VPN Connectivity	$25,000	4	.25	
Dell Servers—Pentium 4's	$32,000	2	.25	
Linux Servers	$20,000	2	.25	
End-User Workstations (HW & SW)	$300,000	1	.05	
Microsoft SQL Server	$20,000	3	.50	
Oracle SQL Data (Customer Data)	$500,000	5	.90	

Conducting a Threat Analysis

With the calculations completed for SLE, the next step is to determine the ARO. This is the average number of times you might expect this to happen in a year. Here's an example: Galveston typically gets hit with a hurricane at least once every ten years. Therefore, the chance for a hurricane is .10.

Take a moment to review Table 1.1.3. You will need to complete this table based on the following information:

Stolen equipment   Based on information provided by actuary tables, there is the possibility that your organization will lose equipment, or have its equipment compromised, once in a five-year period.

Hardware failure   By examining past failure rates of equipment, you have determined that it has happened twice in the last eight years.

Computer virus   Historical data shows that the company has been seriously affected only once in the last two years.

DoS attack   Your research has shown that the average company in your field is affected by denial of service (DoS) up to three times every 12 years.

Short-term outage   Trouble tickets from the help desk indicate that three-fourths of all trouble tickets in one year are related to some type of outage.

TABLE 1.3   Annualized Rate of Occurrence (ARO)

Threat Level or Vulnerability	ARO Value
5=STOLEN or COMPROMISED DATA	.2
4=HARDWARE FAILURE	.25
3=VIRUS or MALWARE	.5
2=DoS ATTACK	.25
1=SHORT-TERM OUTAGE	.75

Determining the Annual Loss Expectancy

Armed with SLE values and ARO values, you are now ready to complete the final steps of the risk assessment process:

1. To calculate ALE you will use the following formula: ALE = Single Loss Expectancy (SLE) × Annualized Rate of Occurrence (ARO). As an example, if the SLE is $1,000 and the ARO is .25, the formula would be $1000 × .25 = $250 ALE.

2. Using the information gathered earlier in this task, complete Table 1.1.4.

Given the risk calculated for Table 1.1.5, note that the customer's database has the largest ALE.

The answers for Table 1.1.4 can be found in Table 1.1.5.

TABLE 1.4   Calculating Single Loss Expectancies

IT Asset Name	SLE Value	Threat	ARO Value	ALE Value
Symantec's Enterprise Firewall	$6,250	2=DoS ATTACK	.25	
WAN Circuits (3 remote call centers)	$6,250	4=HARDWARE FAILURE	.25	

TABLE 1.4   Calculating Single Loss Expectancies *(continued)*

IT Asset Name	SLE Value	Threat	ARO Value	ALE Value
Cisco 6500 Switch/Router	$40,000	4=HARDWARE FAILURE	.25	
LAN Connectivity	$25,000	4=HARDWARE FAILURE	.25	
LAN VPN Connectivity	$6,250	4=HARDWARE FAILURE	.25	
Dell Servers—Pentium 4's	$8,000	2=DoS ATTACK	.25	
Linux Servers	$5,000	2=DoS ATTACK	.25	
End-User Workstations (HW & SW)	$15,000	1=SHORT-TERM OUTAGE	.75	
Microsoft SQL Server	$10,000	3=VIRUS or MALWARE	.5	
Oracle SQL Data (Customer Data)	$450,000	5=STOLEN or COMPROMISED DATA	.2	

TABLE 1.5   Calculating Single Loss Expectancies Results

IT Asset Name	SLE Value	Threat	ARO Value	ALE Value
Symantec's Enterprise Firewall	$6,250	2=DoS ATTACK	.25	$1,562.50
WAN Circuits (3 remote call centers)	$6,250	4=HARDWARE FAILURE	.25	$1,562.50
Cisco 6500 Switch/Router	$40,000	4=HARDWARE FAILURE	.25	$10,000
LAN Connectivity	$25,000	4=HARDWARE FAILURE	.25	$6,250
LAN VPN Connectivity	$6,250	4=HARDWARE FAILURE	.25	$1,562.50
Dell Servers—Pentium 4's	$8,000	2=DoS ATTACK	.25	$2,000
Linux Servers	$5,000	2=DoS ATTACK	.25	$1,250
End-User Workstations (HW & SW)	$15,000	1=SHORT-TERM OUTAGE	.75	$11,250

TABLE 1.5   Calculating Single Loss Expectancies Results *(continued)*

IT Asset Name	SLE Value	Threat	ARO Value	ALE Value
Microsoft SQL Server	$10,000	**3**=VIRUS or MALWARE	.5	5,000
Oracle SQL Data (Customer Data)	$450,000	**5**=STOLEN or COMPROMISED DATA	.2	$90,000

Criteria for Completion

You have completed this task when you have calculated the SLEs, ALEs, and AROs for a range of IT products.

Task 1.2: Determining Which Security Policy Is Most Important

Security policies are the lifeblood of any organization. Once you've performed a risk assessment, you can begin to lock in these findings in the security policy. The policy should spell out what should be protected, how it should be protected, and what value it has to senior management. Be sure to specify these concerns in *written* documents. You must also verify that the policies comply with all federal, state, and local laws.

Policies play such an important role because they put everyone on the same page and make it clear where senior management stands on specific issues. Policies help define how security is perceived by those within an organization. Policies must flow from the *top* of the organization because senior management is ultimately responsible.

Scenario

Management was pleased with your recent risk assessment, and you have been asked to make some basic security policy recommendations. Any given company only has a limited amount of funds so you real task is to determine when the funds you can spend on security will have the most benefit. The risk assessment process discussed previously is one way to place a value to assets and to the threats those assets face.

Scope of Task

Duration

This task should take about 10 minutes.

Setup

For this task you only need read through the scenario and determine what you think is the best solution.

Caveat

Well-written policies should spell out who's responsible for security, what needs to be protected, and what's an acceptable level of risk. When writing policies you should make sure that what is written is something that users can really do. For example you may want policy to state that users must select complex passwords but will the operating system support that feature?

Procedure

In this task, you will learn to write and assess the security of an organization and determine where to start in the security policy process.

Equipment Used

For this task you must have:

- A pen or pencil

Details

This task will introduce you to basic policy design and help you understand the importance of specific policies to the organization. The following organization and company profile will be used to complete this task.

Company Profile

Your company has all of its future potential pinned to the fact that it has several unique products in FDA-approved trials. If the products are approved for use, the company will be able to obtain additional funding. Recently, a sensitive internal document was found posted on the Internet. The company is worried that some of this information may have ended up in the hands of a competitor. If key proprietary information was leaked, it could endanger the future of the company.

Company Overview

Your talks with senior management revealed the following. The company is betting everything on the success of these products. Most of its key employees have been stolen away from competing firms. These employees were originally attracted by the promise of huge stock options. HR has all these records and they have to keep track of any payouts if they occur.

The company has been lucky—venture capital has poured in. All of this capital has been invested in research and development (R&D). Once a design is pulled together, the company locks in the documentation. It doesn't actually build the product in the United States; a subsidiary in South Korea assembles the design. The finished product returns to the United States for final tests, and then the product is submitted for FDA trials.

Because the company is new and poised for growth, the rented office and lab space is full. There are several entrances to the building, and people can come and go through any of them. Employees often work from home. Employees connect to the office from home via virtual private networks (VPNs). They have been required to sign an acceptable-use policy that specifies for what purposes they can use the network and its resources.

There is no full-time network administrator; those responsibilities fall on a research assistant that has experience managing systems in a college environment (but not in a high-security environment). The network consists of one large local area network (LAN) connected to the Internet through a firewall appliance—except for the VPNs, where the firewall still has its factory-default configuration. Employees must use two-factor authentication to log into local computers, and laptops have biometric authentication.

Because a storm last year wiped out a competitor, the company called in a disaster recovery expert and backup policies were developed. It also contracted with a service bureau for its backup services, should the network go down because of a disaster. This led the company to set up policy templates for other major areas, but policies have not been completed.

Policy Development Overview

Once an organization has decided to develop security polices, the question that usually comes to mind is "What's next?" The best place to start is to frame the policies within some type of existing framework.

Two examples of such a framework are ISO 17799 and BS7799. BS7799 is a recognized standard that breaks security policy into ten categories. These include the following:

Business continuity planning   Addresses business continuity and disaster recovery

System access control   Addresses control of information, protection of network resources, and the ability to detect unauthorized access

System development and maintenance   Addresses the protections of application data and the safeguards associated with confidentiality, integrity, and availability of operational systems

Physical and environmental security   Addresses the physical protection of assets and the prevention of theft

Compliance   Addresses the controls used to prevent the breach of any federal, state, or local law

Personal security   Addresses the protection of individuals and the protection from human error, theft, fraud, or misuse of facilities

Security organization   Addresses the need to manage information within the company

Computer and network management   Addressees the need to minimize the risk of system failure and protect network systems

Asset classification and control   Addresses the need to protect company assets

Security policy   Addresses the need for adequate policies to maintain security

Based on the information provided in the Details section of this task and the BS7799 categories, you should complete Table 1.2.1. In the table you will find a listing for each of the BS7799 categories. Beside each category, list the level of importance of each of these items. Use the following scale:

- 1—Low importance, should not be an immediate concern
- 2—Medium importance, requires attention
- 3—High importance, should be a priority

Answers for Table 1.2.1 can be found in Table 1.2.2.

TABLE 1.6   Policy Action Items

Category	Level of Concern
Business Continuity Planning	
System Access Control	
System Development and Maintenance	
Physical and Environmental Security	
Compliance	
Personal Security	
Security Organization	
Computer and Network Management	
Asset Classification and Control	
Security Policy	

NOTE   Answers will vary but should be similar to what is found in Table 1.2.2.

TABLE 1.7   Policy Action Items

Category	Level of Concern
Business Continuity Planning	1
System Access Control	3
System Development and Maintenance	1
Physical and Environmental Security	3
Compliance	3
Personal Security	3
Security Organization	2
Computer and Network Management	2
Asset Classification and Control	3
Security Policy	2

NOTE   The SANS Institute has a great resource that can be used to develop specific policies. You'll find it at http://www.sans.org/resources/policies/. Best of all, it's free!

Criteria for Completion

You have completed this task when you have completed Table 1.2.1 determined which security concerns are most important.

Task 1.3: Establishing a User Awareness Program

Policies are not enough to protect an organization. Employees must develop user awareness programs so that other employees know about specific policies and are trained to carry out actions specified in security policies. The overall process to accomplish this task is usually referred to as security education, training, and awareness (SETA).

Take, for example, a policy dictating that employees should access the Internet for business use only. Management can dictate this as a policy, but how are end users going to know? That's where employee awareness comes in. Employee awareness could include asking employees to sign an acceptable-use statement when they are hired; it might also include periodic training, and could even include warning banners that are displayed each time an employee accesses the Internet. Awareness is about making sure that employees know security policies exist, what they are, and what their purpose is.

Scenario

Your company has established basic security policies based on BS7799 standards. They have now turned to you for help in developing an awareness program.

Scope of Task

Duration

This task should take about 10 minutes.

Setup

For this task you will need to have performed a risk assessment and developed policies. Once policies are in place you can then start the training process.

Caveat

A study conducted by Ernst and Young found that more than 70 percent of companies polled failed to list security awareness and training as top company initiatives. These same companies reported that 72 percent of them had been affected by infected e-mails and computer viruses. Good training and awareness would have reduced these numbers. You can read more about this at: `http://www.ey.com/global/download.nsf/UK/Survey_-_Global_Information_Security_04/$file/EY_GISS_%202004_EYG.pdf`.

Procedure

In this task, you will be required to categorize and design a basic user awareness program.

Equipment Used

For this task you must have:

- A pen or pencil

Details

This task will provide you with details on how a security awareness program is developed and give you the opportunity to develop key portions of the procedure.

User Awareness

It is sad but true that one of the least implemented and yet most useful parts of a security policy is user awareness. Security must be kept at the forefront of employees' minds for a security program to work. This overall program is typically referred to as security education, training, and awareness (SETA).

SETA is the responsibility of the chief security officer and consists of three elements: education, training, and awareness. While these items can be categorized in many ways, The National Institute of Standards and Technology (NIST) has developed some benchmark procedures that perform such services. One such document is NIST 800-12. Table 1.3.1 contains the information found in that document.

Based on the information provided in Table 1.3.1, identify the following items shown in Table 1.3.2 and place them into the proper category of education, training, or awareness.

TABLE 1.8   Security Awareness, Training, and Education

Item	Education	Training	Awareness
Trinkets printed with security slogans			
Newsletters			
Security + certification			
Bachelor's degree in Computer Security			
SANS 3- day seminar			
CISSP certification			
T-shirts provided for good security practices			

TABLE 1.8   Security Awareness, Training, and Education *(continued)*

Item	Education	Training	Awareness
1- day security seminar at the local college			
Quarterly security quiz with prize			
2 -year degree in Associates of Security			

Based on Table 1.3.2, which of the items do you feel would be most useful to keep security awareness at the forefront of users' minds as they work day to day?

Answers may vary but may include anything that keeps people focused on security, such as mousepads printed with security slogans, coffee cups, T-shirts, pens, or other objects that would be used during the workday.

Answers to questions in Table 1.3.2 can be seen in Table 1.3.3.

TABLE 1.9   Security Awareness, Training, and Education

Item	Education	Training	Awareness
Trinkets printed with security slogans			X
Newsletters			X
Security + certification		X	
Bachelor's degree in Computer Security	X		
SANS 3- day seminar		X	
CISSP certification		X	
T-shirts provided for good security practices			X
1- day security seminar at the local college		X	
Quarterly security quiz with prize			X
2- year degree in Associates of Security	X		

Criteria for Completion

You have completed this task when you have analyzed the items needed for a SETA program and determined which are most useful for a user awareness program.

Task 1.4: Reviewing a Physical Security Checklist

The value of physical security cannot be overstated. Physical security is also the oldest aspect of security. Even in ancient times, physical security was a primary concern of those who had assets to protect. Just consider the entire concept of castles, walls, and moats. While primitive, these controls were clearly designed to delay attackers. Physical security is a vital component of any overall security program. Without physical security you can have no security at all. Any time someone can touch an asset, there is a good chance they can control it. Usually, when you think of physical security items such as locks, doors, and guards come to mind, but physical security is also about employees. What can they bring to work—iPods, USB thumb drives, camera phones? Even these items can pose a threat to security. One good way to start building effective physical security is by creating a checklist of items employees are allowed (or not allowed) to bring with them to work.

Scenario

Your organization may soon be subject to a security audit. Your manager would like to get ahead of this process and have you investigate the current physical security practices.

Scope of Task

Duration

This task should take about 20 minutes.

Setup

In real life security audits don't happen in a void. They occur with the support and under the direction of senior management. End users may or may not be informed ahead of time. Either way you would most like have a memo or letter of authorization authorizing you to perform such activities.

Caveat

Physical security is sometimes overlooked in the mostly logical world of IT. That can have catastrophic consequences.

Procedure

In this task, you will learn how to go through a physical security checklist.

Equipment Used

For this task you must have:

- A pen or pencil

Details

This task will step you through a physical security checklist. It will highlight the value of physical security. Physical security is different from the security controls focused on hackers and crackers. Logical security addresses controls designed to prevent disclosure, denial, or alteration of information. Both are important and, when combined, a holistic view of security can be adopted.

Reviewing a Physical Security Checklist

One of the best ways to check the physical security of your network infrastructure is to conduct a physical security review.

Use Table 1.4.1 to measure your company's level of security. For each item that is present, note a score of 1. If the control is not present, rate that item a 0.

TABLE 1.10   Physical Security Checklist

Item	Score (Yes=1 / No=0)
Is there perimeter security?	
Is a security fence is present?	
Is exterior lighting used to deter intruders?	
Is CCTV being used?	
Are exterior doors secured?	
Is access control in use at building entries?	
Are dumpsters in an area where the public can access?	
Are sensitive items shredded or destroyed before being discarded?	

TABLE 1.10   Physical Security Checklist *(continued)*

Item	Score (Yes=1 / No=0)
Do interior areas have access control?	
Are the servers in a secure location?	
Does the server room have protection on all six sides?	
Is access to the server room controlled?	
Are network cables the lines protected from tapping, cutting, or damage from digging	
Are there "deadman" doors at each of the entrances to prevent piggybacking?	
Is old media degaussed, shredded, and destroyed?	
Are confidential documents marked?	
Is visitor access controlled?	
Are UPS, surge protectors, and generators user?	
Are visitor badges different than regular employees?	
Are end-users allowed uncontrolled access to USB ports or CD/DVD burners?	
Total Score	

After filling in Table 1.4.1, add up the score and compute the total:

- A score of 18 or higher is good.
- A score of 16 to 17 is fair.
- A score of 15 or below is poor.

In real life, physical security takes much more work. This rating system doesn't take into account the issue of reliability or assurance but should give you an idea of the types of items you will want to examine.

Criteria for Completion

You have completed this task when you have reviewed a physical security checklist.

Task 1.5: Understanding the Value of Documents

Identifying the value of the documents you company has is an important task. Documents have value—some more than others. You might lose a quote from a vendor for the new server you have requested and have little to worry about. But what if you lost a client list that had credit card and other personal information? Clearly, some documents and the information they contain are more valuable than others. Factors that impact organizations and how they handle information include:

Government regulations such as the Health Insurance Portability and Accountability Act (HIPAA) and the Gramm-Leach-Bliley Act hold corporations accountable for the privacy, integrity, and security of information.

- Industry is more dependent than ever on the Internet. Many organizations use it for critical and sensitive communications.

- Identity theft and loss of personal information is at an all-time reported high.

These issues are affecting businesses and placing an increased emphasis on how they handle information.

Scenario

You organization recently lost a laptop with sensitive company information. The data on the drive was not encrypted. This has started a big debate at work on the value of documentation and data. Your boss has asked you to investigate a system that could be used to value documents and the information they hold. You will be asked to make recommendations at the next staff meeting.

Scope of Task

Duration

This task should take about 15 minutes.

Setup

For this task you need a group of people from throughout the organization working with you. While you may be an expert on IT systems, you may not know the value of documents or information in the HR department. Gathering date from different people in different departments will provide better results.

Caveat

Documents and data, whether in paper or electronic form, need adequate protection. Sometimes this fact is grossly overlooked.

Procedure

In this task, you will learn how to categorize and place a value on documents and data.

Equipment Used

For this task you must have:

- A pen or pencil

Details

This task will introduce you to some of the methods of information classification. You will be required to take specific documents and determine which category they belong in. This will allow you to specify the level of protection needed.

Information Classification

All companies must take steps to protect the integrity and confidentiality of their information assets. An information classification system is one way to do this. Information classification helps identify sensitive information and can assist an organization in meeting government regulations, such as the Health Insurance Portability and Accountability Act (HIPAA), and other regulatory requirements. Such a system also helps prevents identity theft.

Two systems are primarily used to classify information:

- Governmental classification
- Commercial classification

This task will look at commercial classification, which is broken into the following four lcategories:

Confidential   This is the most sensitive rating. This is the information that keeps a company competitive. This information is for internal use, and its release or alteration could seriously affect or damage the corporation.

Private   This category of restricted information is considered of a personal nature and might include medical records or human resource information.

Sensitive   This information requires controls to prevent its release to unauthorized parties. Damage could result from its loss of confidentiality or its loss of integrity.

Public   Disclosure or release of information in this category would cause no damage to the corporation.

By using the categories as described in Table 1.5.1, place the following items in Table 1.5.2 into their proper categories.

After completing Table 1.5.1, compare it to the results shown in Table 1.5.2.

TABLE 1.11   Commercial Information Classification

Item	Classification
Employee Medical Records	
Trade Secrets	
Prototypes of Next Year's Products	
Schedule of Public Events	
Customer Database	
Pending Sales Events	
Salesmen Call List	
Monthly Customer Profit Reports	
Router Configuration	
Network Diagrams and Schematics	

TABLE 1.12   Commercial Information Classification

Item	Classification
Employee Medical Records	Private
Trade Secrets	Confidential
Prototypes of Next Year's Products	Confidential
Schedule of Public Events	Public
Customer Database	Confidential
Pending Sales Events	Sensitive
Salesmen Call List	Sensitive

TABLE 1.12   Commercial Information Classification *(continued)*

Item	Classification
Monthly Customer Profit Reports	Confidential
Router Configuration	Sensitive
Network Diagrams and Schematics	Sensitive

Did the answers agree with what you felt was the adequate level of protection? Were you more conservative than the answers shown in Table 1.5.2? Although your answers may vary from the chart, the goal is to see how certain documents, data, and information have more value than others. Part of the job of a security professional is to determine that value and work with management to develop adequate protection.

NOTE   Computer security is not just about networks. It also encompasses the technological and managerial procedures applied to protect the confidentiality, integrity, and availability of information.

Criteria for Completion

You have completed this task when you have placed the various documents into their proper categories.

Phase

2

Hardening Systems

The objective of hardening a system is to reduce the attack surface of the system, minimizing the opportunities for an attacker to exploit your system. Every system should be hardened to a standard, baseline level of security. The servers holding your most sensitive information assets and services should be hardened to a higher level.

In addition to implementing security controls, such as having and enforcing a security policy, physically securing your sensitive servers, providing regular user security awareness training, implementing a strong password policy, and implementing security following the principle of least privilege, the hardening of systems should include configurations and controls such as the following:

- Disable and lock down unnecessary services

- Close all unnecessary ports

- Implement a standard operating system (OS) and application patching routine

- Implement security controls on the OSs, the users, and the network

- Manage the launching of applications

- Implement antivirus filtering and updates of virus definitions

- Implement antispyware filtering and updates of spyware definitions

In addition to the tools presented here, many tools are available to help you, the security administrator, perform tasks related to analyzing, understanding, and hardening your systems. Websites with several handy tools include:

- Gibson Research Corporation (http://www.grc.com/default.htm)

- GFI Software (http://www.gfi.com/)

- Sysinternals (http://www.sysinternals.com/)

Microsoft's new Defender application (in beta 2 at the time of this writing) provides a wealth of system information as well.

The tasks in this phase map to Domains 1 and 3 in the objectives for the CompTIA Security+ exam (http://certification.comptia.org/security/).

Task 2.1: Managing Services

Several attack vectors are aimed at exploiting system services. Services are applications and processes that run at system startup. These services perform many beneficial tasks, such as the

Server service (File and Printer Sharing), or the World Wide Web Publishing service, required to run a web server.

Services often open doorways, or *ports*, into a system. It is through these open ports that an attacker can attempt to penetrate your system with known, potential exploits.

Another attack vector on services is aimed at privilege escalation. All processes, including services, must run under the context of a user account. These services have an associated user account that is granted rights and permissions (known as *privileges*) sufficient to perform the work that the service is designed to accomplish. These user accounts are automatically "logged on" during system startup so that the services can be started, even without any human user logging onto the system.

Many services run under the context of the System account, a built-in user account that is granted quite a bit of privilege. During installation, many applications build a service account and grant that user account appropriate privileges to do the work of that application.

If an attacker can execute a successful exploit against a service, the attacker now has access to the system at the privilege level of the user account running the service that was exploited. If this is the System account, the attacker now has quite a bit of system access and can strengthen his hold on your system. This is what was referred to as *escalation of privilege*.

For these reasons, any and all services that are not essential for the operation and performance of a system should be disabled, stopped, and locked down by Group Policies. A diligent administrator may even schedule a task to regularly kill these services, just in case an attacker has been able to get one running.

Further, service accounts for applications should be granted only the minimum level of privilege required to perform the work of the application, following the principle of least privilege. It is usually a mistake to run services under the context of the Administrator account. This account almost always has too many privileges, more than are required to perform the work of the application.

The decision on what services to have started or stopped will vary greatly and will depend on the specific requirements of the individual system being configured.

Scenario

You are configuring a new system to be used as a file and print server that will hold sensitive data. You must reduce the attack surface of the system by disabling unnecessary services and ensure that they cannot be started inappropriately.

Scope of Task

Duration

This task should take about 90 minutes.

Setup

For this task, you will need a Windows workstation or server. Both of these operating systems have a Server service and may be used for file and printer sharing.

Workstation-class operating systems allow for a maximum of 10 inbound connections to the Server service. In the corporate environment, this is usually considered insufficient and therefore a server-class operating system is preferred.

Caveat

While you want to stop any and all unnecessary services, services are created to provide good benefit to users. Disabling services will reduce the utility of a system and many potentially desirable features of a system will no longer function. It may not be immediately obvious what features will stop working as you disable a given service. Services have relationships (known as *dependencies*) to other services. As you look at the properties of a service, you may discover that other services are required to run this service, and that other services may require this service to be running.

   You must proceed cautiously and test the system to ensure the desirable features are still functional while stopping as many nonessential services as you can.

Procedure

In this task, you will disable services that aren't required for the given functional requirements of a system. You will minimize privilege levels, and implement controls to keep nonessential services disabled.

Equipment Used

For this task, you must have:

- A Windows XP or Windows Server–class system
- A Local Administrator account

If you have access to an Active Directory environment and a Domain Administrator account, the task on Group Policy Object (GPOs) can be completed.

Details

The following sections guide you through identifying any dependencies related to a given service, both upstream and downstream. Next, you will examine how to disable and stop a service. You will then identify which service account is being used for each service and consider how you might change this account to follow the principle of least privilege.

   In an Active Directory environment, you can implement a Group Policy Object (GPO) to further lock down a service. These GPOs refresh on a regular basis and will maintain control over the service continuously.

Finally, you will write a batch file to disable a service and schedule it to run every four hours, in case an attacker has been able to reconfigure a disabled service to run.

Using the Computer Management Tool

1. After logging on as a Local Administrator, from the Start menu, select Programs ➤ Administrative Tools ➤ Computer Management.

2. Expand Services and Applications.

3. Select Services and maximize the window.

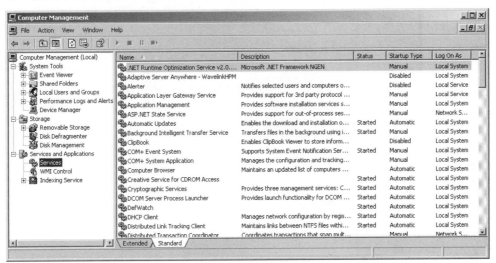

The services are listed in alphabetical order by default. You can click on the column title to re-sort ascending/descending by any column. This will be useful to view what services are running, set services to start automatically, and identify the user account a service is running under. Click on the column title to sort by Startup Type to see which services are set to start automatically at system startup.

    You can also build a Services Microsoft Management Console (MMC) by adding the Services snap-in. To do this, click Start ➤ Run and type **MMC**. Then click OK. In the Console Root window, select File ➤ Add/Remove Snap-in and click the Add button. Then, select Services from the snap-in list and click Add. Click Close and then click OK.

    The Services MMC is also available by clicking Start ➤ Programs ➤ Administrative Tools ➤ Services.

Examining Dependencies between Services

1. In the Computer Management window, double-click any service, and select the Dependencies tab.

This tab may take a few moments to populate.

2. Observe the two fields: This Service Depends On The Following System Components and The Following System Components Depend On This Service.

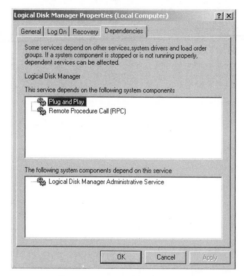

It is the components in the The Following System Components Depend On This Service field that you need to be most concerned about when disabling a service. Any services listed in this field will fail to start if you disable the selected service.

3. Select additional services to get a feel for their dependencies.

4. Close all service property pages.

Disabling and Stopping Services

1. In the Computer Management console Services window, double-click on the Windows Time service. The Windows Time service is used to synchronize the system clock with the system clock on its authentication server.

You must reset this service to its default configuration—Automatic and Started—at the completion of this task.

2. Select the Dependencies tab.

This tab may take a few moments to populate.

3. Observe the lower field: The Following System Components Depend On This Service. Notice that, by default, no services depend on this service. Be aware that on other services, if this field is populated, the dependent service will fail as you complete this task.

4. On the General tab, select the Startup Type drop-down control. Notice that the Startup Type options are Automatic, Manual, and Disabled. Automatic starts at system startup; Manual starts this service if another service or application starts that depends on this service; Disabled means that this service will be prohibited from starting.

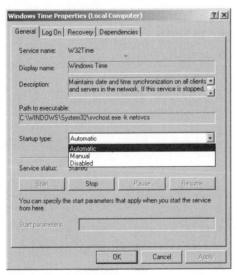

5. Set the Startup type to Disabled. Click Apply.

Notice that the Service status is still Started. Disabling a service does not stop the service if it had been started. You must manually stop the service.

6. Click Stop to shut down the service. You will see a progress bar as the service is being stopped.

7. Confirm that the Service status is now stopped.

8. You have now successfully disabled and stopped a service.

For proper system operation you must reset this service to its default configuration: Automatic and Started.

9. Set Startup type to Automatic. Click Apply.

10. Click Start. You will see a progress bar as the service is being started. Confirm that the Startup type is Automatic and the Service status is Started.

11. Click OK to close the property pages for the Windows Time service.

Identifying the Service Account Used to Start a Service

1. With the Computer Management Tool open, click on the Log On As column to sort its contents.

2. Scroll down this list and notice the various user accounts used to start each service. Most services run under the context of the Local Service, Local System, or the Network Service account. If your system has an application installed that requires a service account, you will see those accounts listed as well. Whatever account is utilized, it should have just the bare minimum level of privilege to perform the work of the application, process, or service. If you see the Administrator account listed here, this privilege level is probably too high and should be changed to an account of lesser but sufficient privilege.

3. As a demonstration of how to change the service Log On As account, you will use the ClipBook service.

At the end of this task, you will reset the service account to the default Local System account. Failure to reset the Log On As account may cause desirable services to fail.

Double-click the ClipBook service. Select the Log On tab. Notice that this service defaults to the Local System account.

4. Select This Account, and then click Browse.

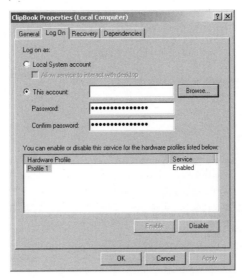

5. Click Advanced.

6. Click Find Now and highlight the Administrator account.

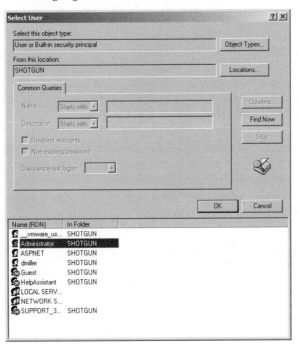

Click OK twice, which selects the Administrator account as the account to be Logged On As for this service.

7. In the ClipBook Properties dialog box, select the Log On tab, type the Administrator's password in the Password field, and then retype it in the Confirm Password field. Click Apply to complete the process.

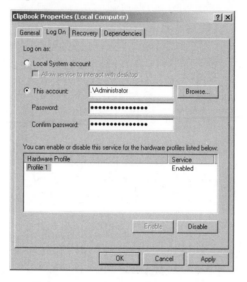

 Be aware that if this account password is changed—and it should be changed regularly—you must change the password in this dialog box as well. If you do not keep this dialog box synchronized with the account password, the service will fail to start.

8. You have now successfully changed the Log On As service account for a service.

 For proper system operation of the ClipBook service, you must reset this service to its default configuration, Local System.

9. Set Log On As to the Local System account. Confirm that the Allow Service To Interact With Desktop checkbox is cleared. Click Apply.

10. Confirm that the Local System account is selected.

11. Click OK to close the property pages for the ClipBook service.

Locking Down Services with Group Policy Objects

Computer GPOs are applied at system startup and are refreshed by default every 90–120 minutes on member servers and workstations and every 5 minutes on domain controllers.

This task requires access to an Active Directory (AD) environment and you must have Domain Administrator privilege. If you do not have these components, you cannot complete this task. In a well-developed AD environment, you may need to build a security group with administrators that you want to be able to manage system services. In this task, you will be granting only this elite group of Administrators the privilege of managing system services on your hardened servers.

1. After logging on as a Domain Administrator on either a domain controller or on a Windows XP system with Adminpak.msi installed, select Start ➢ Programs ➢ Administrative Tools, and launch Active Directory Users And Computers (ADUC).

2. Expand the domain object. Select and right-click on the Users OU. Select New ➢ Group.

3. Name the group **Service Admins**. Confirm that Group Scope is set to Global and that Group Type is set to Security. Click OK to create the security group. This group will now be populated with the elite group of domain administrators that you wish to allow to configure services.

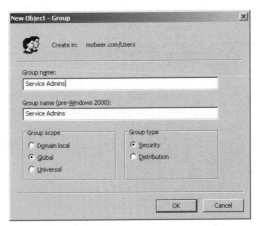

4. In ADUC, select the domain name. Then right-click on the domain name and select New ➤ Organizational Unit.

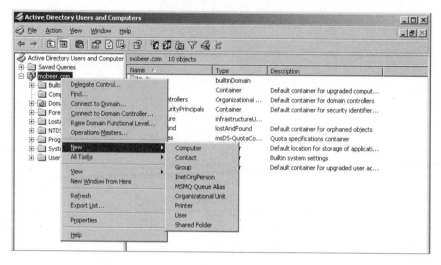

5. Name the new organizational unit (OU) **Hardened Servers**. Click OK. Place into this OU the computer account objects for all servers you are attempting to harden with these GPOs.

6. Right-click on the Hardened Servers OU and select Properties. Select the Group Policy tab.

7. Click New and rename the new GPO **Services Lockdown**.

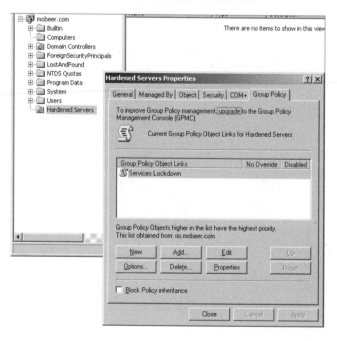

8. Click Edit,

9. Inside the new Services Lockdown GPO, in the left pane expand Computer Configuration ➢ Windows Settings ➢ Security Settings. Select System Services.

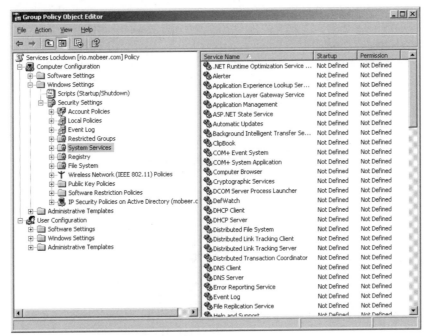

10. In the right pane, double-click the ClipBook service.

11. Select Define This Policy Setting, and then select Disabled. This configures the ClipBook service to disabled during system startup.

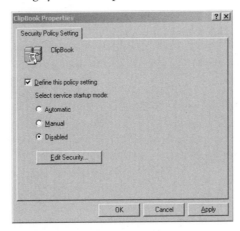

12. Click Edit Security. You must first add your elite group of administrators—the Service Admins global group—then remove the administrators from the access control list (ACL). To do this, first click Add.

13. In the resulting dialog box, click Advanced, then click Find Now and select the Service Admins global group.

14. Click OK twice. This adds the Service Admins global group to the Security For ClipBook ACL. Confirm that all Allow permissions are selected, except Special Permissions.

15. Select the Administrators Group in the Group Or User Names field. Click Remove.

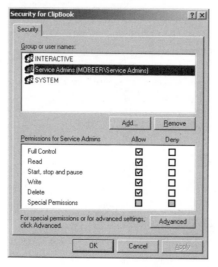

16. Click OK to close the Security For ClipBook dialog box. Click OK in the ClipBook Properties dialog box.

17. Close the GPO.

You have now successfully created a GPO that will, at startup, reset the ClipBook service on all computers in the Hardened Servers OU to Disabled, and only the members of the Service Admins security group have the privilege to make any changes to the Startup type and Service status of this service.

You have only configured one service: ClipBook. If you were hardening a system, you would configure this GPO with additional service settings defined for all services you wish to control.

Resetting Services with Task Scheduled Scripts

1. In Windows Explorer, create a new folder in the root of C: called **Scripts**.

2. Open the Scripts folder. In the right-hand pane, right-click the white space in the Scripts folder and select New ➢ Text Document.

3. Rename the text document **StopAlerter.cmd**. Notice that there are no spaces in the filename. You will be prompted with a warning about changing the file's extension. Click Yes to accept the filename with the new extension.

4. Right-click StopAlerter.cmd and select Edit. If prompted, select Notepad as the application used to open this document.

5. In the Notepad application, type the command **net stop alerter**, and then press Enter.

 To determine the name of the services on a system, launch Regedit (Start ➢ Run ➢ and type **Regedit**. Then click OK.). In the Registry Editor application, expand the registry to HKEY_LOCALMACHINE\SYSTEM\CURRENTCONTROLSET\ SERVICES. The folder names in this folder are (usually) the correct service names to use with the NET STOP command. Test these at a command prompt to be certain. Another option for locating service names is to boot into Recovery Console and type the command **LISTSVC**. Then scroll through the services available on the system to identify the service name.

6. Select File ➢ Save, and then close Notepad.

7. In the Control Panel (Start ➢ Settings ➢ Control Panel), select Scheduled Tasks ➢ Add Scheduled Task.

8. Build a Scheduled Task to run the StopAlerter script every four hours. When the Task Scheduler Wizard launches, click Next.

9. Browse to C:\Scripts\StopAlerter.cmd. Click Next.

10. Schedule the task to run daily. (You'll fix this later.) Click Next.

11. Set the start time to 9:00 A.M. every day and the start day to tomorrow's date. Click Next.

12. Enter the credentials (username and password, which you enter twice) of either the local administrator, the domain administrator, or in the case of a service controlled by the Services Lockdown GPO, the credentials of a member of the Service Admins security group (someone with a privilege level sufficient to configure the service). Click Next.

13. Select Open Advanced Properties and click Finish.

14. In the Task Properties dialog box, select the Schedule tab.

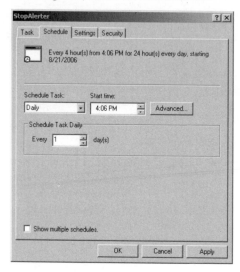

15. Click Advanced, and then select the option to repeat the task every 4 hours and set the duration to 24 hours.

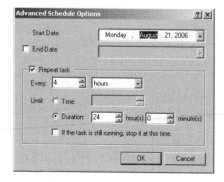

16. Click OK twice.

You have now scheduled the StopAlerter task to run every 4 hours, every day. If an attacker managed to get this service to start, this task would stop the service when it runs. This means that the attacker would have to break into your system every 4 hours and restart this service (assuming he could accomplish such a feat!), essentially starting over with his devious activities.

WARNING You should carefully consider resetting all changes that you've made to their original default configuration. You have stopped and disabled services. You have locked services down, perhaps to a point where desirable system operations may fail. You have scheduled a task that stops a service to run every 4 hours, forever. Evaluate the changes you've made and determine whether you should undo these changes before you proceed.

Criteria for Completion

You have completed this task when you know how to determine a service's dependencies, how to disable and stop services, how to set the service account to a user account with the minimum level of privilege to run the service, how to lock down the services by GPO, and how to regularly stop services in case they do somehow get started.

Task 2.2: Managing Ports

Ports represent services available on a system, such as File And Printer Sharing, Domain Name System (DNS), and Windows Internet Name Service (WINS). These services provide a good benefit to clients and the network infrastructure as a whole. Ports are also the path into the system for an attacker. To harden a system against attackers, you want to close all ports except those that are required to provide the desired services on a system.

Task 2.1 covered how to manage services. You learned how to view which services are running, how to disable and stop those services, how to lock down the services by managing who can make changes to the services, and how to continuously stop unwanted services from running. This is a big first step in managing ports.

The next step in managing ports is to install, enable, and configure the firewall service on your systems.

Scenario

You are configuring a new system to be used as a workstation with limited file and print sharing and a personal website. You must reduce the attack surface of the system by implementing Windows Firewall and configuring it correctly to close unnecessary ports.

Scope of Task

Duration

This task should take about 60 minutes.

Setup

For this task you will need a Windows workstation with Service Pack 2 (SP2).

Windows Firewall was provided in Windows Server 2003 SP1 and in Windows XP SP2. Workstation class operating systems allow for a maximum of 10 inbound connections to the server service.

To perform testing of open ports using a port scanner, you will need a second Windows XP system. You will need to make sure the following applications are installed on this system (in order):

- WinPCap version 3.1 for Windows XP (http://www.winpcap.org/install/default.htm)

- Nmap port scanner (http://insecure.org/nmap/download.html)

Caveat

Although you want to close any unnecessary ports, ports are opened to provide a benefit to users. Enabling the Windows Firewall and closing ports will reduce the utility of a system, and many potentially desirable features of a system will no longer function.

You must proceed cautiously and test the system to ensure the desirable features are still functional while making sure that you've closed as many ports as you can.

Procedure

You will implement Windows Firewall and close ports that aren't required for the given functional requirements of a system. You will then test the system, both internally and externally, and confirm that you've achieved the desired results.

Equipment Used

For this task, you must have:

- A Windows XP SP2 system with Internet Information Services (IIS) web services installed and started

- A Local Administrator account

To perform testing of open ports using a port scanner, you will need a second Windows XP system. This system will need the following applications downloaded and installed, in order:

- WinPCap version 3.1 for Windows XP
- Nmap port scanner

Details

The following sections guide you through the configuration of Windows Firewall. This firewall closes all inbound ports except those you allow. You will configure the firewall to allow file and printer sharing (ports 137, 138, 139, and 445) and HTTP (port 80) for the personal web server. Then you will test the system to identify ports that the system is utilizing and the applications associated with the open ports. You will then use a port scanner (Nmap) to interrogate the system from an external vantage point.

Configuring Windows Firewall on XP SP2

1. On the Windows XP SP2 system, right-click on My Network Places and select Properties. If there is no icon on the desktop, you can go to the Control Panel and launch Network Connections.

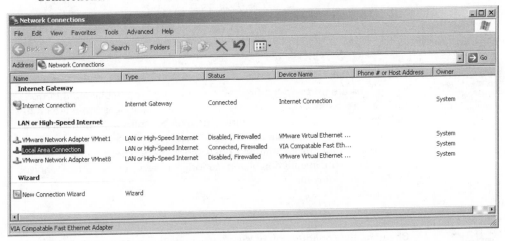

2. Right-click on Local Area Connection and select Properties. Select the Advanced tab and click Settings.

3.   On the General tab of the Windows Firewall dialog box, if Firewall is not enabled, select On (Recommended).

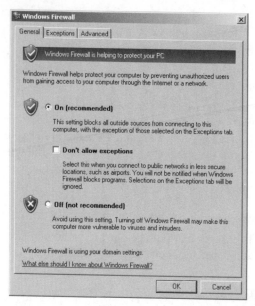

4.   Select the Exceptions tab.

Exceptions are ports on the firewall that are open to unsolicited inbound frames. These inbound frames are trying to reach services provided on the system behind the firewall. If there is no exception for a port, the firewall simply rejects the unsolicited inbound frame. Your Exceptions tab may contain different entries than the ones shown here. These entries are the by-product of the installation of applications and services that are recognized by Windows Firewall.

Changing the configuration of Windows Firewall may cause some services and applications to fail. Further, it may leave your system vulnerable to attack. If you are not sure of the proper configuration for the firewall, do not make any changes to the firewall.

5. Notice that File And Printer Sharing is enabled, as well as UPnP (Universal Plug and Play) Framework. Highlight File and Printer Sharing and click Edit.

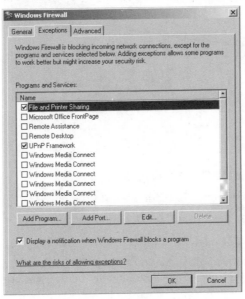

 Notice that Windows File and Printer Sharing utilized UDP port 137 (NetBIOS Name Service), UDP port 138 (NetBIOS Datagram Service), TCP port 139 (NetBIOS Session Service), and TCP port 445 (Microsoft Directory Services). These services are required to support File and Printer Sharing for NetBIOS/ SMB (Microsoft and Samba) clients. By default, ports that are opened are available to receive inbound frames from any source. To restrict allowed inbound frames to one or a few systems, you can change the scope of the exception.

6. In the Edit A Service dialog box, click Change Scope.

 You can restrict allowed inbound frames to My Network (subnet) only or produce a custom list of IP addresses and ranges.

Leave the default Any Computer setting and click Cancel in the Change Scope dialog box.

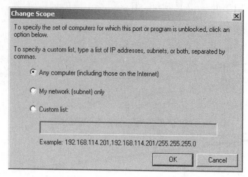

Click Cancel again in the Edit A Service dialog box.

7. Highlight other entries on the Exception list of Programs And Services and examine the details by clicking Edit.

 To identify applications and services related to port numbers, check out the excellent reference tool Port Authority: http://www.grc.com/PortDataHelp.htm.

8. Notice that (at least in our example) there is no exception for the web service. It is currently being blocked by this firewall. To add an exception, select Add Port.

9. In the Add A Port dialog box, enter the following information:

- Name: Web Server
- Port Number: 80

Enable TCP and click OK.

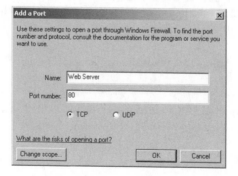

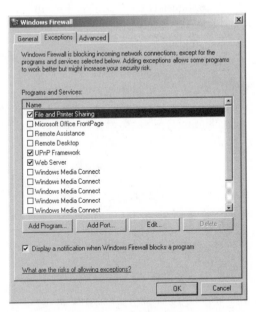

10. Select the Advanced tab in the Windows Firewall dialog box. On this tab you can enable or disable the firewall on any of the network interfaces in the system, configure the logging details for the firewall, allow or drop ICMP frames (used for the PING application—which is good—but also used in many attacks—which is bad!), and reset the firewall to its default configuration, just in case you're not sure what damage you may have done.

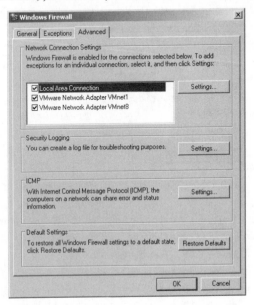

11. Click OK to close the Windows Firewall properties dialog box.

You have now enabled and configured the Windows Firewall. You have also enabled inbound frames for Windows File And Printer Sharing, UPnP, and web services. Next, you'll test the system for open ports.

Testing Open Ports

1. Open a command window by selecting Start ➤ Run, typing **CMD**, and clicking OK.

2. Open Netstat, a command-line tool that interrogates the system for open ports, connections, and protocol usage. Simply type **netstat /?** at the command prompt. You should see the following:

```
C:\>netstat /?

Displays protocol statistics and current TCP/IP network
    connections.

NETSTAT [-a] [-b] [-e] [-n] [-o] [-p proto] [-r] [-s] [-v]
    [interval]

    -a        Displays all connections and listening ports.
    -b        Displays the executable involved in creating each
              connection or listening port. In some cases well-known
              executables host multiple independent components, and in
              these cases the sequence of components involved in
              creating the connection or listening port is displayed.
              In this case the executable name is in [] at the bottom,
              on top is the component it called, and so forth until
              TCP/IP was reached. Note that this option can be time-
              consuming and will fail unless you have sufficient
              permissions.
    -e        Displays Ethernet statistics. This may be combined with
              the -s option.
    -n        Displays addresses and port numbers in numerical form.
    -o        Displays the owning process ID associated with each
              connection.
    -p proto  Shows connections for the protocol specified by
              proto; proto may be any of: TCP, UDP, TCPv6, or
              UDPv6. If used with the -s option to display per-
              protocol statistics, proto may be any of: IP, IPv6,
              ICMP, ICMPv6, TCP, TCPv6, UDP, or UDPv6.
    -r        Displays the routing table.
    -s        Displays per-protocol statistics. By default, statistics
              are shown for IP, IPv6, ICMP, ICMPv6, TCP, TCPv6, UDP,
              and UDPv6; the -p option may be used to specify a subset
```

of the default.

-v   When used in conjunction with -b, will display sequence
         of components involved in creating the connection or
         listening port for all executables.

interval   Redisplays selected statistics, pausing interval
           seconds between each display. Press CTRL+C to stop
           redisplaying statistics. If omitted, netstat will
           print the current configuration information once.

3. At the command prompt, type **netstat -a -n -o**.

This command displays all open ports and connections, places them in numeric or alphabetic order, and shows the process ID (PID) that opened the port. Your results should look something like this:

```
C:\>netstat -a -n -o

Active Connections

  Proto Local Address     Foreign Address     State      PID
  TCP   0.0.0.0:21        0.0.0.0:0           LISTENING  3984
  TCP   0.0.0.0:80        0.0.0.0:0           LISTENING  3984
  TCP   0.0.0.0:135       0.0.0.0:0           LISTENING  1060
  TCP   0.0.0.0:443       0.0.0.0:0           LISTENING  3984
  TCP   0.0.0.0:445       0.0.0.0:0           LISTENING  4
  TCP   0.0.0.0:2268      0.0.0.0:0           LISTENING  3984
  TCP   0.0.0.0:2869      0.0.0.0:0           LISTENING  1472
  TCP   127.0.0.1:1047    0.0.0.0:0           LISTENING  672
  TCP   192.168.222.201:139 0.0.0.0:0         LISTENING  4
  TCP   192.168.222.201:445  192.168.222.218:3274   ESTABLISHED 4
  TCP   192.168.222.201:1161 192.168.222.200:3268   CLOSE_WAIT  3740
  TCP   192.168.222.201:2256 192.168.222.218:445    ESTABLISHED 4
  UDP   0.0.0.0:445       *:*                            4
  UDP   0.0.0.0:500       *:*                            824
  UDP   0.0.0.0:1025      *:*                            1252
  UDP   0.0.0.0:1026      *:*                            1252
  UDP   0.0.0.0:1425      *:*                            1252
  UDP   0.0.0.0:3456      *:*                            3984
  UDP   0.0.0.0:4500      *:*                            824
  UDP   127.0.0.1:123     *:*                            1188
  UDP   127.0.0.1:1027    *:*                            824
  UDP   127.0.0.1:1041    *:*                            768
  UDP   127.0.0.1:1075    *:*                            1600
  UDP   127.0.0.1:1160    *:*                            3740
```

```
UDP    127.0.0.1:1269        *:*                              2752
UDP    127.0.0.1:1419        *:*                              2416
UDP    127.0.0.1:1577        *:*                              3204
UDP    127.0.0.1:1900        *:*                              1472
UDP    127.0.0.1:2165        *:*                              2908
UDP    127.0.0.1:2229        *:*                               660
UDP    127.0.0.1:2302        *:*                              3292
UDP    127.0.0.1:2373        *:*                              1884
UDP    127.0.0.1:2383        *:*                               556
UDP    127.0.0.1:2603        *:*                              1212
UDP    192.168.222.201:123 *:*                                1188
UDP    192.168.222.201:137 *:*                                   4
UDP    192.168.222.201:138 *:*                                   4
UDP    192.168.222.201:1900 *:*                               1472
```

4. Review some of these port numbers on the Port Authority website: `http://www.grc.com/ PortDataHelp.htm`.

5. Launch Task Manager by right-clicking on the taskbar and selecting Task Manager. Select the Processes tab. Then choose View ≻ Select Columns.

6. Enable the following columns:

- PID
- CPU Usage
- CPU Time
- Memory Usage
- User Name
- Base Priority

Click OK.

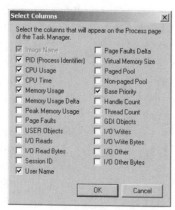

7. Click on the PID column title to sort ascending by the Process ID.

By comparing the PID value in the results from the `netstat` command to the PID value in Task Manager, you can identify which processes opened which ports, as well as who launched the process. This may help you identify desirable versus undesirable processes and ports that your system is running. Don't worry if you don't know how these processes were launched; we'll cover that later in this phase.

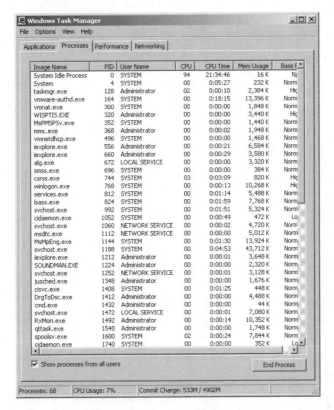

These Testing Open Ports processes, Steps 1 through 7, have taken a look at the processes and ports that the system has available—a sort of self-perspective from behind the firewall. Next you'll take a look at how the system appears from outside the firewall from an external system looking at the firewall.

1. On the second XP system, if you haven't already downloaded WinPCap version 3.1 and Nmap version 4.11 (or the latest versions), download them from the websites referenced earlier into a folder on the hard drive. A reference guide for Nmap is available at `http://insecure.org/nmap/man/`.

2. Install WinPCap v3.1. This step must be performed first.

3. Install Nmap.

4. Open a command window.

5. At the C:\ prompt, enter **nmap**.

   This will show you a quick summary of switches to use with Nmap. If you get an error message that **nmap** is not a recognized command, change your focus to the **nmap** installation directory, specified during the Nmap installation.

6. At the C:\ prompt, enter **nmap -sS -O <*IP Address of the first XP system*>**.

   The command is case sensitive. This command tells your machine to run a port scan on the first XP system, utilize the Stealth Scan mode, and attempt to identify the operating system. Here is the result of this scan on our system, named Shotgun, IP address 192.168.222.201:

```
C:\>nmap -sS -O 192.168.222.201


Starting Nmap 4.11 ( http://www.insecure.org/nmap )
at 2006-08-22 15:10 Eastern Standard Time
Warning: OS detection will be MUCH less reliable because you did
not find at least 1 open and 1 closed TCP port
Interesting ports on shotgun (192.168.222.201):
Not shown: 1677 filtered ports
PORT  STATE SERVICE
80/tcp open http
139/tcp open netbios-ssn
445/tcp open microsoft-ds
MAC Address: 00:0C:76:C0:21:BE (Micro-star International CO.)
Device type: general purpose
Running: Microsoft Windows NT/2K/XP
OS details: Microsoft Windows XP SP2


Nmap finished: 1 IP address (1 host up) scanned in 25.567 seconds
```

Notice that Ports 139 and 445 are open to support file and printer sharing and port 80 is open to support the website. No other ports are shown to be available externally because of the firewall. If other ports are open, identify their source(s) and determine whether they are desirable or undesirable. If undesirable, disable the application(s) and service(s) related to these ports, and reconfigure your Windows firewall to block these ports correctly.

Criteria for Completion

You have completed this task when you have enabled and configured Windows Firewall in your XP SP2 system; configured services through the firewall; tested the system internally for services, ports, connections and protocols; and tested the system from an external XP system by running a port scanner against the firewall.

Task 2.3: Patching the Operating System

Many appraisals of operating system and applications estimate that there are typically somewhere between 10 and 50 bugs per 1,000 lines of code. Windows XP has an estimated 40 million lines of code, and Vista is expected to have approximately 50 million lines of code. These bugs are doorways for attackers to enter and exploit your systems, potentially compromising the confidentiality, integrity, and availability of your information services. This translates to the need for a diligent and continuous patching routine to minimize the potential exposure of these vulnerabilities in your operating system and applications.

Scenario

You are responsible for maintaining an XP 10-user workgroup in your corporate environment. You are also responsible for maintaining 100 XP systems in an Active Directory environment. You need to periodically spot-check patching processes, and you must provide a patching routine to satisfy these maintenance needs.

Scope of Task

Duration

This task should take approximately 1 hour.

Setup

You will need to perform manual patching from the Windows Update website, configure automatic patching for the workgroup, and configure automated patching of your domain member workstations.

Caveat

Patches are intended to correct bugs in the operating system and applications. They replace buggy system and application files with new, corrected versions. These versions are often released with minimal, if any, testing in the real world. Patches can cause functioning applications and services to fail. Patches should be tested in a lab environment prior to implementation on corporate production systems.

Procedure

For the workgroup environment, where the users are local administrators, you can configure Windows Updates to run automatically. You can run update checks manually to perform spot-checking to ensure that the patching system is working correctly. Further, for the Active Directory (AD) environment, you will install Windows Server Update Services (WSUS) on a Windows Server 2003 and then deploy the approved patches via a Group Policy Object (GPO) to your AD clients.

Equipment Used

For this task, you need the following equipment:

- Windows XP SP2 system in Workgroup mode
- Windows XP SP2 as a domain member
- Windows Server 2003 SP1, domain controller with IIS and WSUS installed
- Internet connectivity

Details

Manual Patching of the Operating System

1. On the XP system in Workgroup mode, log on as a Local Administrator.
2. Launch Internet Explorer and ensure that you have Internet connectivity.
3. Select Tools ➤ Windows Update.

 Depending on the status of your system, Windows Update may need to install an ActiveX application to aid with the testing of the patch status of the system. Allow this application to be installed.

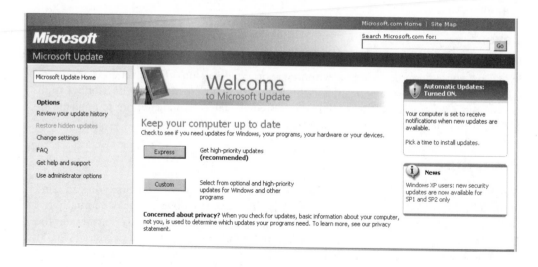

4. Click Custom.

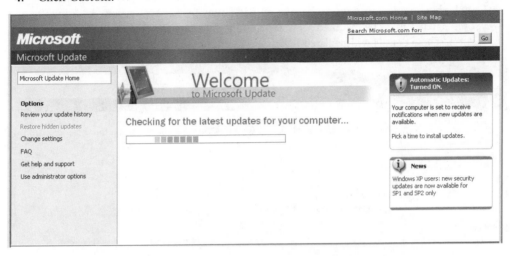

5. Your system is now downloading a file from the Windows Update website called MSSecure.xml, which is a list of all released patches. Windows Update will compare the status of your system with this downloaded list. Anything your system is missing from this list is presented for download in the resulting web page.

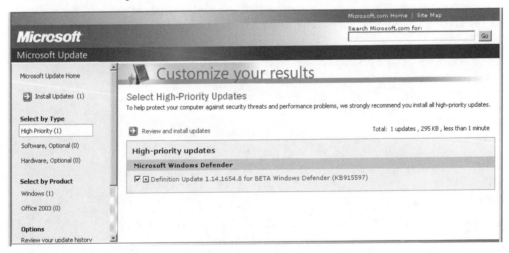

 Notice in the left-hand column of this web page that Windows Update identifies High Priority patches, patches for the hardware in the system and patches for Microsoft software, as well as patches for Microsoft Office, if it is installed on the system.

6. Click Review and Install Updates. By expanding the details on the patch(es) you may identify how valuable—or how dangerous—a patch may be to your system. Additionally, some patches must be installed separately and the system must be rebooted after installation. These details will be listed here.

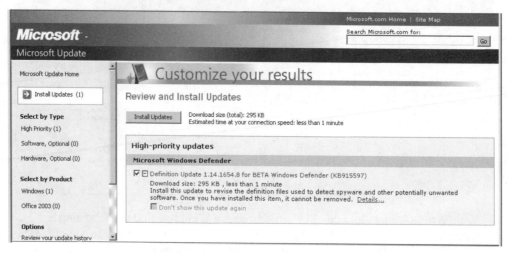

7. If after reviewing the details of the patch you are confident that the patch is desirable and you don't expect it to cause other processes to fail, confirm that the patch(es) are selected by placing a check mark in the box to the left of the patch title, and then click Install Updates.

8. A Windows Update progress dialog box is presented.

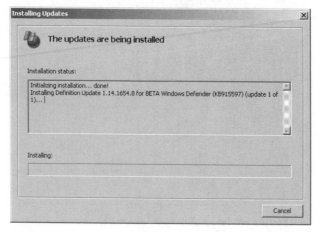

9. Upon completion of the installation of the patch(es) you will be presented with a completion dialog box. This dialog box may indicate that you need to reboot the system. The

patching is not complete until after rebooting in this case. If necessary, you should reboot the system as soon as possible. Click OK.

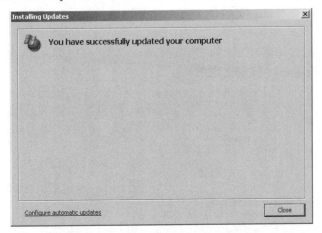

10. An Installation Summary is presented. Close this window to complete the manual patching process.

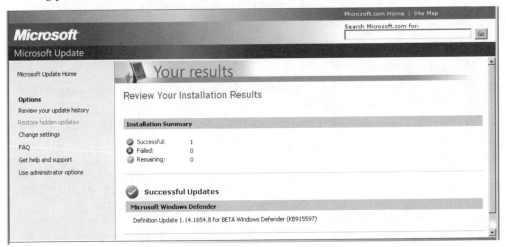

Automated Patching in Workgroup Mode

1. Log on to the XP system in Workgroup mode as a Local Administrator.

 For automated patching to take place correctly, the user of the system must be a local administrator.

2. Right-click on My Computer and select Properties. In the resulting dialog box, select the Automatic Updates tab.

You can also open this dialog box by selecting Control Panel ➤ System ➤ Automatic Updates.

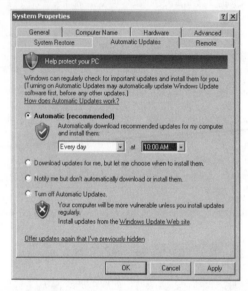

3. The options presented are:

- Automatic (Recommended) – Automatically Download Recommended Updates For My Computer And Install Them

- Download Updates For Me, But Let Me Choose When To Install Them

- Notify Me But Don't Automatically Download Or Install Them

- Turn Off Automatic Updates

4. Select the first option. Specify that you want to perform this task every day at 10 A.M.

 If the system is turned off during a scheduled update, the update will be triggered and will occur when the system is turned on.

 In the scenario, this configuration would need to be performed on each of the 10 systems individually.

5. Click OK.

Automated Patching in Domain Mode: Configuring WSUS

1. On the Windows Server 2003 Domain Controller, log in as a Domain Administrator.

2. You can download WSUS (currently in beta 3 version, 127MB) from http://www .microsoft.com/windowsserversystem/updateservices/downloads/WSUS.mspx.

The user must have a Microsoft Live 1 login account (MSN e-mail or Passport accounts are accepted as well).

Several Overview and Deployment guides are available on this website.

3. WSUS utilizes IIS on the WSUS server for its administration interface. On the Windows Server 2003 domain controller and now WSUS server, open Internet Explorer. Enter the URL **http://localhost/WSUSAdmin**.

You will need to authenticate as a domain administrator. The following administrative interface is presented:

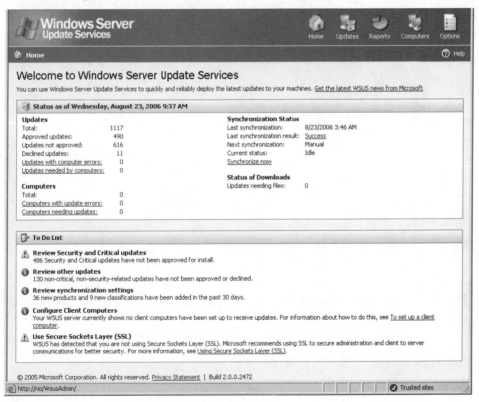

4.   In the upper-right corner, click Options. You are given three configuration choices:

▪   Synchronization Options

▪   Automatic Approval Options

▪   Computers Options

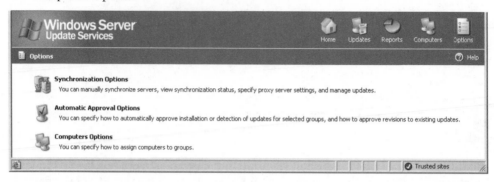

5.   Select Synchronization Options.

Here you can choose to synchronize manually or set a daily synchronization schedule. In the corporate environment, you'll probably want to set this for daily synchronization.

For this task, select Synchronize Manually.

6. In the next section, click the Change button under Products.

   Select the operating systems and applications you are required to support in your environment.

   For this task, select Windows Server 2003 and Windows XP.

7. Click the Change button under Update Classifications.

   Select the types of updates you wish to provide through the WSUS system.

   For this task, select all options.

8. Scroll down to the next sections.

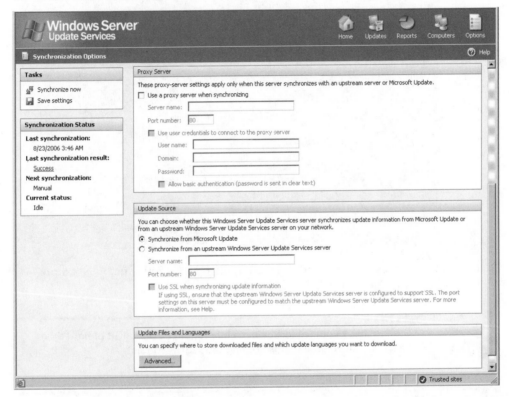

9. If you are not connected to the Internet through a proxy server, deselect the Use A Proxy Server When Synchronizing check box.

   If you are connected to the Internet through a proxy server, enable that check box and configure this section according to the configuration requirements of the proxy server. If you are not sure of the proxy server configuration requirements, contact your network administrator.

   If you are not sure whether you are passing through a proxy server, first try this setting with the Use A Proxy Server setting cleared.

10. In the Update Source section, choose either Synchronize From Microsoft Update or Synchronize From An Upstream Windows Server Update Services Server.

For this task, select Synchronize From Microsoft Update.

11. In the Update Files And Languages section, click Advanced. Review and clear the warning message.

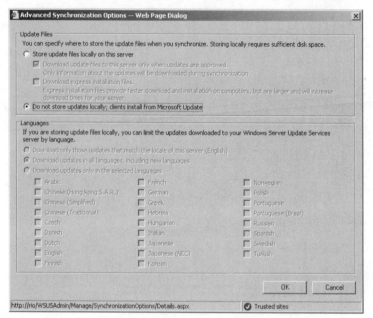

12. Here you can choose to Store Update Files Locally On This Server or Do Not Store Updates Locally; Clients Install From Microsoft Update.

Storing these updates locally currently requires about 6GB of hard drive space on the volume that is holding the WSUS content.

With the setting Do Not Store Updates Locally; Clients Install From Microsoft Update, the WSUS server is only used to configure the Approval log and have clients download only the approved updates directly from Microsoft Update.

If you choose to have clients download updates from Microsoft Update, the list of available updates for administrative approval includes all languages supported by Microsoft Update. Only approve updates for the language(s) required by your environment.

As you can see, this server is configured with the setting Do Not Store Updates Locally; Clients Install From Microsoft Update.

For this task, retain whichever setting the WSUS server was configured with (assuming you have 6GB+ of free space on the volume holding the WSUS content; otherwise select Do Not Store Updates Locally On This Server).

13. If your system is configured to store update files locally on the server, the Languages section is available. Choose only the languages you need to support in your environment.

14. Click OK. In the upper-left corner, in the Tasks section click Save Settings.

15. If your system requires it, you may need to synchronize your WSUS server before you can proceed.

Synchronization can take an extended period of time, potentially several hours, depending on your configuration choices and Internet connectivity bandwidth.

To synchronize your server, click Synchronize Now in the upper-left hand in the Tasks section.

16. Click Updates in the upper-right corner.

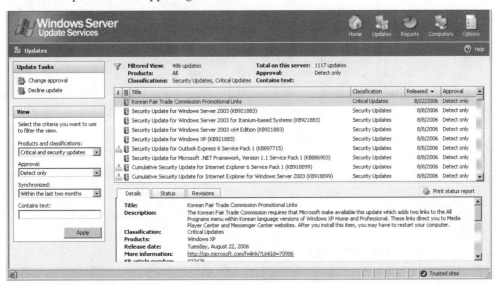

17. Review updates in the right-hand pane, observing the Details, Status, and Revisions below.

In a corporate environment, all updates should be tested for compatibility in a lab environment prior to approving and deploying to the production network.

18. In the left-hand pane, in the View section select the drop-down lists to observe the products and classifications, approval status, and synchronization status.

In the three drop-down lists, select All Updates, All Updates, and Any Time, then click Apply to view all updates.

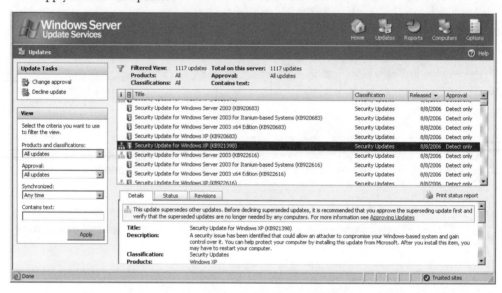

19. Select an update in the right-hand pane. In the left-hand pane, in the Update Tasks section, click Change Approval.

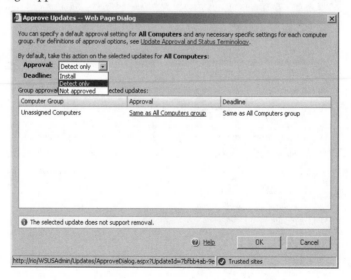

20. Review the contents of the dialog box. In the Approval drop-down list, select
Install. Click OK. You will see this update now configured to install in the
Approval column.

You have now walked through the process of configuring WSUS to synchronize and
download either the approval list of updates or to store updates locally and maintain the
approval list. You have performed an approval of one or more updates.

Next you must configure systems to receive updates from the WSUS server. This is
done by Group Policy Objects (GPOs).

Automated Patching in Domain Mode: Configuring Systems to Update from WSUS

1. On the Windows Server 2003 Domain Controller, log in as a Domain
Administrator.

2. From Administrative Tools, launch Active Directory Users And Computers
(ADUC).

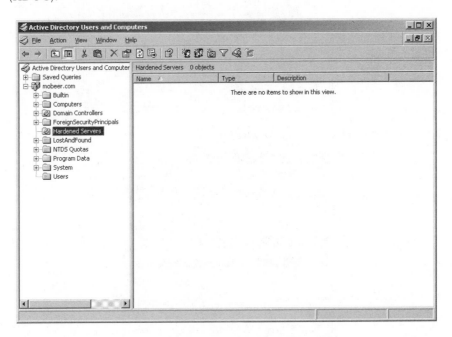

3. Earlier, in Task 2.1, you created an OU called Hardened Servers. Right-click this OU and select Properties. Select the Group Policy tab.

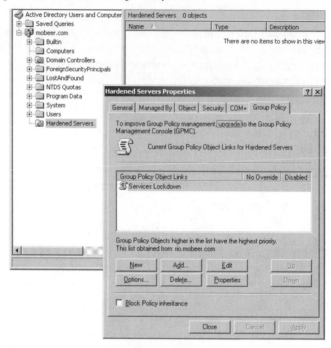

4. Click New and name the new GPO **WSUS Clients**.

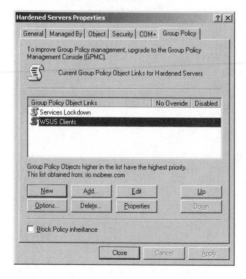

5. Click Edit. Expand the GPO to view Computer Configuration ➤ Administrative Templates ➤ Windows Components ➤ Windows Update. Review the various GPO configuration settings available. Notice the Explain tab on the properties of each setting.

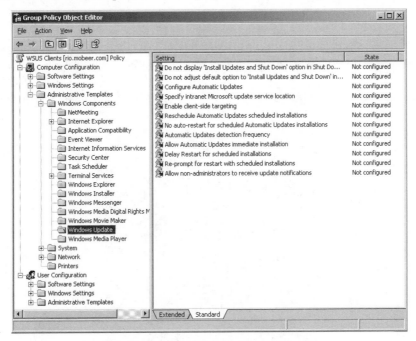

6. Double-click Configure Automatic Updates.

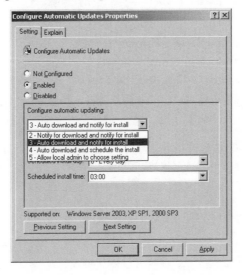

7. Enable the Configure Automatic Updates.

From the Configure Automatic Updating drop-down list, select Auto Download And Schedule The Install.

 The default configuration schedules the install at occur every day at 3:00 A.M. These settings are acceptable for the purposes of this task.

8. Click Next Setting. This brings up the Specify Intranet Microsoft Update Service Location Properties dialog box.

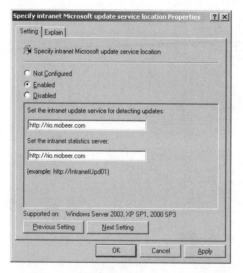

9. Enable the setting. Specify the WSUS server in the two fields. These fields must both be filled in and must follow the specified format:

- http://server: Hostname or IP address minimum
- http://server.domain.com: Fully qualified domain name (FQDN) preferred

 If the WSUS server is specified by name, name resolution services must be configured properly in your network environment.

10. Click OK.

These two are the minimum required settings to configure clients to use the WSUS services. Feel free to configure additional settings as desired in your environment. When you have completed configuring these settings as desired, close the GPO by clicking the X in the upper-right corner.

 Only computer objects that reside in the Hardened Servers OU are subject to this GPO and these settings. Move the appropriate computer objects into this OU.

You have now configured systems to utilize the WSUS services and automatically receive approved updates.

Criteria for Completion

You have completed this task when you have manually performed updates by going to the Microsoft Update website; configured clients to automatically download and install updates; configured WSUS to synchronize the update list; approved selected (and tested) updates; and configured clients to receive WSUS approved updates by GPO.

Task 2.3 addresses several objectives of the Security+ Exam, including objectives 3.1 and 3.5. The Security+ Exam Objectives can be downloaded from CompTIA's website at http://certification.comptia.org/security/.

Task 2.4: Security Templates

In a large network environment, the challenge of configuring security on many systems can be daunting. Configuring a security template and deploying this standardized security configuration simultaneously to many systems can simplify this process substantially.

Scenario

You have just completed assembling 20 Server 2003 systems for a new department. These systems require a specialized and uniform security configuration. You must develop and deploy a custom security template to these systems.

Scope of Task

Duration

This task should take 90 minutes.

Setup

Security templates can be reviewed, developed, and deployed from a single system in the environment. A convenient system to use for this process is a domain controller, since it has all of the required tools already installed.

Caveat

The deployment of security templates can cause serious problems in networks. These are powerful controls, which can severely restrict functionality of the systems. Use caution and test these templates prior to deployment. If you've ever locked yourself out of your car or house, you understand the seriousness of this caveat.

Procedure

You will configure a custom security template and incorporate it into a GPO for deployment to your specialized systems.

Equipment Used

For this task, you need the following equipment:

- Windows Server 2003 system, domain controller

Details

You will first build an MMC with the proper security-related snap-ins. You will then do a quick review of the default templates supplied by Microsoft. Then you will launch the Security Configuration and Analysis Tool (SCAT), and create a custom template that meets your specialized security needs. Lastly, you will deploy the security template by GPO to the target systems for a uniform security configuration.

Security MMC and Default Templates

1. Log on to the Windows Server 2003 domain controller as a Domain Administrator.
2. From the Start menu, select Run. Type **MMC** and click OK.
3. In the MMC – Console1, select File ➤ Add/Remove Snap-in.
4. Click Add.
5. In the Add Standalone Snap-in dialog box, scroll down and select Security Configuration and Analysis, then click Add.

6. In the Add Standalone Snap-in dialog box, select Security Templates and click Add.

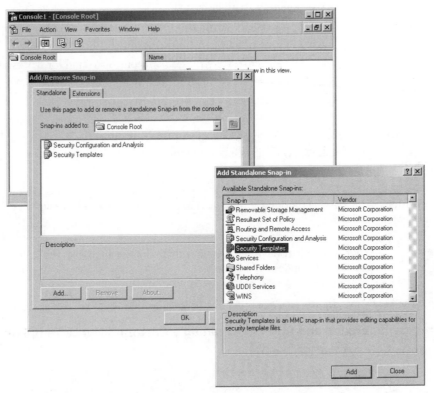

7. Click Close, then click OK.

8. Expand Security Templates: C:\WINDOWS\security\templates.

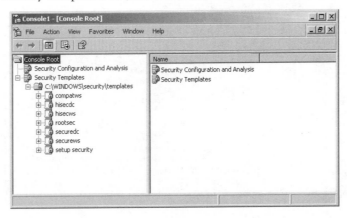

9. Microsoft provides several default security templates during installation. They are contained in files with an .inf extension in the path indicated.

    ▪   Setup Security—Configures security settings to match a fresh install of the operating system.

    ▪   Securedc and Securews—Stronger security for domain controllers and for workstations and servers, respectively.

    ▪   Hisecdc and Hiscews—Still stronger security for domain controllers and for workstations and servers, respectively.

    ▪   Compatws—Weakens permissions on the files and folders under the Windows folder to match that of Windows NT 4. This level of permissions may be required to run legacy (NT 4) applications.

    ▪   Rootsec—Resets folder permissions on the root of volumes to the original, default permissions. This may be required if these permissions have gotten erroneously adjusted.

NOTE   Your system may have slightly different templates available. These, however, are a fairly standard collection.

10. Save the MMC by selecting File ➢ Save As, then name the file **Security.msc** and click Save.

Security Configuration and Analysis: Creating a Custom Security Template

1. Click on Security Configuration And Analysis.

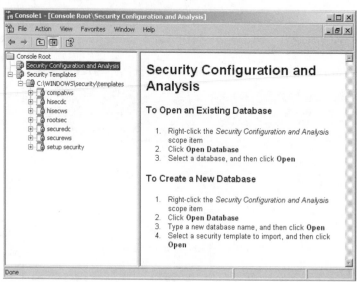

2.   In the left-hand pane, right-click on Security Configuration And Analysis and select Open Database. Type the name **Hardened Servers**, and click Open.

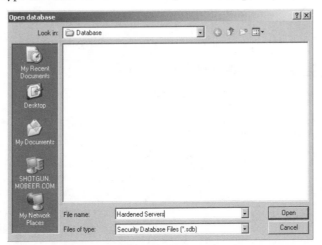

3.   Next, select the `securews.inf` default security template.

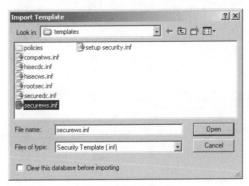

4.   Click Open.

WARNING   Do not select Configure Computer Now. Doing so would implement this strong security template on the system you are currently working on. This could cause the failure of desired functionality and could disable you from accessing the system.

5. In the left-hand pane, right-click on Security Configuration And Analysis and select Analyze Computer Now.

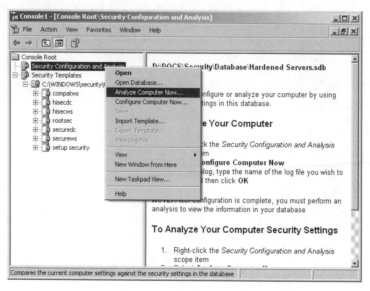

6. Accept the default path for log files by clicking OK.

7. Once the analysis is complete (this should take just a few seconds), expand Local Policies and select Audit Policy.

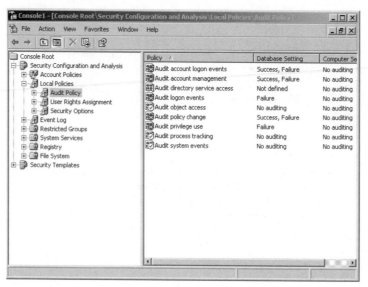

8. Double-click Audit Process Tracking Policy in the right-hand pane. Enable the policy and configure it for Success and Failure.

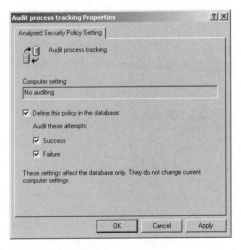

9. Click OK.

You have just customized the security template. You could make additional configuration changes, as desired, for this new, custom template.

10. Once you have introduced all of the desired security configuration parameters for the new, custom template, in the left-hand pane right-click on Security Configuration And Analysis and select Save.

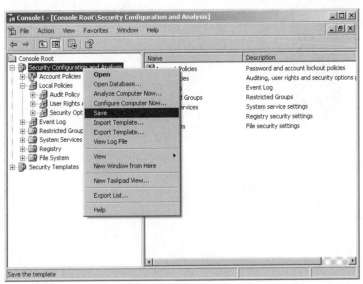

11. Right-click on Security Configuration And Analysis and select Export Template.

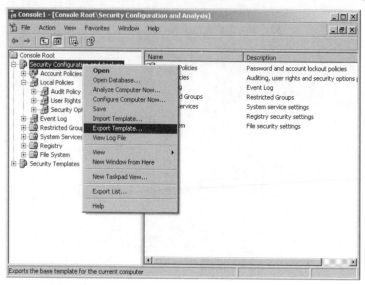

12. Type the name **Hardened Servers** and accept the default extension .inf by clicking Save.

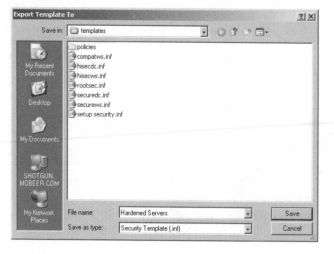

 This template is now available in the folder C:\WINDOWS\security\templates.

Security Template Deployment by GPO

1. From Administrative Tools, launch Active Directory Users And Computers.

2. Earlier, you created an OU called Hardened Servers. Right-click this OU and select Properties. Select the Group Policy tab.

3. Click New and name the new GPO **HS Security Template**.

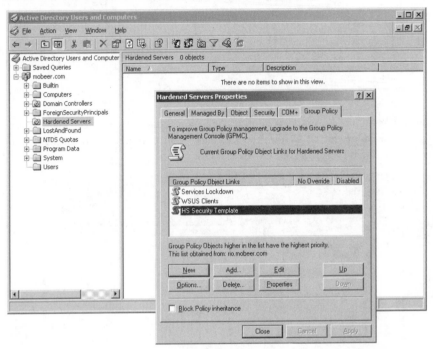

4. Click Edit. Expand the GPO to view Computer Configuration ➢ Windows Settings and click on Security Settings.

5. Right-click on Security Settings and select Import Policy.

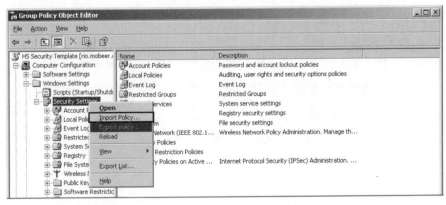

6. Select the Hardened Servers.inf template and click Open.

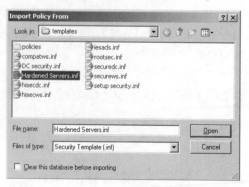

7. Expand Local Policies and select Audit Policy. You should observe your custom setting of Success and Failure for the Audit Process Tracking audit policy. Confirm the presence of any other template settings you may have configured.

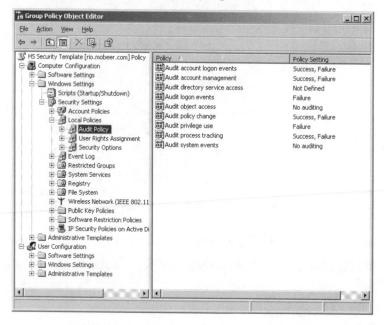

8. Close the GPO by clicking the X in the upper-right corner.

Any computer account you place in the Hardened Servers OU is now subject to this new security template.

Criteria for Completion

You have completed this task when you have built the Security MMC and reviewed the default security templates; imported a template into the SCAT tool; analyzed the local system security; modified, saved, and exported the new, custom template; and then imported the custom template into a GPO for mass deployment of these custom security settings.

Task 2.4 addresses several objectives of the Security+ Exam, including objectives 3.1 and 3.5. The Security+ Exam Objectives can be downloaded from CompTIA's website at http://certification.comptia.org/security/.

Task 2.5: Securing Autoruns

Autoruns are applications and processes that are configured to launch at boot-up or at logon. There are several ways to cause this to happen. These applications and processes are generally performing desirable activities; however, they may contain vulnerabilities, be specifically planted to introduce vulnerabilities, or even perform destructive processes. It is therefore a wise thing for an administrator or security professional to understand exactly what applications and processes are configured to autorun and to control these processes carefully.

In addition to the procedures outlined in Task 2.5, there are several utilities that may be useful in the identification and management of auto-running applications and processes.

In Microsoft's recently released Windows Defender, on the Tools and Settings page, Software Explorer presents several categories of programs that are currently running on a system including Startup Applications. Windows Defender can be downloaded from http://www.microsoft.com/athome/security/spyware/software/default.mspx.

Another worthy tool to assist with this administrative task is from Sysinternals called Autoruns. This freeware tool can be downloaded from http://www.sysinternals.com/Utilities/Autoruns.html.

Scenario

You are an administrator responsible for the maintenance and security of several servers holding sensitive data. You want to identify the autorun applications and processes and be certain that no undesirable applications or processes are running on these systems.

Scope of Task

Duration

This task should take 60 minutes.

Setup

You will interrogate a system for any autorun applications or processes and attempt to identify them. To accomplish this you will utilize several utilities and look in several locations on the system. You will also interrogate a domain controller to identify any startup, logon, logoff, and shutdown scripts that may be configured.

Caveat

Removing any autorun applications or processes may cause desirable applications and processes to fail. Often, these executables are not obviously named to identify their function. Remove these autorun applications or processes cautiously and test the system after the removal process.

Procedure

You will begin the system interrogation by launching MSConfig, the System Configuration Utility. You will then use Regedit to identify any Run, RunOnce, and RunOnceEx settings. You'll look at the Startup folders for users on the system, the Config.sys and Autoexec.bat files (for Win16 applications, processes, and drivers), and finish by looking at a domain controller to identify any startup, logon, logoff, and shutdown scripts that may be configured.

Win16 applications were written to run on Windows For Workgroups, version 3.11. All versions of Windows provide support for these legacy applications. Win16 apps use the Config.sys and Autoexec.bat files to configure the system environment for these applications.

Equipment Used

For this task, you need the following equipment:

- Any Windows XP or Server 2003 system
- For the startup, logon, logoff, and shutdown scripts that may be configured, access to a Server 2003 domain controller
- Local or Domain Administrator access

Details

MSCONFIG: THE MICROSOFT SYSTEM CONFIGURATION UTILITY

1. Log on to a system as a Local or Domain Administrator.

2. Select Start ➤ Run and type **MSConfig**. Click OK.

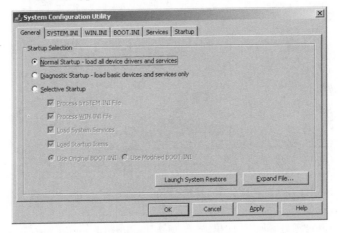

3. On the General tab, notice the various startup options available.

4. Select the SYSTEM.INI tab. This file is processed any time a Win16 application is launched.

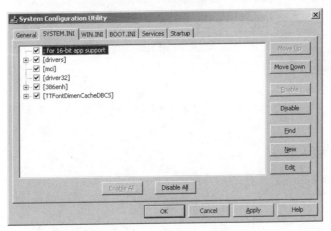

5. Select the WIN.INI tab. This file is also processed any time a Win16 application is launched.

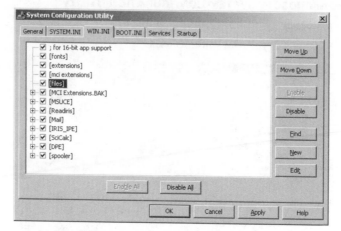

6. Review these files to identify any applications, processes, or drivers that may be undesirable.

7. Select the BOOT.INI tab. This file provides the Startup menu as you power on a system. Confirm that the paths and default are mapped to desired instances of the operating system.

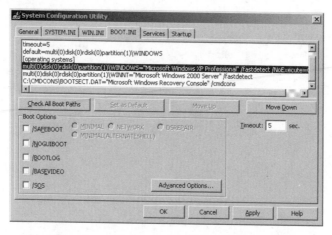

8. Select the Services tab. Review these services to identify any that may be undesirable. Managing services was covered in Task 2.1.

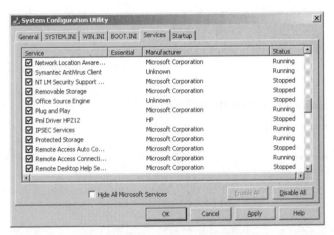

9. Finally, select the Startup tab. This is a list of applications and processes that launch at startup or logon, configured in the Registry and in the All Users Startup folder.

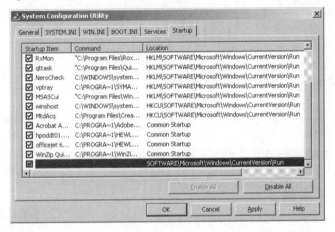

Review this list. Any applications or processes that you do not recognize can be further researched at the following website: http://www.processlibrary.com/.

Another website that may be able to identify unknown processes is http://www.windowsstartup.com/wso/search.php.

10. Clear the checkbox for any applications or processes that are undesirable.

If the executable is identified as being malicious in nature, it might be prudent to uninstall the application, delete the entry from the Registry, and/or delete the content from the hard drive.

11. Notice the Location column. This identifies the source of execution for the process: the Registry and the All Users Startup folder.

12. Click OK to apply your changes and close the MSConfig application. For your changes to take effect immediately, reboot the system as prompted. Otherwise, select Don't Reboot.

REGEDIT RUN, RUNONCE, AND RUNONCEEX

1. Select Start ➤ Run and type **regedit**. Click OK.

Improper editing of the Registry could cause your system, applications, and/or processes to fail. Make changes *only* if you are certain of your actions.

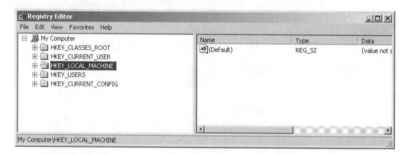

2. Expand HKEY_LOCAL_MACHINE ➤ SOFTWARE ➤ Microsoft ➤ Windows ➤ Current-Version ➤ Run.

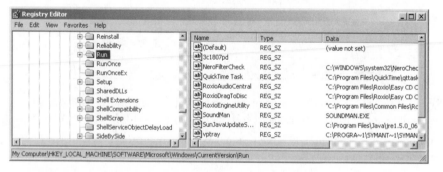

3. Expand HKEY_LOCAL_MACHINE ➤ SOFTWARE ➤ Microsoft ➤ Windows ➤ Current-Version ➤ RunOnce.

4. Expand HKEY_LOCAL_MACHINE ➤ SOFTWARE ➤ Microsoft ➤ Windows ➤ Current-Version ➤ RunOnceEx.

5. Review the entries in these three locations to identify applications and processes that launch at system startup.

6. After a careful review, in the right-hand pane, right-click on any undesirable applications or processes and select Delete.

 Improper editing of the Registry could cause your system, applications, and/or processes to fail. Make changes *only* if you are certain of your actions.

7. Expand HKEY_USERS ➤ DEFAULT ➤ Software ➤ Microsoft ➤ Windows ➤ Current-Version ➤ Run.

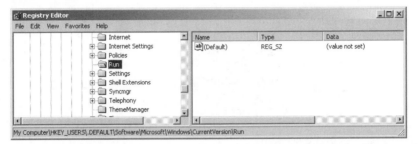

8. Review this location to identify applications and processes that launch at every user logon.

9. After a careful review, in the right-hand pane right-click on any undesirable applications or processes and select Delete.

 Improper editing of the Registry could cause your system, applications, and/or processes to fail. Make changes *only* if you are certain of your actions.

10. Expand HKEY_CURRENT_USER ➤ Software ➤ Microsoft ➤ Windows ➤ Current-Version ➤ Run.

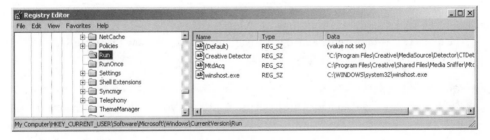

11. Expand HKEY_CURRENT_USER ➤ Software ➤ Microsoft ➤ Windows ➤ Current-Version ➤ RunOnce.

12. Review these two locations to identify applications and processes that launch at user logon.

13. After a careful review, in the right-hand pane right-click on any undesirable applications or processes and select Delete.

 WARNING Improper editing of the Registry could cause your system, applications, and/or processes to fail. Make changes *only* if you are certain of your actions.

14. Close Regedit.

STARTUP FOLDER

1. Right-click on the Start button and select Explore All Users.

2. Expand Programs and select Startup.

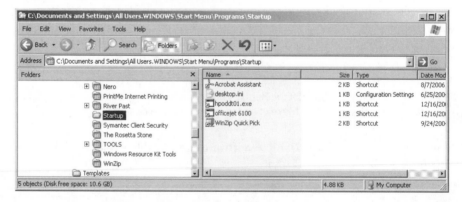

3. The items in this folder will launch with every user logon. Review these items and delete any that are undesirable by right-clicking on the item and selecting Delete.

 WARNING Improper editing of the Registry could cause your system, applications, and/or processes to fail. Make changes *only* if you are certain of your actions.

4. Right-click on the Start button and select Explore.

5. Expand Programs and select Startup.

6. The items in this folder will launch when the currently logged-on user logs on. Review these items and delete any that are undesirable by right-clicking on the item and selecting Delete.

Improper editing of the Registry could cause your system, applications, and/or processes to fail. Make changes *only* if you are certain of your actions.

AUTOEXEC AND CONFIG FILES

1. `Autoexec.nt` and `Config.nt` are in the `Windows\System32` folder and are triggered when a DOS or Win16 application is launched. They configure the DOS or Win16 (`WoWExec`) environment. These files can be used to launch applications or processes, drivers, or services.

   `Autoexec.bat` and `Config.sys` are in the root of the `C:\` drive and are used when the system is booted into down-level operating systems. These files can be used to launch applications or processes, drivers, or services.

2. Launch Explorer. Select the root of the `C:\` drive. In the right-hand pane, locate and click once on `Autoexec.bat`. Right-click on `Autoexec.bat` and select Edit.

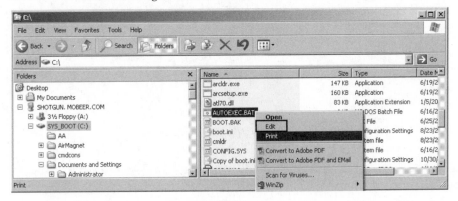

3. Review `Autoexec.bat` to identify any applications and processes that are being launched. If you identify any undesirable applications or processes, you can remark out the line by placing REM as the first characters of the line followed by a tab, or you can delete the line.

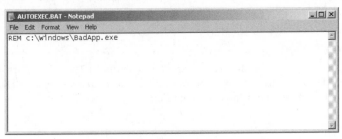

4. Select File ➢ Save.

5. Close the `Autoexec.bat` file in Notepad.

6. Repeat this process for `C:\Config.sys`, `C:\Windows\System32\Autoexec.nt`, and `C:\Windows\System32\Config.nt`.

STARTUP, LOGON, LOGOFF AND SHUTDOWN SCRIPTS

1. For this task, you will need to log on to a domain controller as a Domain Administrator.

2. After logging in to a domain controller as a Domain Administrator, launch Explorer.

3. Expand the drive containing the system files. Drill down to the following path:

   `Windows\SYSVOL\sysvol\DomainName.com\scripts`

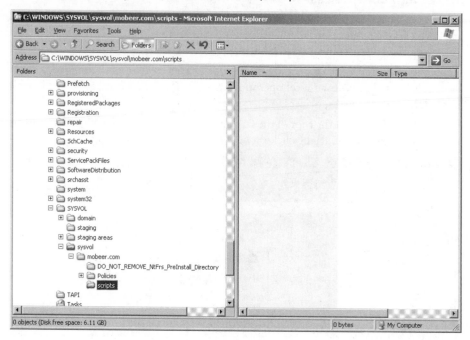

WARNING   Inappropriate modification or deletion of these scripts may cause system services and/or processes to fail. Do not modify any script that you do not fully understand.

NOTE   This folder should already be shared as the NETLOGON share. This folder may be empty in your environment, but it is the location for all startup, logon, logoff, and shutdown scripts to be deployed by GPOs.

NOTE   Any scripts located here should be interrogated to confirm that they execute desired processes and do not execute undesirable processes. Edit these scripts as appropriate.

4. When you have interrogated and confirmed the validity of all entries in all scripts, save your work and close Explorer.

5. Log off the domain controller.

Criteria for Completion

You have completed this task when you have reviewed and appropriately adjusted autorun applications and processes located in the Registry, startup folders, and initialization (.INI, .BAT, .SYS, and .NT) files and scripts.

Task 2.5 addresses several objectives of the Security+ Exam, including objectives 1.3 and 3.1. The Security+ Exam Objectives can be downloaded from CompTIA's website at http://certification.comptia.org/security/.

Phase

3

Protecting Against Malware

This phase of the book addresses some of the threats a security administrator must deal with on a day-to-day basis. Just one of these concerns is *malware*, which includes viruses, worms, Trojans, and spyware.

In this phase, we will teach you the hands-on skills you need to address these concerns and show you how to tackle them. Specifically, you will learn how to use antivirus software, run a rootkit checker, and check for various types of spyware.

The tasks in this phase map to Domains 1 and 2 objectives in the CompTIA Security+ exam (http://certification.comptia.org/security/).

Task 3.1: Installing, Updating, and Running Antivirus Software

Viruses date back to the 1980s when Fred Cohan originated the term. Viruses depend on people to spread them. Worms, while closely related to viruses, spread without human intervention. Viruses propagate through three basis means:

Master boot record infection   The original method of attack that works by attacking the master boot record (MBR) of floppy disks or the hard drive. It's now considered ineffective because so few people pass around floppy disks.

File infection   A slightly newer form of virus propagation that relies on the user to execute the file. Extensions such as .com and .exe are typically used. Social engineering is needed to get the user to execute the program.

Macro infection   This is the most modern of the three types and began appearing in the 1990s. Macro viruses exploit scripting services installed on your computer. The "I Love You" virus was a prime example of a macro infector. It was released in 2000.

Protection against computer viruses is one of the most important and basic security countermeasures that you can deploy. Some individuals think that deployment of an antivirus is enough. Well, that is not true—having an out-of-date antivirus program is little better than none at all.

Scenario

You have just completed the building of a new system for a client. You are now going to install and update the antivirus program. You will then make an initial scan with the antivirus program to make sure the system is clean and ready to be delivered to the client.

Scope of Task

Duration

This task should take about 30 minutes.

Setup

For this task, you will need a Windows workstation or server. You will also need to download the free avast! antivirus software from `http://www.avast.com`.

Caveat

Most antivirus programs do not scan for or prevent spyware. Make sure you understand what the antivirus will and will not prevent.

Procedure

In this task, you will install, update, and scan a system for viruses using the avast! antivirus scanning software. avast! is an example of a signature-scanning antivirus program. Signature-scanning antivirus programs work in a similar fashion as intrusion detection system (IDS) pattern-matching systems. Signature-scanning antivirus software looks at the beginning and end of executable files for known virus signatures. Signatures are nothing more than a series of bytes found in the virus's code.

Equipment Used

For this task, you must have:

- A Windows XP or Windows Server class system
- A Local Administrator account

Details

The following sections guide you through installing, updating, and running an antivirus program.

Downloading and Installing the avast! Antivirus Tool

1. After logging on as a Local Administrator, open Internet Explorer and go to `http://www.avast.com/eng/download-avast-home.html` and download the current version of the software.

2. You will be prompted to open or save the application. Click Open.

3. When the download is completed you will be prompted with the avast! setup screen. Click Next to continue.

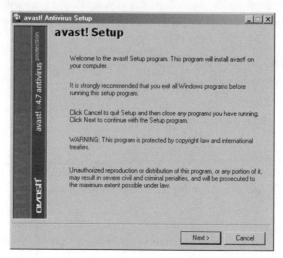

4. You will be prompted to read the avast! Read Me file. This file contains basic information, such as the minimum requirements for installation. Take a few minutes to review this information.

5. You will be prompted to review the license agreement. Click Agree to continue.

6. avast! will now prompt you to choose a destination directory. Please leave it as suggested, `C:\program files\alwil software\avast4`.

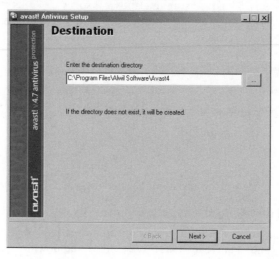

7. Before the installation, the program will prompt you to select the installed configuration. Click Typical.

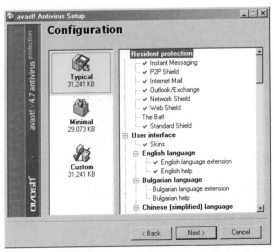

8. Once the installation is completed you will be prompted to reboot the computer. Please do so now.

Updating avast! Antivirus

Although most antivirus programs periodically check for updates, it is still a good idea to make sure you have the most recent version. This is particularly important when performing a new installation or when you have been asked to check a system for viruses.

1. To begin the update process, right-click the avast! icon that is located on the desktop tray at the bottom-right corner of the screen.

2. You should now see a menu of options, which includes updating. There are two options: AVS Update, which allows you to update the signature file, and Program Update, which is the antivirus program file. As you have just downloaded the program, you should have the most current version of the program. Click iAVS Update.

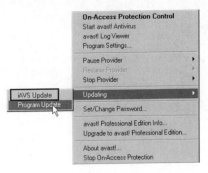

3. After waiting a short period of time, you should receive a message that the signatures have been updated.

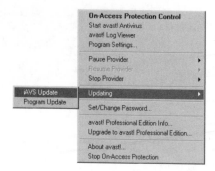

4. Click Close in the summary window to complete this task.

Performing an Antivirus Scan

1. Right-click on the avast! icon that is located on the desktop tray at the bottom-right corner of the screen and select Start avast! Antivirus. The avast! antivirus scan will start by examining the memory.

2. Once the memory check is completed, you'll be presented with the avast! antivirus user interface. There are six icons on this interface (via the three located on each side of the center information display). These include:

Virus Chest   Examines quarantined files

Resident Scanner   Sets the sensitivity of the scanner

iAvs   Updates the antivirus definitions

Local Disks   Chooses local disks to scan

Removable Media   Chooses removable media to scan

Folder Selection   Chooses specific folders to scan

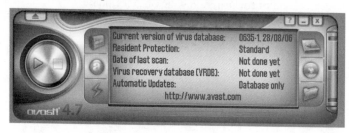

3. Select the Local Disks option. Select Standard Scan, and then click the Start button located on the left side of the interface. The program will then start scanning the selected drive. If a virus is found, a warning will appear.

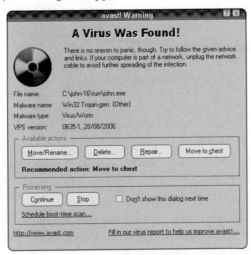

4. Once the scan is completed, you will be prompted with a report telling you what was found. In this example scan, eight programs were found.

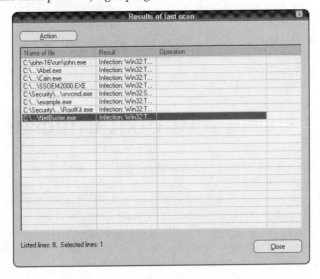

Testing the avast! Antivirus Tool

The purpose of this portion of the exercise is to give you a better understanding of how signature antivirus works.

1. Copy the following into a text file and rename it **samplevirus.exe**:

   X5O!P%@AP[4\PZX54(P^)7CC)7$EICAR-STANDARD-ANTIVIRUS-TEST-FILE!$H+H*

2. Start avast! and scan for viruses. In a few moments you should notice that avast! finds the file and identifies it as a virus.

While it is not actually a virus and the code is harmless, it does match a known virus signature. The code was developed by the European Institute of Computer Antivirus Research (EICER) to use to test the functionality of antivirus software.

In real life, virus creators attempt to circumvent the antivirus signature process by making viruses polymorphic.

Criteria for Completion

You have completed this task when you have accomplished the steps in this exercise. You will then know how to install an antivirus, how to update an antivirus, and how to use an antivirus program to scan for viruses.

Task 3.2: Using a Rootkit Checker

As a security professional it is of the utmost importance that you maintain control of your systems and be able to detect whether an attacker has compromised any of your systems. One of the most common tools an attacker will use is a *rootkit*. Rootkits are nasty pieces of malware. Attackers use rootkits to gain control of a victim's system. Rootkits contain tools to replace executables for many of the operating system's critical components. Once an attacker has installed a rootkit, it can be used to hide evidence of the bad guy's presence and gives them backdoor access to the system at will. Once the rootkit is installed, the attacker can come and go at any time and their activities will be hidden from the administrator. Some rootkits even contain log cleaners that attempt to remove all traces of an attacker's presence from the log files.

Rootkits can be divided into two basic types. Traditionally, rootkits replaced binaries, such as ls, ifconfig, inetd, killall, login, netstat, passwd, pidof, or ps with Trojaned versions. These Trojaned versions have been written to hide certain processes or information from the administrator. The second type of rootkit is the loadable kernel module

(LKM). A kernel rootkit is loaded as a driver or kernel extension. Both types can be a real problem. If you suspect that a computer has been infected with a rootkit, you will need to run a rootkit checker on the system to ensure that it has not been compromised. This will be the objective for this task.

Scenario

You have been asked to examine a Linux server by one of your clients. Your client is worried that a former employee may have compromised the system by installing a rootkit on it before quitting. Your task will be to examine the system and verify its integrity.

Scope of Task

Duration

This task should take about 30 minutes.

Setup

For this task you will need a Linux computer and an Internet connection, and you must have the ability to download files.

Caveat

When working with the Linux system, you will need access to the root account. You will want to use this account carefully. The root account has full and complete control of the Linux system. The root account has complete access to all files and commands and can modify the system in any way desired and to grant and revoke any permissions. Unlike with Windows systems, you may not be prompted several times before a critical change is made.

Procedure

In this task, you will learn how to run a rootkit checker on a Linux system.

Equipment Used

For this task, you must have:

- A Linux system (such as Red Hat or equivalent)
- A CD-based version of Linux such as BackTrack or Knoppix
- Access to the root account

Details

This task will progress through several steps. First, you must download the rootkit checker and install it. Then you will execute it and examine its various options. The tool used in this task is Rootkit Hunter. Rootkit Hunter is an open source tool that checks machines running Linux for the presence of rootkits and other unwanted tools. You can learn more about Rootkit Hunter by visiting the site at `http://www.rootkit.nl/projects/rootkit_hunter.html`.

Downloading and Installing Rootkit Hunter

1. Once you have accessed your Linux system, you will need to open a root terminal and download the Rootkit Hunter. To do so, you must enter the following at the command-line shell:

```
wget http://downloads.rootkit.nl/rkhunter-version.tar.gz
```

The *version* syntax will require you to enter the current version of the software. As an example, at the time of this writing version 1.2.8 is the most current version, so you would enter **rkhunter-1.2.8.tar.gz**.

2. Once the download is completed, you will need to unpack the archived file. Enter the following from the command line:

```
tar zxf rkhunter-version.tar.gz
```

This will extract the Rootkit Hunter files.

3. To install Rootkit Hunter, you first will need to change directories. This will be the one below your current location. Enter **cd rkhunter**.

4. Once you are in the proper directory, you now will need to run the installer. This will complete the installation. Enter **./installer.sh**.

5. You should be able to see that the installation was successfully completed. This code shows the type of syntax of a successful installation:

```
Rootkit Hunter installer 1.2.4 (Copyright 2003-2005, Michael
Boelen)
----------------
Starting installation/update

Checking /usr/local... OK
Checking file retrieval tools... /usr/bin/wget
Checking installation directories...
- Checking /usr/local/rkhunter...Exists
- Checking /usr/local/rkhunter/etc...Exists
- Checking /usr/local/rkhunter/bin...Exists
- Checking /usr/local/rkhunter/lib/rkhunter/db...Exists
```

```
- Checking /usr/local/rkhunter/lib/rkhunter/docs...Exists
- Checking /usr/local/rkhunter/lib/rkhunter/scripts...Exists
- Checking /usr/local/rkhunter/lib/rkhunter/tmp...Exists
- Checking /usr/local/etc...Exists
- Checking /usr/local/bin...Exists
Checking system settings...
- Perl... OK
Installing files...
Installing Perl module checker... OK
Installing Database updater... OK
Installing Portscanner... OK
Installing MD5 Digest generator... OK
Installing SHA1 Digest generator... OK
Installing Directory viewer... OK
Installing Database Backdoor ports... OK
Installing Database Update mirrors... OK
Installing Database Operating Systems... OK
Installing Database Program versions... OK
Installing Database Program versions... OK
Installing Database Default file hashes... OK
Installing Database MD5 blacklisted files... OK
Installing Changelog... OK
Installing Readme and FAQ... OK
Installing Wishlist and TODO... OK
Installing RK Hunter configuration file... Skipped (no
overwrite)
Installing RK Hunter binary... OK
Configuration already updated.

Installation ready.
See /usr/local/rkhunter/lib/rkhunter/docs for more
information.
Run 'rkhunter' (/usr/local/bin/rkhunter)
```

Running Rootkit Hunter

1. Once Rootkit Hunter is installed, you are ready to run it. A variety of options are available to you. To perform a complete check of the system, run Rkhunter --checkall.

2.   Rootkit Hunter can search for many different types of rootkits. Here is a partial list:

5808 Trojan—Variant A	Ni0 Rootkit
Ambient (ark) Rootkit	NSDAP (Rootkit for SunOS)
Apache Worm	Optic Kit (Tux)
Balaur Rootkit	Oz Rootkit
Beastkit	Portacelo
beX2	R3dstorm Toolkit
BOBKit	RH-Sharpe's rootkit
CiNIK Worm (Slapper.B variant)	RSHA's Rootkit
Devil Rootkit	Scalper Worm
Dica	Shutdown
Dreams Rootkit	SHV4 Rootkit
Duarawkz Rootkit	SHV5 Rootkit
Flea Linux Rootkit	Sin Rootkit
FreeBSD Rootkit	Slapper
GasKit	Sneakin Rootkit
Heroin LKM	SunOS Rootkit
HjC Rootkit	Superkit
ignoKit	TBD (Telnet BackDoor)
ImperalsS-FBRK	TeLeKiT
Irix Rootkit	T0rn Rootkit
Kitko	Trojanit Kit
Knark	URK (Universal Rootkit)
Li0n Worm	VcKit
Lockit/LJK2	Volc Rootkit
mod_rootme (Apache backdoor)	X-Org SunOS Rootkit
MRK	zaRwT.KiT Rootkit

3. Once the scan is completed, you should receive a message that is similar to the following:

```
-------------------------- Scan results ----------------------

MD5
MD5 compared: 0
Incorrect MD5 checksums: 0

File scan
Scanned files: 342
Possible infected files: 0

Application scan
Vulnerable applications: 4

Scanning took 15748 seconds


--------------------------------------------------------------


Do you have some problems, undetected rootkits, false
positives, ideas or suggestions?
Please e-mail me by filling in the contact form
(@http://www.rootkit.nl)


--------------------------------------------------------------
```

In this example you were lucky to find the system had not been infected, but if it had been, you would be faced with additional challenges. This is primarily due to the fact that it is almost impossible to clean up a rootkit. Since hiding is the main purpose of the rootkit, it is difficult to see whether all remnants of the infection have been removed. You should always rebuild from well-known, good media. Should you find a rootkit, the program will return a message similar to this:

```
-------------------------- Scan results ----------------------

MD5
MD5 compared: 0
Incorrect MD5 checksums: 0

File scan
Scanned files: 362
Possible infected files: 1
```

```
Netstat possible infected


  Application scan
  Vulnerable applications: 4


  Scanning took 14631 seconds


--------------------------------------------------------------------


  Do you have some problems, undetected rootkits, false
  positives, ideas or suggestions?
  Please e-mail me by filling in the contact form
  (@http://www.rootkit.nl)
```

Criteria for Completion

You have completed this task when you have downloaded Rootkit Hunter, installed it on a Linux system, and scanned the system for rootkits.

Task 3.3: Using Adware Checker

The Internet has certainly lived up to its reputation for being known as a dangerous place. We make this statement because by simply going to the wrong website or downloading the wrong program, you can end up with a system full of *adware*. Adware is usually bundled with a shareware of free programs. And from a programmer's point of view, it is a way to recoup some of the program's development cost.

What is particularly annoying about most adware is the way it causes constant pop-ups on your computer, or redirects you to other sites for which you do not care to visit. These programs can even degrade system performance to the point of being unusable. Recent studies estimated that adware and anti-spyware protection solutions will rise to over $300 million by 2008.

Scenario

Your battle with malicious software is continuing. A manager has asked if you can look over several of his employees' computers. They are complaining that when they access the Internet their browsers subject them to an endless stream of pop-ups. You suspect their systems have been infected with adware.

Scope of Task

Duration

This task should take about 30 minutes.

Setup

For this task, you will need a Windows computer, access to the Administrator account, Internet connection, and the ability to download files.

Caveat

While removal programs for adware are quite efficient, you must be careful when asked to remove programs or components since this can cause a lack of functionality or can sometimes disable required components.

Procedure

In this task, you will learn how to install and run Ad-Aware.

Equipment Used

For this task, you must have:

- A Windows computer
- Access to the Administrator account
- An Internet connection

Details

This task will show you how to install and run Lavasoft's Ad-Aware. This program will allow you to remove adware and other types of malicious software. It has the ability to examine the registry, hard drives, and even system RAM for known data-mining, advertising, and tracking components.

Installing and Running AD-Aware

1. Once you have accessed your Windows computer and have logged in as Administrator, open your browser and go to `http://www.lavasoftusa.com/support/download/`.

   Once the program has completed downloading, execute it from the folder to which it was saved. This will start the installation process.

2. During the installation you will be prompted to accept the licensing agreement. You must accept this to complete the installation. Accept all other default settings to complete the installation. Once the installation is completed, Ad-Aware will then start.

3.   Upon startup, Ad-Aware will ask you to configure General Settings.

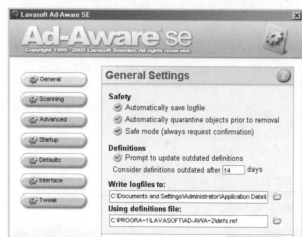

4.   You are now ready to start a scan. You can start by clicking the Scan Now button. After clicking Scan Now you will be prompted as to what type of scan you would like to perform.

▪   Smart scan

▪   Full system scan

▪   Custom scan

▪   Scan for alternate data streams (ADS)

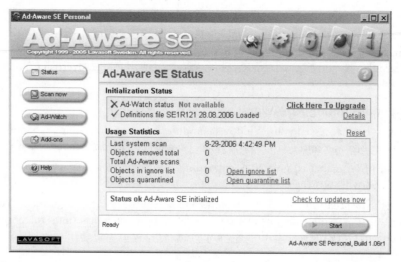

5. Depending on the size of the hard drive being scanned and the type of scan being performed, the scan can take 10 to 20 minutes. Once it's completed, you will receive a report that shows any recognized objects.

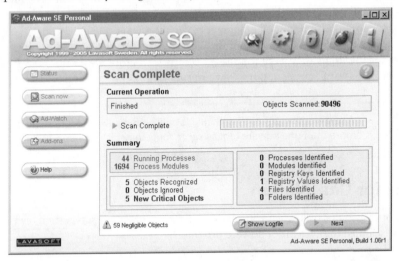

6. The next screen gives a more detailed listing of findings and will allow you to look a little closer as to what was discovered. You'll notice four tabs on this menu, which include:

Scan Summary   A summary of events

Critical Objects   Critical objects found are items that may pose a risk or have been identified to be associated with adware.

Negligible Objects   Objects found that pose little danger

Scan Log   A log of all scans that were run, including the date and time of each scan

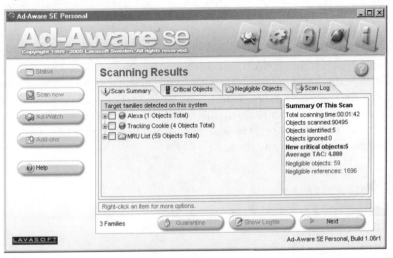

7. The final step in this process is to check for items you wish to remove. Review each item carefully before marking them for removal.

Ad-Aware is designed to report all possible suspicious content present on your system. This does not mean that everything that was detected by Ad-Aware should be removed. A security professional must use good judgment in deciding what must go or stay. To help you in this process, Ad-Aware has developed the Threat Assessment Chart (TAC). It lists the threat level for the items that were found. You can learn more about the TAC by visiting http://www.lavasoft.com/support/securitycenter/threat_analysis.php.

 When working with a system that is badly infected, we recommend that you use more than one adware tool as some tools may pick up items others may miss.

Criteria for Completion

You have completed this task when you have downloaded Ad-Aware, installed it on a Windows system, and scanned the system for adware programs.

Task 3.4: Using Spyware Checker

Spyware is much like adware except that has the ability to track your activities as you move about the Internet, as well as capture your keystrokes. This information can be returned to hackers or advertisers, who use it to track your visits to specific sites and to monitor your activity. Spyware programs have become increasingly intelligent. Many have the capability to install themselves in more than one location, and like a malignant disease, removing one piece of the malicious code triggers the software to spawn a new variant in a uniquely new location.

Spyware is capable of changing Registry entries and forcing a system to reinstall itself when the computer reboots. What are some of the worst spyware programs that you might be exposed to? Well, Webroot.com has compiled a list, and its top ten includes titles such as KeenValue, a program that collects user information to target them with specific pop-up ads. PurityScan is another; it advertises itself as a cleaner that removes items from your hard drive. Finally, there is CoolWebSearch. This program is actually a bundle of browser hijackers united only to redirect their victims to targeted search engines and flood them with pop-up ads. As a security professional, dealing with these types of programs is something you will be faced with many times.

Scenario

A coworker believes their computer is acting strangely and may be infected with spyware. You have been asked to investigate.

Scope of Task

Duration

This task should take about 30 minutes.

Setup

For this task, you will need a Windows computer, access to the Administrator account, an Internet connection, and the ability to download files.

Caveat

While spyware-removal programs are quite efficient, you must be careful when asked to remove programs or components since this can cause the lack of functionality of a required component.

Procedure

In this task, you will learn how to install and run Spybot-S&D.

Equipment Used

For this task, you must have:

- A Windows computer
- Access to the Administrator account
- An Internet connection

Details

This task will show you how to install and run Spybot-S&D. This program will allow you to remove spyware and other types of malicious software. It has the ability to do a thorough examination of your system, hard drive, Registry, and system RAM for known malicious programs.

Installing and Running Spybot-S&D

1. Once you have accessed your Windows computer and have logged in as Administrator, open your browser and go to http://www.safer-networking.org/en/download/index.html. Once you download the program, execute it from the folder to which it was saved. This will start the installation process.

2. During the installation you will be prompted to accept the licensing agreement. You must accept this to complete the installation. Continue with the setup and accept all other default settings to complete the installation. Once the installation is completed, Spybot-S&D will then start.

3. Upon startup, Spybot-S&D will start a wizard that will ask you several questions, including whether you would like to make a backup of your Registry settings. While this is not necessary, it is a good idea because it can offer an added level of protection should the program remove a component that another program needs.

4. At the main menu of the program are five options on the far-left side of the application:

    Search & Destroy   Searches for spyware and other malicious code.

    Recover   Allows you to undo any changes made.

    Immunize   Blocks known spyware and adds some preventive measures against malicious code.

    Update   Looks for program updates.

    Donations   As the program is provided freely, you can choose whether to make donations to the creator.

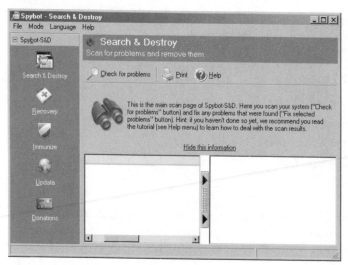

 With any antivirus, spyware, or malicious code scanner, you should always make sure you have the most current version.

5. From the main menu, begin the scan by selecting Search & Destroy and then clicking Check For Problems. The scan will start at this point.

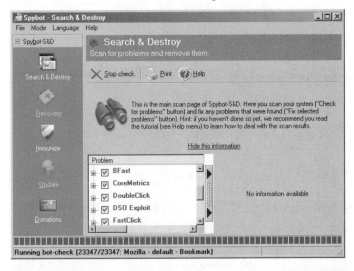

6. Once the scan is completed, you will have a list of the problems detected. Spend time looking through these. As you review each item you will be offered more details. This should give you what you need to make an intelligent choice about whether to remove or keep the item.

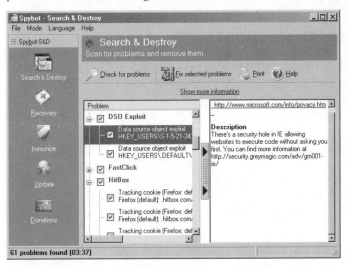

7. The final step in this process is to click the Fix Selected Problems button to check the items you wish to remove.

When working with a system that is badly infected, we recommend that you use more than one spyware tool as some tools may pick up items others may miss.

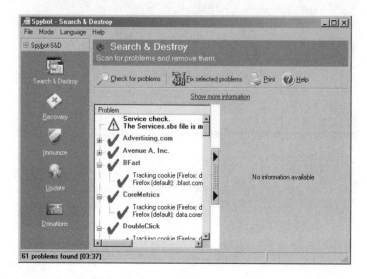

Criteria for Completion

You have completed this task when you have downloaded Spybot-S&D, installed it on a Windows system, and scanned the system for spyware programs.

Phase

4

Secure Storage

An important aspect of protecting your information and information systems has to do with the secure storage of your valuable information assets. In addition to the implementation of physical security controls, such as a locked server room, sensitive information should have tight permissions, and also be encrypted while in storage (on the hard drive). Therefore, encryption protects the confidentiality of your information assets. Further, because unauthorized users cannot access the encrypted information, they cannot make unauthorized changes to the information, thus protecting the integrity of the information.

Many encryption utilities and even devices are available that can help you secure your critical and sensitive information assets. One is GuardianEdge Technologies at www.guardianedge.com/. Another is PGP Corporation at www.pgp.com/. A manufacturer of encryption devices is L3 Titan Group at www.titan.com/.

Another aspect of protecting your information assets has to do with ensuring the availability of the information assets. You should be knowledgeable about fault-tolerant disk arrays, or RAID systems, and know how to perform routing backups and data recovery from backups to increase the availability of these assets.

The tasks in this phase map to Domains 2, 3, 4, and 5 objectives in the CompTIA Security+ exam (http://certification.comptia.org/security/).

Task 4.1: The Encrypting File System

Windows 2000 and above provides for this service on NTFS volumes. This is called the Encrypting File System (EFS). EFS operates as an additional layer of security, complementing both the NTFS and share point permissions on Windows systems.

EFS should be implemented for any sensitive data. Because of the increased frequency of portable devices being lost or stolen, it is especially important to implement EFS on laptop computers.

Scenario

You are responsible for the protection of sensitive information that often gets produced and utilized on company-owned laptop computers. On occasion, these laptops and sensitive files must be shared among several top-level executives of the company.

Scope of Task

Duration

This task should take approximately 2 hours.

Setup

You will create secured (encrypted) content and confirm that it is secure. Then you will provide access to this content for selected other user(s).

Caveat

With the addition of any securing technology, there will be an increase in administrative overhead to support that technology. It is possible that users will lock themselves out of their sensitive content, requiring a preconfigured data recovery agent (Local Administrator for Workgroup mode systems, configured manually, or the administrator of the domain for domain members, automatically configured) to decrypt the content.

 See Task 4.2 for detailed instructions on the data recovery procedure.

Further, there are combinations of events that can prevent decryption of the content. Data can be lost permanently.

As an administrator, implement EFS with care. If you implement EFS for your users, provide proper training and warnings to those users regarding these issues.

Procedure

For this task, you must first create the Data Recovery Agent policy.

Then you will need to create two users: User1 and User2. User1 will create and secure sensitive content. You will then log on as User2 and confirm that even though NTFS permissions should allow access to the content, EFS does not allow User2 to access the content.

Next you'll log on as User1 again, and add User2 to the list of users who can access the encrypted file.

Then you'll log back on as User2 and confirm that you now can access the encrypted content as User2.

Equipment Used

For this task, you need the following equipment:

- Windows XP Pro system with the following configuration:
    - A member of a workgroup (not a member of a domain)
    - At least one NTFS volume
- Local Administrator access

Details

Configuring the Volume for EFS

1. Log on the Windows XP Pro system as the Local Administrator.

2. Launch Explorer by right-clicking the Start button and selecting Explore.

3. Select the root of the C:\ drive in the left pane.

> You may have to enable viewing of the folders and files on the C:\ drive by selecting Show The Contents Of This Folder in the right pane.

4. Right-click on the C:\ drive and select Properties.

5. Confirm that the volume's filesystem is NTFS, then click OK.

> EFS is not available on any FAT filesystems, including floppy disks. It is only available on volumes formatted with NTFS.

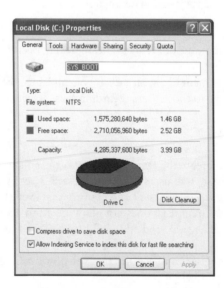

6. In the right pane, right-click in the white space and select New ➢ Folder. Name the folder **GOODSTUFF**.

7. Right-click the new GOODSTUFF folder and select Properties.

8. In the Properties dialog box, select the Security tab. Under Group Or User Names, select *ComputerName*\Users on the list of Group Or User Names, where *ComputerName* is the name of your computer.

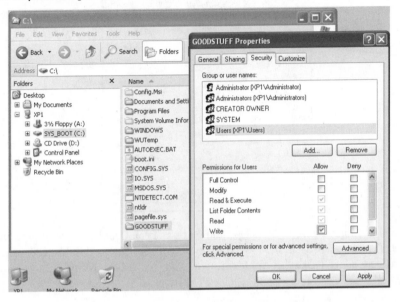

 In the case shown, the computer name is XP1.

9. Enable the Write permission under Permissions For Users. Click OK. You have now confirmed that the volume supports EFS and you have created a storage location for the local users of the system.

Creating Users

1. Right-click on My Computer and select Manage to open the Computer Management console.

2. Expand Local Users And Groups. Select the Users subfolder.

3. In the right pane, right-click in the white space and select New User.

4. Type **User1** for both User Name and Full Name. Type **Password1** in the Password and Confirm Password fields. Clear the option User Must Change Password At Next Logon,

and enable the options User Cannot Change Password and Password Never Expires. Click Create.

5. You will get a new, empty, New User dialog box. Type **User2** for User Name and Full Name. Type **Password1** in the Password and Confirm Password fields. Clear the option User Must Change Password At Next Logon, and enable both User Cannot Change Password and Password Never Expires. Click Create.

6. Click Close. Confirm the existence of the two new user accounts for User1 and User2.

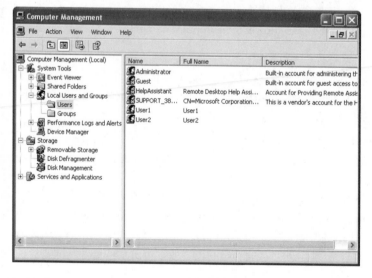

7. Minimize the Computer Management console by clicking the X in the upper-right corner.

Creating the EFS Data Recovery Agent Policy

1. To define an EFS Data Recovery Agent (DRA) policy, you must produce a DRA certificate for the local administrator. Still logged on as the local administrator, open a command window by selecting Start ➤ Run and entering **CMD**. Then click OK.

2. You will create a location to hold the certificates and view the properties of the command (Cipher) used to create the certificates. At the command prompt, enter the command **cd**. Press Enter, which returns you to the root of the C:\ drive.

3. At the command prompt, enter the command **md AA**. Press Enter to create a new folder called C:\AA.

4. At the command prompt, enter the command **cd AA**. Press Enter to place your focus in the new C:\AA folder.

5. At the command prompt, enter the following command and view the results:

   `Cipher /?`

6. To create the certificates required for EFS Data Recovery, at the command prompt enter this command:

   `cipher /R:c:\AA\AdminEFSDRA`

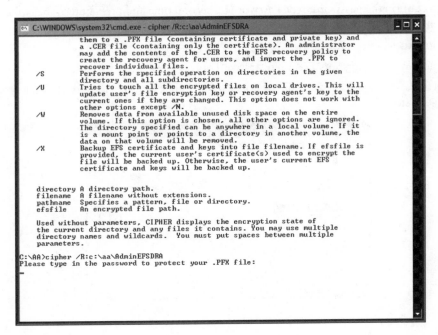

7. Type the password **Password1** and press Enter.

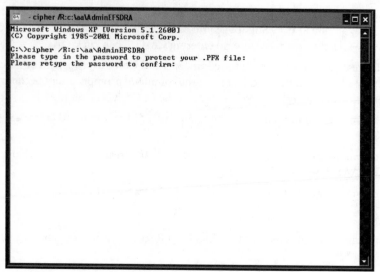

8. To confirm the password, type **Password1** a second time and press Enter. The two certificates for DRA are produced in the C:\AA folder.

9. Close the command window.

10. Select Start ➤ Programs ➤ Administrative Tools ➤ Local Security Policy.

11. In the Local Security Settings dialog box, expand Public Key Policies and select Encrypting File System.

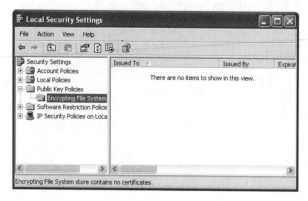

12. Right-click on Encrypting File System and select Add Data Recovery Agent. This launches the Add Recovery Agent Wizard. Click Next.

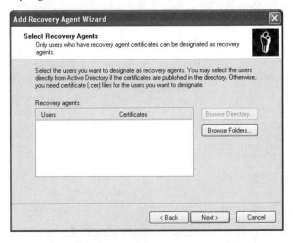

13. On the Select Recovery Agents screen, click the Browse Folders button and browse to C:\AA.

14. Select the file AdminEFSDRA.cer file that you just created with the Cipher command. Click Open. This pulls the certificate file into the Add Recovery Agent Wizard.

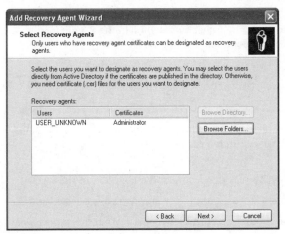

15. Click the Next button, and then click Finish.

16. Close the Local Security Settings dialog box.

17. Right-click the Start button and select Explore.

18. Open the folder C:\AA.

19. Right-click on the file `AdminEFSDRA.pfx` and select Install PFX.

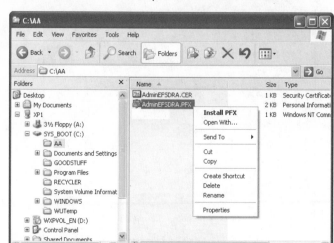

20. In the Certificate Import Wizard, click Next.

21. Confirm the certificate file with the `.PFX` extension is entered in the File Name field. Click Next.

The file name may be presented in the 8.3 file format: `C:\AA\ADMINE~1.PFX`. This is acceptable.

22. Enter the password **Password1** to access the private key associated with the certificate.

This password was implemented in the two certificates created with the `Cipher` command earlier.

23. Leave the two checkboxes deselected and click Next in the wizard.

24. Allow the Certificate Store location to be automatically selected and click Next in the wizard.

25. Click Finish. You should see a message reporting that the import was successful. Click OK to clear the message.

26. Log off as the Local Administrator by selecting Start ➢ Log Off Administrator.

27. You have now confirmed and configured the `C:\` drive for EFS, you created two users to implement EFS, and you have successfully configured the local administrator as the EFS Data Recovery Agent.

Creating EFS Content as User1

1. Log on to the local computer as User1 with the password Password1.

2. Launch Explorer by right-clicking the Start button and selecting Explore.

3. Select the root of the C:\ drive in the left pane.

> You may have to enable viewing of the folders and files on the C:\ drive by selecting Show The Contents Of This Folder in the right pane.

4. In the right pane, double-click the folder GOODSTUFF.

5. Right-click in the white space in the right pane and select New ➢ Text Document.

6. Rename the text document **Secrets.txt**.

7. Open `Secrets.txt` with Notepad and type a message.

8. Save `Secrets.txt` with the new content.

9. Close Notepad.

10. Right-click `Secrets.txt` and select Properties.

11. In the Properties dialog box, on the General tab click Advanced.

12. In the Advanced Attributes dialog box, enable the option Encrypt Contents To Secure Data.

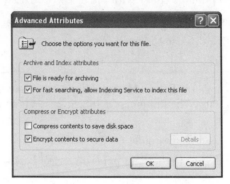

 Notice that if you also try to enable compression, the Encrypt Contents To Secure Data checkbox clears. Encryption and compression are mutually exclusive for content on NTFS volumes.

13. Click OK.

14. Click Apply in the Properties dialog box. You will be prompted to select between encrypting the folder and all content, or encrypting just this one file. Select Encrypt The File Only.

 EFS can be implemented for a single file at a time, or can be implemented at the folder level. When EFS is implemented at the folder level, any newly created files or folders in the EFS folder inherit the encryption attribute and will be encrypted with the key of the Owner/Creator of the new content.

15. Select the Security tab of the Properties dialog box. Select the Users group in the top pane. Notice that users of the local system have Read & Execute, Read, and Write permissions inherited from parent folders. Click OK,

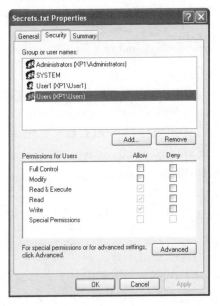

Notice in Explorer that Secrets.txt is displayed in green (the default color and settings).

16. Open Secrets.txt with Notepad and view your message to confirm that you can access the data, even though the file is now encrypted.

17. Close Notepad.

Attempting Access of EFS Content as User2

1. Log on to the local computer as User2 with the password Password1.

2. Launch Explorer by right-clicking the Start button and selecting Explore.

3. Select the root of the C:\ drive in the left pane.

You may have to enable viewing of the folders and files on the C:\ drive by selecting Show The Contents Of This Folder in the right pane.

4. In the right pane, double-click the folder GOODSTUFF.

5. Attempt to open Secrets.txt. Notepad launches, but even though you just confirmed that you have permission to read the Secrets.txt document, you get the error message Access is denied. EFS has this document encrypted so that only User1 can decrypt the file.

6. Click OK to clear the error message, and then close Notepad.

Creating EFS Content as User2

1. Still logged on as User2, in the GOODSTUFF folder in Explorer, right-click in the white space in the right pane and select New ➢ Text Document.

2. Rename the new text document **User2Secrets.txt**.

3. Open User2Secrets.txt with Notepad and type a message.

4. Save User2Secrets.txt with the new content.

5. Close Notepad.

6. Right-click User2Secrets.txt and select Properties.

7. Click Advanced.

8. Enable Encrypt Contents To Secure Data.

9. Click OK in the Advanced Attributes dialog box.

10. Click Apply in the User2Secrets.txt Properties dialog box. You will be prompted to select between encrypting the folder and all content, or encrypting just this one file. Select Encrypt The File Only.

In order for User1 to enable User2 to decrypt Secrets.txt, User2 must, at least on one file, enable EFS on this system. This generates the encryption key for User2, so that User1 can enable the access of Secrets.txt using User2's encryption key.

11. Select the Security tab of the Properties dialog box. Select the Users group in the top pane. Notice that users of the local system have Read & Execute, Read, and Write permissions inherited from parent folders.

12. Click OK.

13. Notice in Explorer that both files, Secrets.txt and User2Secrets.txt, are now displayed in green (the default color and settings).

14. Open User2Secrets.txt with Notepad and view your message to confirm that you can access the data, even though the file is now encrypted.

15. Close Notepad.

16. Log off as User2.

Sharing EFS Content to User2

1. Log on to the local computer as User1 with the password Password1.

2. Launch Explorer by right-clicking the Start button and selecting Explore.

3. Select the root of the C:\ drive in the left pane.

4. In the right pane, double-click the folder GOODSTUFF.

5. Open Secrets.txt with Notepad to confirm that User1 has access to the EFS content.

6. Close Notepad.

7. In Explorer, attempt to open User2Secrets.txt. Once again, Notepad launches, but even though you just confirmed that User1 has permissions to read the User2Secrets.txt document, you get the error message Access is denied. EFS has this document encrypted so that only User2 can decrypt the file.

8. Click OK to clear the error message, and then close Notepad.

9. In Explorer, right-click on Secrets.txt and select Properties.

10. Click Advanced.

11. Select Details. Notice that User1 is the only user listed as Users Who Can Transparently Access This File. Also notice that Administrator is listed as the Date Recovery Agent for Secrets.txt. This is the due to the EFS Data Recovery Agent policy you implemented earlier in this task.

12. Click Add.

13. Highlight User2.

14. Click View Certificate. This certificate for User2 holds User2's encryption key. With this key, User1 can grant User2 access to the EFS content, Secrets.txt. Close the certificate.

15. Click OK in the Select User dialog box.

16. Notice that now both User1 and User2 are listed as Users Who Can Transparently Access This File.

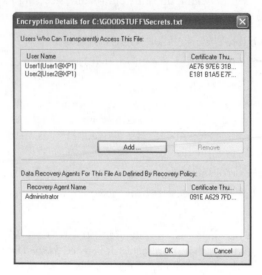

17. Click OK in the Encryption Details dialog box.

18. Click OK in the Advanced Attributes dialog box.

19. Click OK in the Secrets.txt Properties dialog box.

20. Open and view `Secrets.txt` to confirm that you still have access to the data.

21. Close `Secrets.txt`.

22. Log off as User1.

Attempting Access of EFS Content as User2

1. Log on to the local computer as User2 with the password Password1.

2. Launch Explorer by right-clicking the Start button and selecting Explore.

3. Select the root of the `C:\` drive in the left pane.

 You may have to enable viewing of the folders and files on the `C:\` drive by selecting Show The Contents Of This Folder in the right pane.

4. In the right pane, double-click the folder GOODSTUFF.

5. Attempt to open `Secrets.txt`. You now have access to the contents of `Secrets.txt` as User2.

6. Log off as User2.

Criteria for Completion

You have completed this task when you have created secure content and then confirmed that, even with appropriate permissions to view this content, other users cannot decrypt the content. After that, you configured the secured content to allow selected other users' access to this sensitive data, and then confirmed that those additional user(s) can access the encrypted data.

Task 4.2: EFS Data Recovery

One of the fundamental responsibilities of an administrator is to protect the company's information. This means that it is your responsibility to be able to recover any lost or inaccessible data. There are several reasons that an administrator may need to recover content encrypted using EFS by users. A user can accidentally delete their decryption key, or a user may forget their password and need to have their password reset. (Resetting a user's password disables a user's ability to decrypt their EFS content.) The decryption key is stored inside the user Profile. If this profile gets deleted, the decryption key is lost.

Since you have been configured as an EFS Data Recovery Agent, you can decrypt their encrypted content and recover the inaccessible data.

Scenario

As a security administrator, you are responsible for protecting sensitive information and implementing EFS. After cleaning up the User Account database, you realize there is critical data that has been encrypted by a deleted user account. You must recover the data and provide access to that data to another user.

Scope of Task

Duration

This task should take 20 minutes.

Setup

EFS is enabled through the use of a Public Key Infrastructure (PKI) and digital certificates that contain an encryption key. If the decryption key is lost, the user may never regain access to the EFS content.

A safety mechanism to minimize data loss is the EFS Data Recovery Agent. By default, the administrator for the domain is the default EFS Data Recovery Agent on a system in Domain mode. Typically the Local Administrator is configured as the EFS Data Recovery Agent on a system in Workgroup mode. This must be done manually on a system in Workgroup mode.

Taking advantage of the work performed in Task 4.1, you will delete a user account that had created secured content. You will then confirm that other users cannot access the content. With that completed you will work through the steps to recover (decrypt) the content and grant access of the content to another user. That user would then have access to the secure EFS content utilizing their encryption key.

Caveat

There are combinations of events that can permanently prevent decryption of the content. Data can be lost. Implement EFS with care. If you implement EFS for your users, provide proper training and warnings to those users regarding these issues.

Procedure

For this task, you will delete a user (User2) that you created in Task 4.1. User2 created a secure data file called User2Secure.txt. You then log on as User1 and confirm that even though permissions should allow access to the content, EFS does not allow User1 to access the User2 secured content.

You will then walk through the steps to decrypt the content and grant ownership of the critical data to another user. This new owner should implement EFS using their encryption key to secure this sensitive data.

Equipment Used

For this task, you need the following equipment:

- Windows XP Pro system with the following configuration:
  - A member of a workgroup (not a member of a domain)
  - At least one NTFS volume
- Local Administrator access
- Completion of Task 4.1

Details

Losing an EFS Encryption Key

1. Log on the Windows XP Pro system as the Local Administrator with the password Password1.
2. Right-click on My Computer and select Manage to open the Computer Management console.
3. Expand Local Users And Groups. Select the Users subfolder.

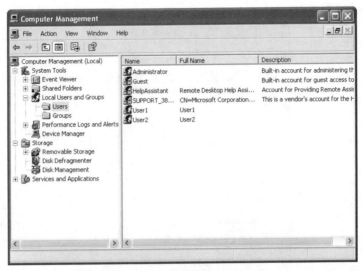

4. In the right pane, right-click on User2 and select Delete.

5. Review the warning regarding the deletion of user accounts. Click Yes to confirm the deletion of User2.

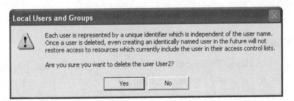

6. Close the Computer Management console. You have just deleted User2, the only account that had access to `User2Secrets.txt`.

Implementing EFS Data Recovery

1. Launch Explorer by right-clicking the Start button and selecting Explore.

2. Select the root of the C:\ drive in the left pane.

3. In the right pane, double-click the folder GOODSTUFF.

4. In Explorer, double-click `User2Secrets.txt`.

5. `User2Secrets.txt` opens correctly in Notepad. This is because the local administrator, by default, has Full Control permissions on all user files and, in Task 4.1, was configured as an EFS Data Recovery Agent for any EFS content produced on the system.

6. Close `User2Secrets.txt` in Notepad.

7. Right-click the file `User2Secrets.txt` and select Properties.

8. Select the Security tab.

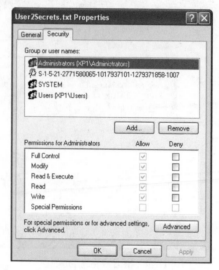

 NOTE Notice that Administrators, a local security group, has full control of the file. The Local Administrator is a member of this group.

9. Select the General tab.

10. Click the Advanced button. This opens the Advanced Attributes dialog. In the Advanced Attributes dialog box, click the Details button, which takes you to the Encryption Details dialog box. To transfer access to User1, you must add User1 to the Users Who Can Transparently Access This File list. Click the Add button.

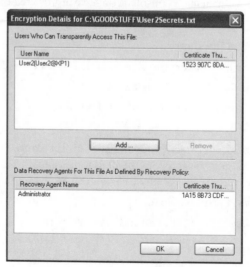

11. Select User1 in the Select User dialog box and click OK.

12. To tighten up the EFS security on this sensitive file, select User2, the deleted user, in the Users Who Can Transparently Access This File list, and then click the Remove button.

13. Click OK in the Encryption Details dialog box.

14. Click OK in the Advanced Attributes dialog box.

15. Click OK in the User2Secrets.txt `Properties dialog box.`

16. Log off as Administrator.

Testing the EFS Data Recovery

1. Log on the Windows XP Pro system as User1 with the password Password1.

2. Launch Explorer by right-clicking the Start button and selecting Explore.

3. Select the root of the C:\ drive in the left pane.

4. In the right pane, double-click the folder GOODSTUFF.

5. In Explorer, double-click `User2Secrets.txt`. `User2Secrets.txt` opens correctly in Notepad. This is because User1 has sufficient permissions on all GOODSTUFF files and was added to the list of Users Who Can Transparently Access This File EFS content by the EFS Data Recovery Agent.

6. Close `User2Secrets.txt` in Notepad.

7. Log off as User1.

Criteria for Completion

You have completed this task when you have removed User2 from the local system, then successfully transferred access to the EFS content, the `User2Secrets.txt` file, to User1 by implementing EFS Data Recovery. You must have then confirmed this access as User1.

Task 4.3: Implementing Syskey

Syskey is a utility that strengthens security on the user account database on a Windows system. It is built into the Windows operating system and encrypts the Security Accounts Management (SAM) database.

Syskey has three modes of operation:

- Syskey Mode 1 is implemented by default on every Windows 2000, Windows XP, and Server 2003 system. Mode 1 encrypts the SAM database and stores the decryption key securely on the local system. This key can be accessed automatically at system startup.

- Syskey Mode 2 stores the key locally, but requires that a system key password be typed in during the system boot-up process to access the SAM database decryption key just prior to starting any services. Without the proper system key password, system services fail to start, thus crippling the system.

- Syskey Mode 3 stores the key locally, but requires that a system key password be supplied via a floppy disk during the system boot-up process to access the SAM database decryption key. This behaves much like a smart card, only by using a floppy disk. Without the floppy disk containing the system key password, system services fail to start, thus crippling the system.

Scenario

You are responsible for strengthening the security of several of your critical systems. You must configure one of your critical systems with a startup password to be entered by a system administrator. Unfortunately, the BIOS on this system does not provide for this capability, so you must implement Syskey, Mode 2.

Scope of Task

Duration

This task should take 30 minutes.

Setup

You are the administrator of an XP Professional system and wish to strengthen its security.

Caveat

Syskey is a powerful tool that can and will lock you out of your own system!

Do not select to export the key unless you have a functioning A: drive with a usable, formatted, blank floppy disk for it. Once you initiate the export process, the system changes the decryption key and then must complete the export process of the new system key password. There is no cancel feature! If the system changes the decryption key and does not export the new system key password to a floppy, the system cannot be rebooted!

Follow the steps in this procedure carefully.

Procedure

For this task, you will log on to the XP Professional system as the Local Administrator. You will launch Syskey and implement Mode 2.

Equipment Used

For this task, you need the following equipment:

- Windows XP Pro system with the following configuration:
    - A member of a workgroup (not a member of a domain)
- Local Administrator access

Details

Implementing Syskey Mode 2

1. Log on the Windows XP Pro system as the Local Administrator.

2. Select Start ➢ Run and type in **Syskey**. Click OK. This opens the Securing The Windows XP Account Database dialog.

3. Notice that you cannot disable encryption; the option is dimmed in the Securing The Windows XP Account Database dialog box. Click Update.

4. By default, Windows 2000, XP, and Server 2003 are configured to store the startup key locally. Select Password Setup and enter **Password1** in both the Password and Confirm fields.

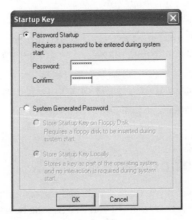

5. Click OK. You will be presented with a success message. Click OK to clear the message.

Testing Syskey Mode 2

1. From the Start menu, select Shut Down.

2. In the Shut Down Windows dialog box, select Restart from the drop-down list.

3. As the system restarts, before any system services are started you will be presented with a Windows XP Startup Password dialog box. Enter the password **Password1** and click OK.

4. Startup will complete and you will be presented with the standard MS GINA dialog box.

 MS GINA is the Microsoft Graphical Identification And Authentication dialog box.

5. Log on normally as the Administrator.

Resetting Syskey to Mode 1

1. Select Start ➢ Run and type in **Syskey**. Click OK.
2. Click Update in the Securing The Windows XP Account Database dialog box.
3. Under System Generated Password in the Startup Key dialog box, select Store Startup Key Locally.

 You could also change the startup password, remaining in Syskey Mode 2, by entering and confirming a new password here.

4. You will be prompted for the startup password. Enter **Password1**, and then click OK.
5. You will receive a success message indicating that the startup key was changed. Click OK to clear the message.

Criteria for Completion

You have completed this task when you have configured the system to operate in Syskey Mode 2 and then tested this with a reboot that requires you to enter the new startup password. You must then reset the system into Syskey Mode 1, Syskey's default mode of operation.

Task 4.4: Converting FAT to NTFS

The original Microsoft filesystem was called FAT (File Allocation Table). Windows NT introduced a more robust and secure filesystem called NTFS (New Technology File System).

FAT uses a linked list to keep track of the files on the partition, like a table of contents, with entries generally listed in the order the files were added to the partition. FAT supports a few attributes, such as Time Saved, Date Saved, Parent Container, Read Only, Archive, System, Hidden, and Directory (vs. File). FAT typically has three possible implementations: FAT12, FAT16, or FAT32.

Floppy disks use FAT12, using a 12-bit cluster addressing scheme.

Partitions on hard drives in systems running DOS, Windows 3x, and 9x, and on Windows NT, 2000, and Server 2003 basic disks can be formatted with FAT16 using a 16-bit cluster addressing scheme.

Optionally on disks in systems running Windows NT, 2000, XP, and Server 2003 basic disks, partitions can be formatted with FAT32, using a 32-bit cluster addressing scheme for larger partitions.

NTFS, the preferred filesystem, is only available on Windows NT, 2000, or XP, or on Server 2003. NTFS uses a Btrieve database to record file locations in order to make searching for files notably faster. It also supports extended attributes, such as Encryption, Compression, Ownership, Permissions, and Auditing.

Scenario

You are responsible for the protection of sensitive information. You discover that two of the partitions used to store this data on an XP Pro system are using the FAT filesystem. You must strengthen the security of this file storage location.

Scope of Task

Duration

This task should take 30 minutes.

Setup

There is a command-line utility, called Convert.exe, used to convert FAT partitions into NTFS partitions. You will use this tool to implement the conversion.

Caveat

The conversion process from FAT to NTFS is a onetime, one-way conversion. NTFS is supported by Windows NT, Windows 2000, Windows XP, and Server 2003. DOS and Windows 9x cannot read NTFS. If the volume you are converting from FAT to NTFS contains any of these down-level (DOS, Windows 9x) operating systems, they will fail to boot ever again.

The conversion process from FAT to NTFS is, theoretically, nondestructive. However, a prudent administrator would never implement such a severe procedure without performing a confirmed, good backup of all data and valuable information assets on the system. Expect the unexpected to occur! You should back up all valuable data on the system before proceeding.

The conversion from NTFS to FAT is a destructive process. You must first perform a backup of all content on the NTFS partition. Then you must delete the NTFS partition, destroying all data; re-create the partition; and format the new partition with the desired FAT file system. You could then restore all content from your backup.

Procedure

For this task, you will initialize a new disk in the system, as necessary. You will then create a new partition, formatted with FAT. You will use the Convert utility to convert the partition to NTFS and confirm successful completion of the conversion.

Equipment Used

For this task, you need the following equipment:

- Windows XP Professional system with the following configuration:
  - A member of a workgroup (not a member of a domain)
- One new disk (basic), installed in the system, with no partitions
- Local Administrator access

Details

Configuring the FAT Partition

1. Log on the Windows XP Professional system as the Local Administrator.

2. Right-click on My Computer and select Manage to open the Computer Management console.

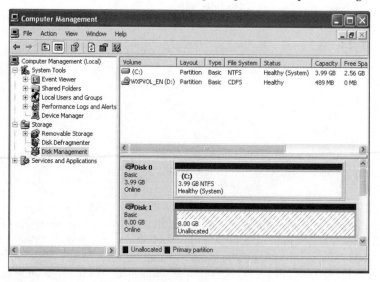

3. Select Disk Management in the left pane.

If the disk has not been initialized before, you will be presented with the Initialize And Convert Disk Wizard. If so, proceed with step 4. If you are not presented with the Initialize And Convert Disk Wizard, skip to step 8.

4. In the Initialize And Convert Disk Wizard, click Next.

5. Be sure your new disk is selected to be Initialized. Click Next.

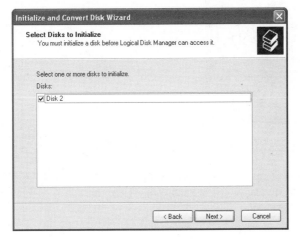

6.   Be sure the checkbox is cleared on the Select Disks To Convert screen of the wizard. Click Next.

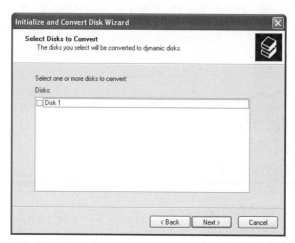

7.   Click Finish to complete the wizard.

8.   In Computer Management ➢ Disk Management, right-click on the new disk in the Unallocated area, and select New Partition.

9. Click Next in the New Partition Wizard.

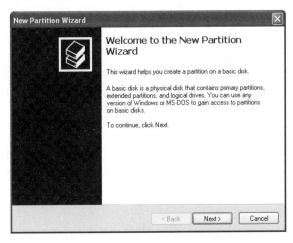

10. In the Select Partition Type screen of the wizard, select Primary Partition. Click Next.

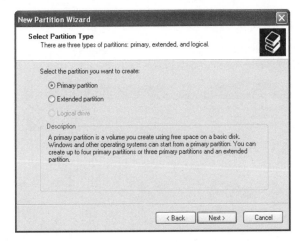

11. In the Specify Partition Size screen of the wizard, enter a desirable partition size. In our example, the partition size will be approximately 1GB. Click Next.

If you select too small a partition size, you will be forced to implement a FAT(16) filesystem on the partition. If free space is available, select between 500MB and 1GB.

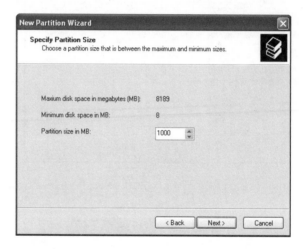

12. Allow the wizard to select the next drive letter (by default). In our example, the partition will be labeled as drive letter E:. Click Next.

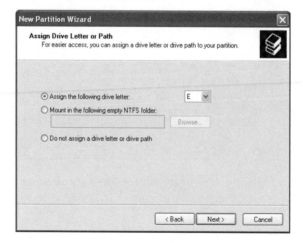

13. In the Format Partition screen, select FAT32 (if available; choose FAT if FAT32 is not available) from the File System drop-down list. Enter **DATA** as the Volume Label. Select the option Perform A Quick Format, as shown.

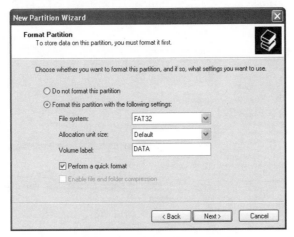

14. Click Next.

15. Click Finish to complete the New Partition Wizard.

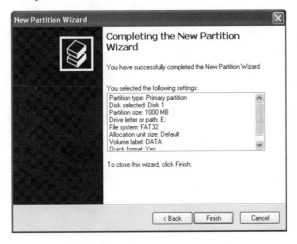

16. In Computer Management ➤ Disk Management, observe your new FAT partition named DATA.

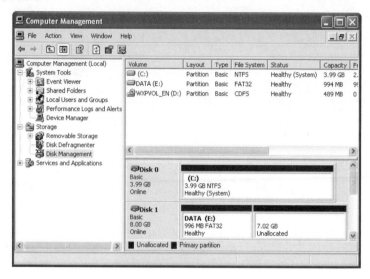

17. Minimize the Computer Management console.

Creating Data on the New FAT Partition

1. Launch Explorer by right-clicking the Start button and selecting Explore.

2. In the left pane, select your new DATA partition.

3. Right-click the white space in the right pane and select New ➤ Text Document.

4. Enter a filename with the .TXT extension.

5. Edit the text document and add some copy that you will recognize later.

6. Save the new document with your new copy.

7. Close Explorer.

Converting the New FAT Partition

1. Still logged on as the Administrator, select Start ➤ Run and enter **CMD**. Then click OK.

2. At the command prompt, enter the command **convert /?**.

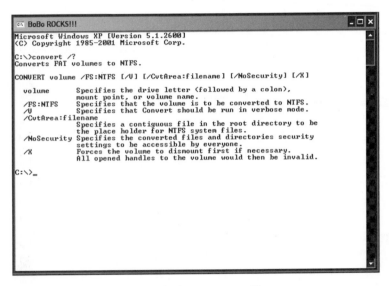

3. Review the switches associated with the Convert utility.

4. At the command prompt, enter the command **CONVERT X: /FS:NTFS**,

   where *X:* is the drive letter for your new DATA partition. In our example, the DATA partition has E: as the drive letter.

5. Where prompted, enter the name of the FAT partition, DATA, and then press Enter.

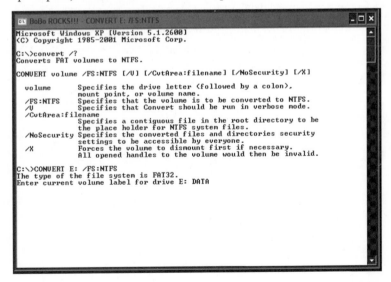

6.   The Convert utility completes with a summary of its progress.

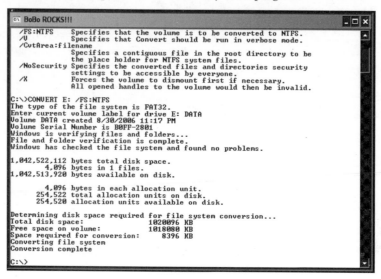

7.   Close the command window.

Confirming the New NTFS Partition

1.   Open the Computer Management console. Notice the DATA partition now shows as NTFS.

2.   Close the Computer Management console.

3.   Launch Explorer by right-clicking the Start button and selecting Explore.

4.   In the left pane, select your new DATA partition. Notice the new System Volume Information folder. This is a component of an NTFS partition.

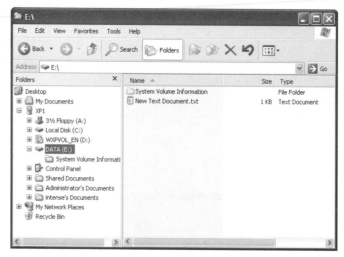

5. Double-click on your `New Text Document.txt` file.

6. Confirm the file is readable.

7. You have successfully converted from a FAT partition to an NTFS partition and could implement folder and file permissions as well as encryption on all of the content on this new volume.

Criteria for Completion

You have completed this task when you have successfully converted your new FAT partition to an NTFS partition, and have confirmed no data loss.

Task 4.5: Implementing Disk Fault Tolerance with RAID

A significant aspect of information systems security relates to protecting against the loss of data and ensuring the data's availability. Data is written on hard disks. These disks can and will fail, resulting in data loss and loss of availability of the data. Fault-tolerant disk arrays are a common approach to mitigating the losses related to disk failure.

Redundant Array of Independent Disks (RAID) systems can be implemented to provide fault tolerance of disks. The two most common implementations of RAID are RAID1 (Mirroring) and RAID5 (Stripe Set with Parity).

RAID1 requires two disks and provides no performance boost or degradation. It provides for one disk to be lost, yet all of the data stored on the Mirrored Volume remains intact and available. The overhead in disk space for this fault tolerance follows the formula $1/n$, where $n =$ the number of disks in the array. In the case of the Mirrored Volume, two disks are used so the overhead is one-half, or 50 percent.

RAID5 requires three disks minimum and can be extended to 32 disks as a typical maximum. It provides increasing performance boost as the number of disks in the array are utilized. It provides for one disk to be lost, yet all of the data stored on the RAID5 Volume remains intact and available. The overhead in disk space for this fault tolerance also follows the formula $1/n$, where $n =$ the number of disks in the array. In the case of a three-disk RAID5 Volume, three disks are used so the overhead is one-third, or 33 percent. In the case of a ten-disk RAID5 Volume, ten disks are used so the overhead is one-tenth, or 10 percent. And in the case of a 32-disk RAID5 Volume, 32 disks are used so the overhead is $1/32$, or 3 percent.

Read and write times in a RAID5 Volume also follow a similar efficiency. The formula for read and write time performance is $t = 1/(n - 1)$ where $n =$ the number of disks in the array. As you increase the number of disks in the volume, the performance gets better and better.

Scenario

You are responsible for ensuring the availability of a critical data set on a file server. While the budget is tight, you must implement a fault-tolerant disk array to protect against loss of data and its availability.

Scope of Task

Duration

This task should take 45 minutes.

Setup

Because of budget concerns, you must provide fault tolerance while keeping spending to a minimum. You have chosen to implement Microsoft's software-based RAID1 to satisfy these issues. You have just added two new disks to your file server.

Caveat

The installation of new hardware and the configuration of partitions or volumes can be risky. Always perform a full backup of the system prior to implementation of any new hardware, software, or changes to the system's configuration.

Procedure

For this task, you will configure the system with a RAID1 Volume to hold your critical data set.

Equipment Used

For this task, you need the following equipment:

- Windows Server 2003 system with the following configuration:
    - Two new disks (basic)
- Local Administrator access

Details

New Disk Initialization and Conversion to Dynamic Disk

1. Log on the Windows Server 2003 system as the Local Administrator with the password Password1.

Fault-tolerant disk arrays are only available on server class operating systems from Microsoft. You cannot build RAID1 or RAID5 arrays in Windows 2000 Pro or Windows XP.

2. Right-click on My Computer and select Manage to open the Computer Management console.

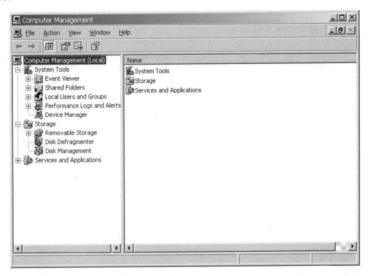

3. In the left pane, select Disk Management. The Initialize And Convert Disk Wizard will launch. Click Next.

4. On the Select Disks To Initialize screen of the wizard, confirm that the two new disks are selected for initialization. Click Next.

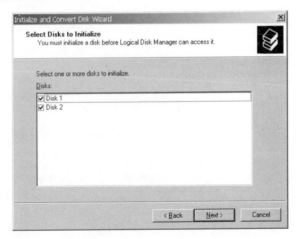

5. On the Select Disks To Convert screen, confirm that the two new disks are selected for conversion to dynamic disks. This is required to assemble a fault-tolerant disk array. Click Next.

6. Confirm that the two new disks are selected for initialization and conversion to dynamic disks. Click Finish.

Creating the RAID1—Mirrored Volume

1. In the Disk Management console, confirm your two new disks are present and are dynamic. Right-click on the Unallocated space on the first new disk and select New Volume.

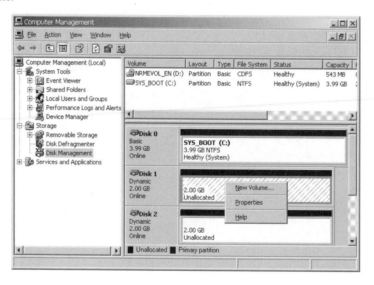

2. This launches the New Volume Wizard. Select Next.

3. In the Select Volume Type screen of the wizard, select Mirrored. Click Next.

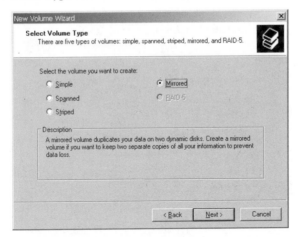

4. In the Select Disks screen, select the second new disk on the left side, and then click the Add button. Click Next.

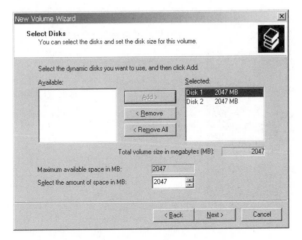

5. In the Assign Letter Drive Or Path screen, allow the system to assign the next available drive letter. Click Next.

6. In the Format Volume screen, format the volume with NTFS, using the default allocation unit size. Add the volume label **MIRROR** and select to perform a quick format. Click Next.

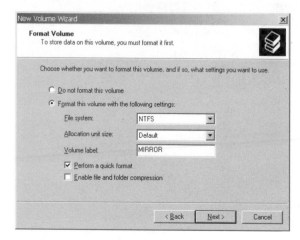

7. Confirm the details of the new volume and click Finish.

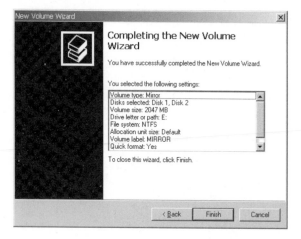

8. In the Disk Management dialog box, you will observe the new volume is formatting, and then resynching.

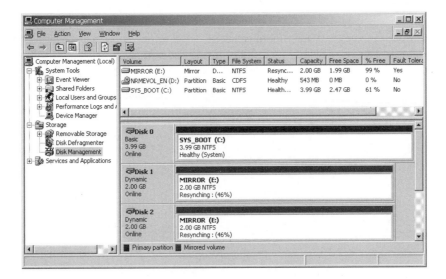

9. The new volume is complete when you see that it is healthy. Notice in the upper-right corner that the new E: drive, MIRROR, is fault tolerant.

10. In Explorer, you can copy your critical data to the new, fault-tolerant, E: drive.

Criteria for Completion

You have completed this task when you have correctly assembled a fault-tolerant RAID1 Volume, and can copy data to it.

Task 4.6: Backing Up Data

Data loss occurs all the time from many different causes, including hardware failure, operating system bugs, application bugs, errors and omissions, and power problems, to name a few. Disaster recovery preparation and procedures should be a routine part of every administrator's concerns and activities. The ability to recover lost data must exist.

Scenario

You are responsible for the protection of mission-critical information. You need to be prepared to recover corrupted or lost data files from any day within the last week. You must establish a backup routine to satisfy these concerns.

Scope of Task

Duration

This task should take 45 minutes.

Setup

Your critical data is on a file server, but you have no tape drive. You plan to perform the backups to the local system on a daily basis. You will manually copy those backups to a remote server over the network, to provide for a remote copy.

Caveat

The process of backing up data can consume massive amounts of system and network resources. The performance of the backup server will degrade substantially during the backup process. Backups are usually performed overnight while the system and network resources are at their lowest levels of consumption.

Backups must be tested regularly to confirm their validity and recoverability. Stepping through the paces of performing the backups may be useless unless you are certain that your data can be restored. You should be performing test restores on a regular basis.

Procedure

For this task, you will identify the data sets that are mission critical and perform an initial, manual backup. This collection of content for backup is referred to as the *catalog*. You will then configure this backup to run, overnight, on a daily basis.

Equipment Used

For this task, you need the following equipment:

- Windows Server 2003 system
- Administrator or Backup Operator access
- Multiple files and or folders identified as critical and requiring backup

Details

Assembling the Catalog

1. Log on the Windows Server 2003 system as the Administrator.
2. Launch Explorer by right-clicking the Start button and selecting Explore.
3. Identify the critical data set requiring backup. Right-click on each of the data folders and select Properties to determine the approximate size of the backup.

 Since you will be backing up to the local drive, be sure you have sufficient free drive space to record the backup. If you have enough free space, you will also be backing up the system state data, which will additionally require approximately 500–600MB.

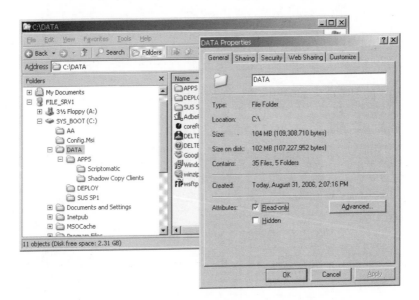

4. Once you have determined the files and folders to contain in the backup, minimize or close Explorer.
5. Launch NT Backup by selecting Start ➤ Programs ➤ Accessories ➤ System Tools ➤ Backup.
6. In the Backup Or Restore Wizard, deselect the Always Start In Wizard Mode checkbox, and select the Advanced Mode, underlined in blue.

7.   In the Backup Utility Advanced Mode screen, select the Backup tab.

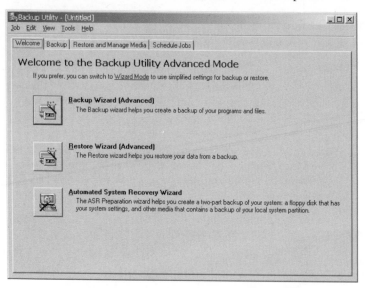

8.   In the Backup Utility, expand the drive where your data set resides. Add content to the catalog by checking the box to the left of the file(s) and/or folder(s) you want to add to the catalog.

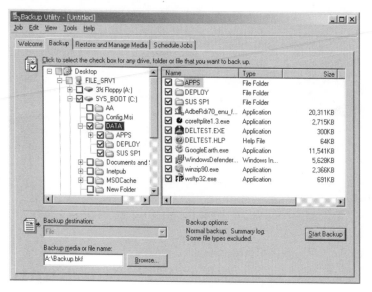

9. Scroll toward the bottom of the left pane and select System State.

Only select System State if your system has sufficient free space for the additional 500–600MB required.

Initializing the Backup

1. Toward the bottom of the Backup Utility, at the Backup Media Or File Name field, click Browse. Clear the Insert A Disk message by clicking Cancel.

2. In the Save As dialog box, select your computer name to select the drive with sufficient free space for the backup.

In our example, the computer name is FILE_SRV1.

3. Once the correct drive is selected, create a new folder called BACKUP by clicking the New Folder button in the upper-right corner. It looks like a folder with a sparkle on it.

4. Name the folder **BACKUP** and then click the white space beside the new folder to set the name.

5. Double-click on the new folder BACKUP. In the File Name field below, enter the backup file name (something like `FS1_DATA_SS.bkf`). This stands for the computer name, FILE_SRV1; DATA to identify this backup contains a data backup; and SS to identify that this backup also includes the system state data for FILE_SRV1.

6. Click Save.

7. In the Backup dialog box, click Start Backup.

8. Review the Backup Job Information dialog box. Accept the default information and click Advanced.

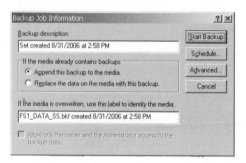

9. Review the settings in the Advanced Backup Options dialog box.

 This is where you would select Verify Data After Backup. This will approximately double the time to complete the backup, and it usually reports errors, since some files have changed since the time they were backed up. This is also where you select the backup type from the drop-down list.

10. Leave the default settings, and click OK to close the Advanced Backup Options dialog box.

11. Click Start Backup in the Backup Job Information dialog box. You will be presented with the Backup Progress dialog box during the backup and a message when the backup has completed.

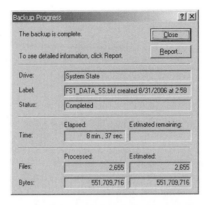

12. 12. Click Report to view the report. This will open the report in Notepad

13. When you are done reviewing the report, close Notepad.

Setting Up the Scheduled Daily Backup

1. In the Backup Utility, on the Backup tab, reselect the files and/or folders you wish to have backed up.

Again, be aware of the free disk space required for the backup, and in this case, the multiple backups if you allow this task to run. Only select System State if your system has sufficient free space for the additional 500–600MB required in each backup.

2. Once you have your catalog selected and the Backup Media Or File Name field defined correctly, click Start Backup.

3. In the Backup Job Information dialog box, click Schedule.

4. You will be prompted to save your selections. Click Yes.

5. Name your selection script something like **FS1_DATA_SS.bks** and click Save.

6. Next you will be prompted to set credentials on the scheduled backup job. The credentials you supply must have the rights to backup files and folders, such as an Administrator or a member of the Backup Operators group. Enter the proper credentials, entering the password twice.

7. In the Scheduled Job Options dialog box, enter a job name and click Properties.

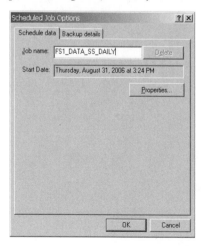

Feel free to review the Backup Details tab as well.

8. In the Scheduled Task drop-down list, select Daily. In the Start Time field, specify a time when the server and resources will have the lowest demand. Select Schedule Task Daily Every 1 Day(s).

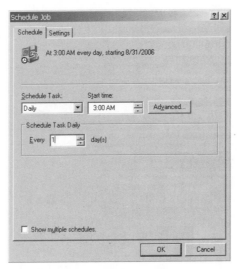

 Feel free to review the Advanced settings and the Settings tab as well.

9. Click OK in the Schedule Job dialog box.
10. Click OK in the Schedule Job Options dialog box.
11. To review the scheduled jobs, select the Schedule Jobs tab in the Backup Utility.

 You may want to disable this scheduled job if you do not need this backup to run daily. This job will continue to consume system resources, especially disk space.

Disabling the Scheduled Daily Backup

1. In the Backup Utility, on the Schedule Jobs tab, click on the backup icon on any of the days that the backup job is scheduled to run on. The cursor turns into the Link Select icon J (pointing finger by default) as you move over the backup icon. This should open the Scheduled Job Options dialog box.

2. Click Properties.

3. Clear the Enabled (Scheduled Task Runs At Specified Time) checkbox at the bottom of this dialog box, and click OK twice.

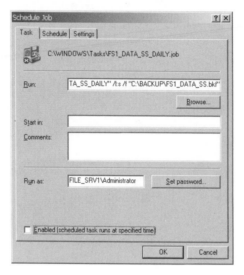

 This keeps the details of the scheduled job intact, but does not trigger to launch the scheduled backup job.

Criteria for Completion

You have completed this task when you have performed a manual backup, reviewed the backup log, scheduled a daily backup, and disabled the daily backup job.

Task 4.7: Restoring Data from a Backup

Every diligent administrator performs regular backups, and that is a fine thing. An excellent administrator also performs practice restores from the backups on a regular basis. Unless you restore data from your backups and verify its integrity, you can never be sure that you can perform appropriate recovery in a real disaster situation.

Scenario

You are responsible for the protection of mission-critical information. You need to be prepared to recover corrupted or lost data files from any day within the last week. You must validate your backup routine by restoring data and verifying its integrity to satisfy these concerns.

Scope of Task

Duration

This task should take 30 minutes.

Setup

You recently established a daily backup routine and it seems to be running well. You must validate this by performing a practice restore, and then testing the restored data.

Caveat

Practice restores should only happen on off-line systems, not in a production environment. It could be disastrous to restore old data over new data, so always perform practice restores to a different location.

Consider the confidentiality requirements of the restored data. If a relatively untrusted administrator is capable of performing these restores, it would be quite easy for them to access confidential information. Always treat your backup media as highly confidential and allow only the most trusted administrators the rights and access to perform these restores.

Consider the appropriate security for storage, or the appropriate destruction, for security purposes, of this restored content.

Procedure

For this task, you will restore several files from an earlier backup to a different location. You will then validate the integrity of that restored content by mounting the data with the appropriate application and determining its readability.

Equipment Used

For this task, you need the following equipment:

- Windows Server 2003 system
- Administrator or Backup Operator access
- Completion of Task 4.6, "Backing Up Data"

Details

Identifying Content to Restore

1. Log on the Windows XP Professional system as the Local Administrator.
2. Launch NT Backup by choosing Start ≻ Programs ≻ Accessories ≻ System Tools ≻ Backup.
3. Select the Restore And Manage Media tab.
4. Expand the folder structure of your earlier backup. Identify and select several files and/or folders to restore.

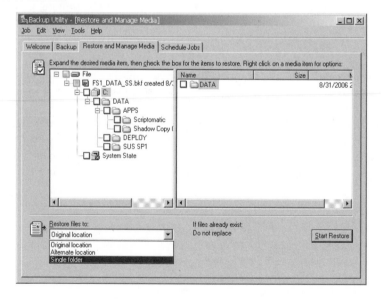

In the real world, you would select the most critical files to practice restore. These would be the most important files to validate and verify.

Be aware of the amount of data you are restoring to the system and the amount of free space on the disk you will be restoring to.

5. In the Restore Files To drop-down list, select Alternate Location, and then identify a folder on a drive with sufficient free space to receive the restored content.

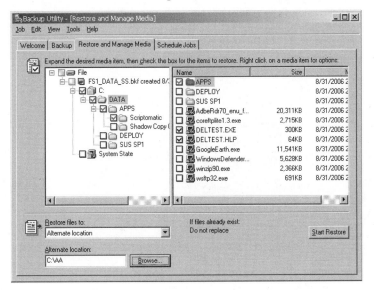

Do not select the original location to restore the old data to. This would over-write newer data with old data. Select to restore to a different location.

In the example, the Alternate Location selected is the C:\AA folder.

Initializing the Restore

1. Click Start Restore. You will be presented with the Confirm Restore dialog box. Click Advanced.

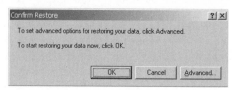

2. The Restore Security checkbox indicates that, assuming the filesystem on the target volume supports it (in other words, if the target volume is formatted with NTFS), the original NTFS permissions will be reapplied to the restored content.

 If this remains enabled, you may not have sufficient permissions to test the content's validity.

The two other active checkboxes indicate that you want to restore any selected folders, that were backed up as mount points, as mount points (as opposed to restoring them as just empty folders), and reconnect the mount points' underlying content to the mount point. Leave the default configuration intact and click OK.

3. In the Confirm Restore dialog box, click OK to proceed with the restore. The Restore Progress dialog box opens, followed by the Restore Is Complete message.

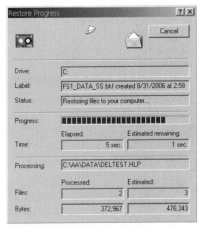

4. Click Report to view the restore report. Notice that it has been appended to the original backup report. Scroll to the bottom of the report to view the restore statistics.

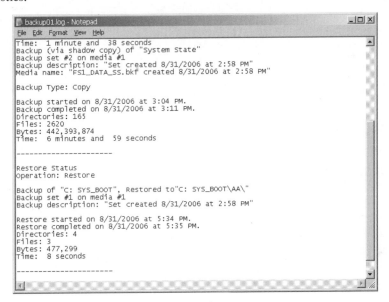

5. Close Notepad.

Testing the Restored Data

1. Launch Explorer.

2. Expand the left pane sufficiently to view the restored content.

 In this case, the restored content was placed in C:\AA.

3. Mount one or more restored files with the appropriate application to validate the restored file's integrity.

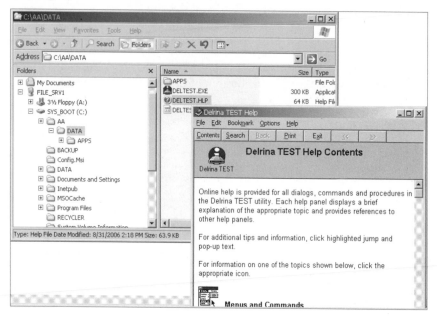

 When the files are mounted properly, or your restored executables launch properly, you have confirmed the validity of your backup.

4. Close all applications.

Criteria for Completion

You have completed this task when you have successfully restored data from an earlier backup, and then tested the validity of the restored content.

Task 4.8: Securing Shares

File and folder resources on a network are accessed through a special opening in a system called a *share point*. These share points are there for good reason, but they are often the doorway that an attacker uses to violate your system security controls. Share points are made possible and managed by the File And Printer Sharing service, otherwise called the Server service.

Only Administrators, members of any of the Operators groups, and Power Users have permissions sufficient to create share points, in an attempt to minimize the potential exposure of vulnerabilities.

Even with this elite and restrictive collection of share point creators, each share point should be carefully configured to implement the principle of least privilege. In other words, only grant the barest minimum level of access to only those who need access.

Scenario

You are responsible for providing appropriate security and access to a new share point on a file server. Users need to be able to read and write content on this share point.

Scope of Task

Duration

This task should take 60 minutes.

Setup

You will create a folder with content to be shared on a file server. Then you will create the proper chain of users and groups to provide appropriate permissions and restrictions to the content within the folder. Then you will create the actual share point.

Caveat

The addition of any share point should be carefully considered. These are holes in the security fortress on a system.

Improper creation of share points can result in the loss of confidentiality, integrity, and/or availability of your information assets and can lead to the compromise of the entire system. The compromise of one system establishes a foothold in your network for the attacker, allowing them to attack your network from within.

Always implement shares with consideration for the principle of least privilege.

Procedure

For this task, you will establish the content to be shared, build the proper AGDLP chain (User Accounts get added to Global Groups; Global Groups get added to Domain Local Groups, Local Groups get granted Permissions) to grant permissions, and then implement the share point.

Equipment Used

For this task, you need the following equipment:

- Windows Server 2003 system in a domain environment

 This can be done with Windows XP Professional as well, but a workstation class operating system can only support ten inbound connections to its Server service. Servers can support unlimited inbound connections to their Server service.

- Domain Administrator access

Details

Pulling Together the Content to Be Shared

1. Log on the Windows Server 2003 system as the Administrator.
2. Launch Explorer by right-clicking the Start button and selecting Explore.
3. In the left pane, select the root of a drive that has sufficient free space to host the shared content.
4. In the right pane, right-click in the white space and select New ➤ Folder.
5. Name the folder **STUFF**.
6. Create or copy content into the STUFF folder.

 For the purposes of this exercise, this content should not contain anything sensitive.

Building AGDLP: Creating the Users and Groups

1. You must first create the groups and users to assemble the AGDLP chain. Launch Active Directory Users And Computers (ADUC) by selecting Start ➤ Programs ➤ Administrative Tools ➤ Active Directory Users and Computers.

NOTE If the system you are logged onto is not a domain controller, you may install these tools by running `Adminpak.msi`, which is located in the `Windows\System32` folder on every server-class system by default.

2. Right-click on the domain name and select New ➤ Organizational Unit.

3. Name the new OU **CLIENTS**.

4. Right-click on the CLIENTS OU and select New ➤ Group.

5. Name the new group **Clients GG,** and select Global for Group Scope, and Security for Group Type. Click OK.

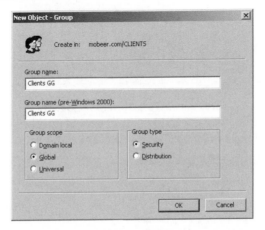

6. Right-click on the CLIENTS OU and select New ➤ Group.

7. Name the new group **Clients DLG,** and select Domain Local for Group Scope, and Security for Group Type. Click OK.

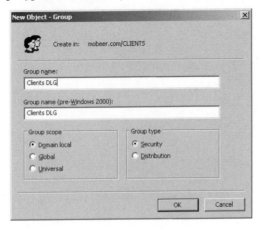

8. Right-click on the CLIENTS OU and select New ➤ User.

9. Type the name **User1** in the First Name field. Type **User1** in the User Logon Name field. Click Next.

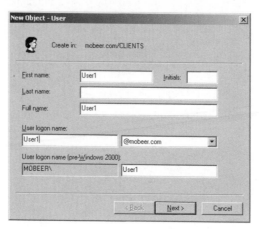

10. Type the password **Password1** in the Password and Confirm Password fields. Clear the User Must Change Password At Next Logon checkbox. Enable the User Cannot Change Password and the Password Never Expires checkboxes. Click Next.

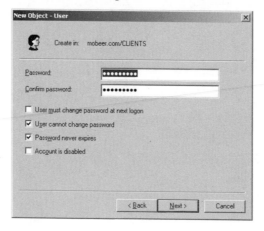

11. Click Finish to create User1.

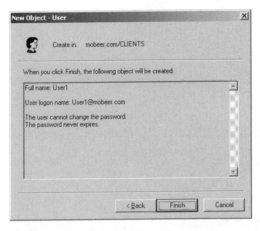

12. Repeat steps 8 through 11 to create User2, User3, and User4.

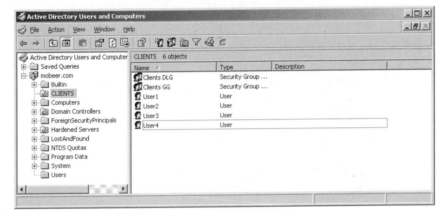

Building AGDLP for the Shared Content

1. Now you will add the four users into the Global Group. Double-click the Global Group named Clients GG. On the Members tab, click Add.

2. Click Advanced.

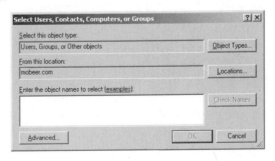

3.   Click Find Now to display all users and groups in the domain.

4.   Select User1 through User4. Then click OK.

 To select all four Users at once, you can click on User1, then press and hold the Shift button on the keyboard and click on User4.

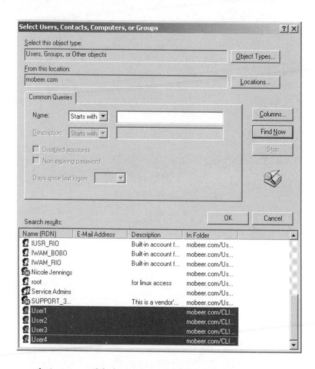

5.   Click OK a second time to add these users to the Clients GG.

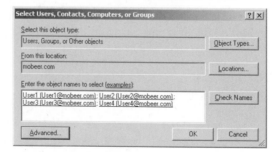

6.   Click OK to close the Clients GG Properties dialog box.

7.   Now you will add the Clients GG into the Domain Local Group called Clients DLG. Double-click on the Domain Local Group named Clients DLG. On the Members tab, click Add.

8. Click Advanced.

9. Click Find Now to display all users and groups in the domain.

10. Select the Clients GG. Then click OK.

11. Click OK a second time to add the Clients GG to the Clients DLG.

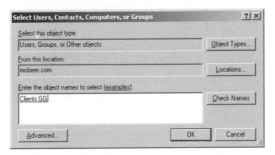

12. Click OK to close the Clients DLG Properties dialog box.

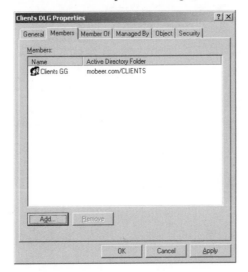

 You have just assembled AGDL of the AGDLP chain for granting permissions (Users into Clients GG; Clients GG into Clients DLG). Next you will grant the Clients DLG permissions, both NTFS and share point permissions.

13. Launch Explorer by right-clicking the Start button and selecting Explore.

14. In the left pane, select the root of a drive that holds the folder STUFF.

15. In the right pane, right-click on the folder STUFF and select Properties. Select the Security tab.

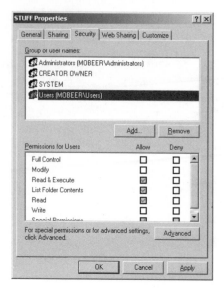

 The security tab is used to set NTFS permissions, that is, permissions that control picking the files up off the NTFS volume. Permissions should always be set following the principle of least privilege.

16. Click Add.

17. Click Advanced.

18. Click Find Now to display all users and groups in the domain.

19. Select the Clients DLG. Then click OK.

20. Click OK a second time to add the Clients DLG to the Access Control List for the STUFF folder.

21. With the Clients DLG selected in the upper pane, check the Allow Write Permission option in the lower pane. This collection of Allow permissions grants the Clients DLG read and write capabilities at the NTFS level for this folder.

22. You do not want all Users of the domain to be able to read these files so you must get rid of the Users group. This group has default permissions inherited from the root of the drive. On the Security tab of the STUFF Properties dialog box, Click Advanced.

23. On the Permissions tab of the Advanced Security Settings For STUFF dialog box, clear the Allow Inheritable Permissions checkbox.

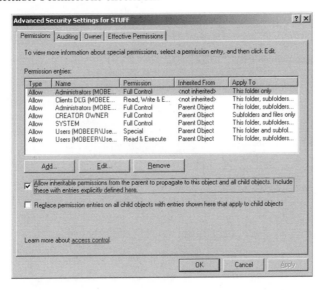

24. Clearing this checkbox immediately prompts you to do one of the following:

- Copy the inherited permissions to make them explicitly assigned at the STUFF folder.
- Remove all permissions.
- Cancel this action.

25. Select to copy the permissions.

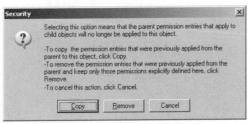

26. Notice in the Inherited From column that the permissions are now shown as <Not Inherited>. Click OK.

27. On the Security tab of the STUFF Properties dialog box, select Users, and then click the Remove button.

28. The Security tab of the STUFF Properties dialog box should appear as shown here. This sets the NTFS permissions on content within the STUFF folder.

29. Next, you must provide the share point permissions for the Clients DLG. This is managed by the Server service on the system. Select the Sharing tab in the STUFF Properties dialog box.

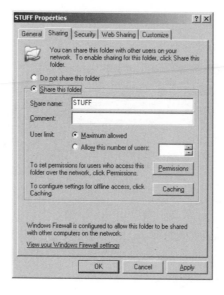

30. Click the Permissions button and observe the default share point permissions provided by the Server service. Click Add.

31. Click Advanced.

32. Click Find Now to display all users and groups in the domain.

33. Select the Clients DLG. Then click OK.

34. Click OK a second time to add the Clients DLG to the Access Control Lost for the Share Permissions.

35. With the Clients DLG selected in the upper pane, check the Allow Change permission in the lower pane. This collection of Allow permissions grants the Clients DLG read and write capabilities at this share point.

36. With the Everyone group selected in the upper pane, click the Remove button to disallow unwanted users from accessing this share point. The resulting Access Control List for the Stuff Share Permissions should appear as shown here.

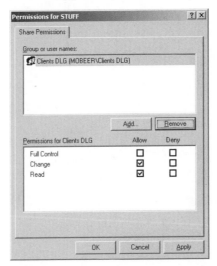

37. Click OK to accept the permissions. Click OK to close the STUFF Properties dialog box.

Criteria for Completion

You have completed this task when you have assembled the proper AGDLP chain for granting permissions. This includes granting NTFS permissions, managed by the NTFS file system, to the proper local group, as well as granting share permissions managed by the Server service to the same local group. You also removed all undesired permissions from the Access Control Lists to remain consistent with the principle of least privilege.

Phase

5

Managing User Accounts

The weakest link in the security of an enterprise is its users. Your job as a security administrator is to implement the strongest security possible. Through user account management, you can introduce security controls that will help to strengthen the security of your information systems.

The user account controls take the form of creating user accounts with a standardized template account to establish the baseline permissions, implementing a strong password policy, auditing failed logons to detect crack attacks, securing default accounts, and implementing Deny groups on sensitive content.

The tasks in this phase map to Domains 1 and 5 objectives in the CompTIA Security+ exam (http://certification.comptia.org/security/).

Task 5.1: Creating User Accounts

To provide as much security as possible while creating user accounts, administrators take advantage of user account templates to establish a minimum baseline of permission required for each role in the enterprise. Only after this baseline is discovered to not have sufficient privilege will an administrator increase the level of privilege by granting only the additional permissions required for the worker to perform the tasks required of their role.

Further, the placement of the user account in the proper organizational unit (OU) within Active Directory (AD) implements user-based security controls by Group Policy Object (GPOs). GPO's can be applied at the AD site, domain, or OU level.

Scenario

You are an administrator in an Active Directory environment. One of your responsibilities includes the creation of all user accounts for the domain. You must perform this task while implementing the utmost security for the environment.

Scope of Task

Duration

This task should take 30 minutes.

Setup

You have just been informed of the need to create five users for a new role today, with another 100 users expected over the next three months. These first five users will begin working next week.

This role of user requires special desktop controls to be implemented on their desktops.

Caveat

As users are created, unless proper security is implemented, attackers can compromise these accounts and gain unauthorized access to many resources.

Also, the implementation of GPOs can adversely affect the operations and security of your information systems. If the implementation is too lax, users gain too much access. If it's too tight, required resources may be unavailable to users.

Procedure

For this task, you will configure a new user template account and secure this template. Then you will create the five users based on this template, secure them properly, and place them into the proper OU. Next you will write the desktop GPO required for these users and link it to the proper OU.

Equipment Used

For this task, you need the following equipment:

- Windows Server 2003 domain controller system
- Domain Administrator access

Details

Building a User Account Template

1. Log on the Windows Server 2003 domain controller system as the Domain Administrator.
2. Select Start ➤ Programs ➤ Administration Tools ➤ Active Directory Users And Computers (ADUC).
3. Expand the domain. Click on the domain name.

4. In the right pane, right-click and select New ➤ Organizational Unit.

5. Name the new OU **Widget Production**. It should become the selected item in the left pane.

6. In the right pane, right-click and select New ➤ User.

7. Assign the new user the name **_WProd_Template** and set the user logon name to **WProd**. Click Next.

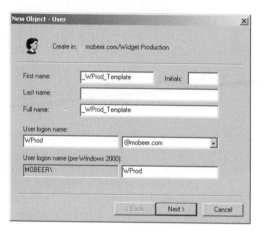

Create the template account with the first character as the underscore _ so it will come first alphabetically, and will be easy to locate as the OU becomes populated with potentially hundreds of user accounts.

8. Enter a strong password for the template account and enable the User Must Change Password At Next Logon (enabled by default) and Account Is Disabled settings. Click Next, and then click Finish to create the account.

A password is typically considered strong when it contains more than seven characters and includes at least one uppercase alpha, at least one lowercase alpha, and at least one numeric or symbol character. You will not need to remember this password. No one should ever log onto this account.

It is important to ensure that this template account is disabled!

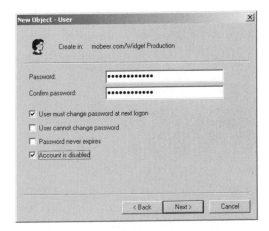

9. Notice the account has a red dot with a white X on it, indicating that it is disabled.

10. In the white space below _WProd_Template, right-click and select New ➢ Group, and create a new Global Security Group named **Widget Production GG**.

11. In the white space below _WProd_Template, right-click and select New ➢ Group, and create a new Domain Local Security Group named **Widget Production DLG**.

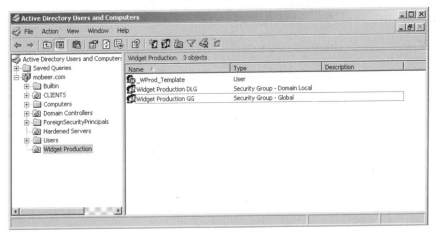

12. Double-click on Widget Production GG and select the Members tab. Click Add.

13. Click Advanced.

14. Click Find Now to display all users and groups in the domain.

15. Click the user account _WProd_Template. Then click OK.

16. Click OK again to add this user into the Widget Production GG.

17. Click OK to close the Widget Production GG Properties dialog box.

Now you will add the Widget Production GG into the Domain Local Group called Widget Production DLG.

1. Double-click on the Domain Local Group named Widget Production DLG. On the Members tab, click Add.

2. Click Advanced.

3. Click Find Now to display all users and groups in the domain.

4. Click the Widget Production GG. Then click OK.

5. Click OK again to add the Widget Production GG into the Widget Production DLG.

6. Click OK to close the Clients DLG Properties dialog box.

You have just assembled AGDL of the AGDLP chain for granting permissions (Users into Widget Production GG, Widget Production GG into Widget Production DLG). Next you will grant the Widget Production DLG permissions, both NTFS and share point permissions, as desired. Any user accounts created from this template will already be a member of this chain of permissions.

The process of building AGLP is detailed in Phase 4, Task 4.8.

You have created a template account in the proper OU to base all Widget Production users on. This account has a strong password, is disabled, will require users based on this template To change their password at first logon, and has been granted membership to the Widget Production GG and the resulting resource accesses.

Creating Users based on the new User Account Template

1. In ADUC, in the Widget Production OU, right-click on the _WProd_Template user object and select Copy.

2. Type **Prod1** in the First Name field and the User Logon Name field. Click Next.

3. Type in a strong password twice. Notice the two settings that are enabled.

- User Must Change Password At First Logon

- Account Is Disabled

Retain these settings and click Next.

You will need to record this username and password and provide it to the worker, Prod1, for their first logon. They will be forced to change this password as they log on for the first time.

4. Click Finish to create the new user Prod1, based on the user template _WProd_Template.

5. Repeat steps 1 through 4 and create users Prod2, Prod3, Prod4, and Prod5 similarly.

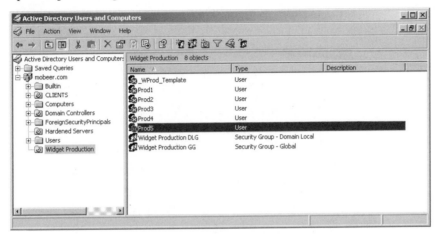

As the new workers show up for work, you would enable the appropriate account and provide the worker with his new username and password. You should advise the worker that he will be forced to change his password at first logon.

6. Double-click on the group Widget Production GG and select Members. Confirm that your five new users are members of this global group.

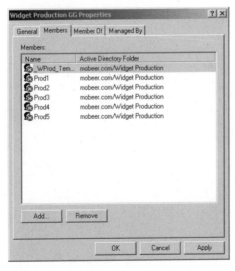

7. Close the Widget Production GG.

Securing the Widget Production Users with a GPO

1. In the left pane of ADUC, right-click on the Widget Production OU and select Properties. Select the Group Policy tab.

2. Select New and name the new GPO **WProd Desktops**.

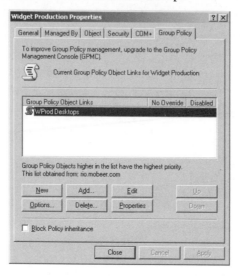

3. Click Edit. Expand the GPO to view User Configuration ➤ Administrative Templates ➤ Desktop.

4. Double-click on Remove My Computer Icon On The Desktop. In the resulting dialog box, select the Enabled radio button, and then click OK.

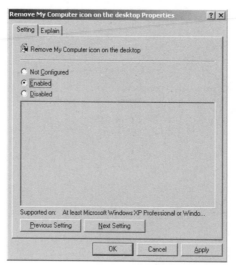

5. Double-click on Prohibit User From Changing My Documents Path. In the resulting dialog box, select the Enabled radio button, and then click OK.

6. Double-click on Prohibit Adjusting Desktop Toolbars. In the resulting dialog box, select the Enabled radio button, and then click OK.

 The Desktop settings selected are simple, representative controls that could be enabled. Any GPO settings in the User Configuration region of this GPO will apply to all users in the Widget Production OU.

7. Close the GPO by clicking the X in the upper-right corner.

Criteria for Completion

You have completed this task when you have built the template account with the proper security controls in place, created several users based on that secure template, and have configured a GPO and linked to the OU containing the new user accounts to further secure those users.

Task 5.2: Implementing the Password Policy

One of the most important components of securing your information systems is implementing a strong password policy. This is accomplished by editing the Default Domain GPO in Active Directory Users And Computers. Setting the password policy at any other location in Active Directory or on the local computer affects the local users' password settings, not their domain user passwords.

Scenario

You are an administrator in an Active Directory environment. You are responsible for the security of all user accounts. You must implement account policies in your domain to enforce the company standard for these password settings.

Scope of Task

Duration

This task should take 15 minutes.

Setup

You need to strengthen the security of the environment, and a strong password policy is your next step in accomplishing this.

Caveat

It is well recognized that a strong password policy is an essential element of strong security in an environment. However, if the policy is set too rigidly, users struggle to remember their passwords. The result is that they continuously lock their accounts, resulting in increased administrative overhead to unlock them, and/or they write down their difficult passwords and store them in a handy location. Unfortunately, this "handy" logon information is also handy for the attacker. By strengthening the password policy too much, you effectively weaken the overall security of the environment.

Modifying any GPO, especially the default domain policy, is a dangerous thing to do. This specific policy affects every computer and every user in the domain. Inappropriate changes to this policy could severely cripple access to your information systems.

Always use caution when modifying any GPO, and be sure you understand the ramifications of your configuration, as well as where you have the GPO linked.

Procedure

For this task, you will configure the password policy in the Default Domain GPO with the following password policy settings:

- The password must consist of at least eight characters.

- A password must contain at least one uppercase alpha character, at least one lowercase alpha character, and at least one number or symbol character in the password.

- Users must change their passwords every 45 days, and cannot change them again for 35 days once set.

- Users cannot reuse a password for the next 24 new passwords.

- If a user types the wrong password three times in a 30-minute period, the user account gets locked and the user must have an administrator unlock the account before the user can log on.

These values can be adjusted up or down to satisfy the specific security levels required in your environment.

Equipment Used

For this task, you need the following equipment:

- Windows Server 2003 domain controller system

- Domain Administrator access

Details

Setting the Password Policy in the Default Domain Policy

1. Log on the Windows Server 2003 domain controller system as the Domain Administrator.
2. Select Start ➢ Programs ➢ Administration Tools ➢ Active Directory Users And Computers.
3. Expand the domain. Right click on the domain name and select Properties.
4. Select the Group Policy tab. Select the Default Domain Policy.

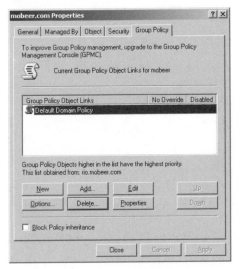

5. Select Edit. Expand the GPO to view Computer Configuration ➢ Windows Settings ➢ Security Settings ➢ Account Policies ➢ Password Policy.
6. Notice that Enforce Password History setting is by default set where you have decided you need it, at 24 Passwords Remembered. The range is from 1 to 24 passwords remembered. A zero setting means you can reuse your same password.
7. Double-click on Maximum Password Age. Set this the Password Will Expire In field to 45 days, and then select OK. The range is from 1 to 999 days. A zero setting means passwords never expire.
8. Double-click on Minimum Password Age. Set the Password Can Be Changed After setting to 35 days, and then select OK. The range is from 1 to 998. A zero setting means passwords can be changed immediately.
9. Double-click on Minimum Password Length. Set the Password Must Be At Least field to 8 characters, and then select OK. The range is from 1 to 24. A zero setting means blank passwords are accepted.

10. Notice that Password Must Meet Complexity Requirements is by default set where you have decided you need it, at Enabled.

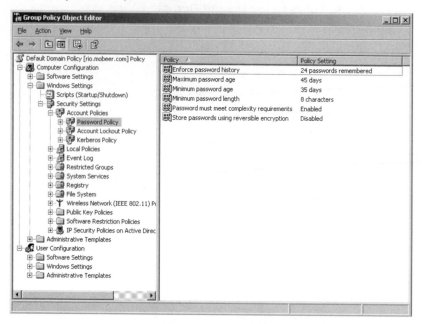

Setting the Account Lockout Policy in the Default Domain Policy

1. In the left pane, select Account Lockout Policy. Notice the default settings.

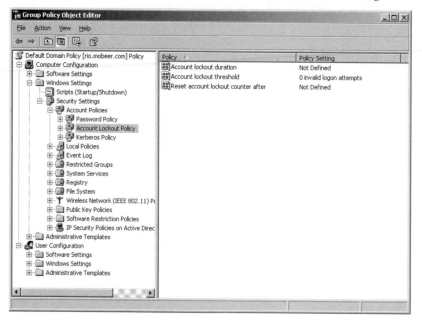

2. Double-click on Account Lockout Duration. Set this to Account Is Locked Out For: 0 Minutes. As you select 0 for the number of minutes, the dialog box changes to read Account Is Locked Out Until Administrator Unlocks It. Click OK. The range is from 1 to 99,999 attempts. A 0 setting means the account is locked out until the administrator unlocks it.

3. Double-click on Account Lockout Thresholds, set Account Will Lock Out After to 3 invalid logon attempts, and then click OK. The range is from 1 to 999 attempts. A 0 setting means the account is never locked out by the Account Lockout Policy.

4. Double-click on Reset Account Lockout Counter After and set Reset Account Lockout Counter After to 30 Minutes; then click OK. The range is from 1 to 99,999 minutes.

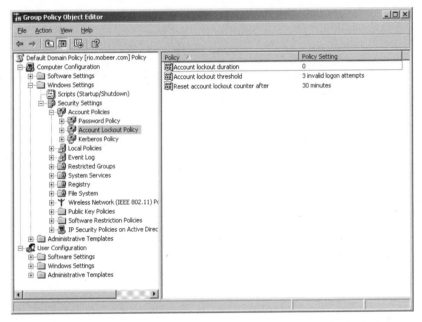

5. Close the GPO by clicking the X in the upper-right corner. Click OK in the DomainName .com Properties dialog box, where DomainName.com is the name of your domain.OTE: DomainName.com is not literally a domain, but is a reference to a variable. The reader should substitute their own domain name for DomainName.com.

This policy should be effective within a few minutes of closing the property pages for the domain. Users will experience these settings with their next password change.

Criteria for Completion

You have completed this task when you have modified the Default Domain GPO to match the specified Password Policy settings and the Account Lockout Policy settings.

Task 5.3: Auditing Logons

It is important to know when users are authenticating on your network. This could reveal such events as a user authenticating at unexpected times of the day or week, or users failing to correctly authenticate. The latter indicates a possibility that a user account is being used in a brute-force logon attack (when an attacker is attempting to guess a user's password by attempting multiple logons so that the attacker can gain unauthorized access to system resources).

Two settings are related to the auditing of logons. The first, Audit Account Logon Events, identifies when a user attempts to authenticate against a domain controller. In other words, a user is attempting to log on as a domain user. This event gets recorded in the authenticating domain controller's security event log.

The second, Audit Logon Events, identifies when a user attempts to authenticate against the local account database. In other words, a user is attempting to log on locally, as a local user. This event gets recorded in the local system's security event log.

Scenario

You are an administrator in an Active Directory environment. You are responsible for the maintenance of security for all domain user accounts. You must be able to track who logs on or attempts to log on, from which system and at what time and day. An appropriately configured audit policy is the proper tool to implement this capability.

Scope of Task

Duration

This task should take 15 minutes.

Setup

You need to generate an audit trail of all domain user logons. You will implement an audit policy for account logons in the Default Domain Policy GPO.

Caveat

Implementing an audit policy is a common approach to monitoring and recording events on your information systems. There are several aspects of auditing that an administrator should be aware of:

- Review the log files, manually or with an automated tool. Monitoring the audit logs of many domain controllers and servers can be an overwhelming task. Third-party applications are often used to collect and filter the logs from numerous servers to make them intelligible to the administrative staff.

- Secure the log files to prevent scrubbing of the logs. An attacker will erase his tracks in the log files if you do not implement proper security on the log files.

- Know when there is a real problem versus when there is just "noise." In this case, from time to time users will be working late or may forget their passwords. This is routine noise, and should be recognized for that, not to be confused with fraudulent activities or brute-force password-cracking attacks.

- Know how to react when you do detect a real problem. You should have an incident response team and plan in place for the occasions when a real threat is perceived.

- Turn the log files and be aware of the log file size, so you don't fill a drive and crash a system. To turn the log files, you save the logs as a file to the hard drive, and then clear all events on the log.

Once again, modifying any GPO, especially the Default Domain Policy, is a dangerous thing to do. This specific policy affects every computer and every user in the domain. Inappropriate changes to this policy could severely cripple access to your information systems.

Always use caution when modifying any GPO, and be sure you understand the ramifications of your configuration, as well as where you have the GPO linked.

Procedure

For this task, you will configure the audit policy in the Default Domain GPO to detect all domain account logons and failed domain logon attempts.

Equipment Used

For this task, you need the following equipment:

- Windows Server 2003 domain controller system
- Domain Administrator access

Details

Setting the Audit Policy in the Default Domain Controllers Policy

1. Log on the Windows Server 2003 domain controller system as the Domain Administrator.

2. Select Start ➢ Programs ➢ Administration Tools ➢ Active Directory Users And Computers (ADUC).

3. Expand the domain. Right-click on the Domain Controllers OU and select Properties.

4. Select the Group Policy tab.

5. Create a new GPO by clicking the New button and typing the name **Audit Account Logon Policy**. Click Edit.

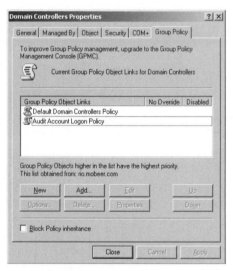

6. Expand the GPO to view Computer Configuration ➢ Windows Settings ➢ Security Settings ➢ Local Policies ➢ Audit Policy.

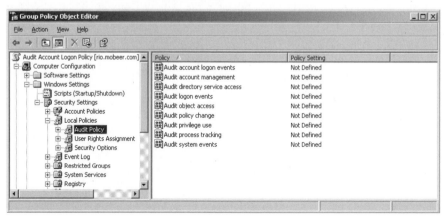

7. In the right pane, double-click on the Audit Account Logon Events.

8. Set the Define These Policy Settings to Success and Failure. Click OK.

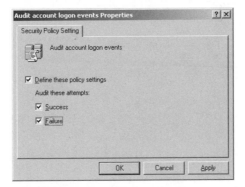

Configuring the Security Event Log in the Default Domain Controllers Policy

1. In the Audit Account Logon Policy, expand the GPO to view Computer Configuration ➢ Windows Settings ➢ Security Settings ➢ Event Log.

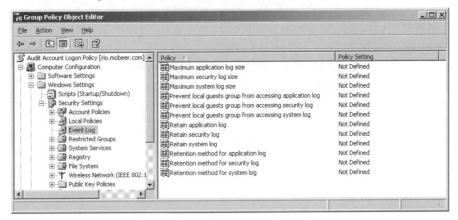

2. Double-click on Maximum Security Log Size.

NOTE   Audit events get written to the security log, viewed and managed in Event Viewer.

3. Define the Policy Setting and configure the size to 100,000 Kilobytes (100MB). The range is from 64KB to 4GB and must be in increments of 64KB. This will be automatically adjusted as you configure the settings. Each event consumes approximately 500B. 100MB allows for approximately 200,000 events written to this security log.

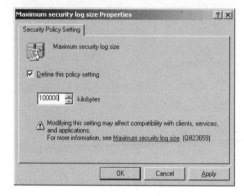

4. Click OK.

5. Double-click on Prevent Local Guests Group From Accessing Security Log.

6. Set This Policy Setting as Enabled. Click OK.

7. Double-click on Retention Method For Security Log.

8. Set This Policy Setting as Do Not Overwrite Events (Clear Log Manually). Click OK.

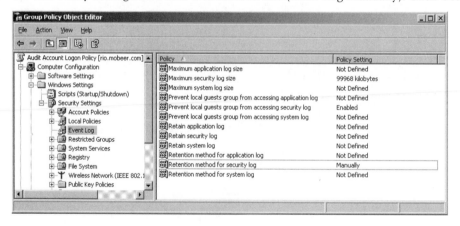

Configuring Security Options for Security Logging in the Default Domain Controllers Policy

 This setting will ensure that you never miss an auditing event by actually shutting down the server, in this case, the domain controller, if the security log gets full. This will kill the domain controller(s) if you do not remember to turn logs regularly.

1. In the Audit Account Logon Policy, expand the GPO to view Computer Configuration ➤ Windows Settings ➤ Security Settings ➤ Local Policies ➤ Security Options.

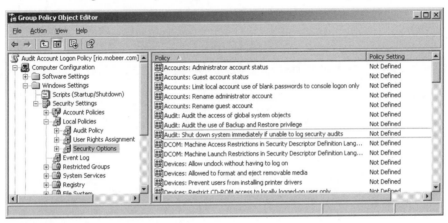

2. Double-click on Audit: Shut Down System Immediately If Unable To Log Security Audits.
3. Set This Policy Setting to Enabled. Click OK.

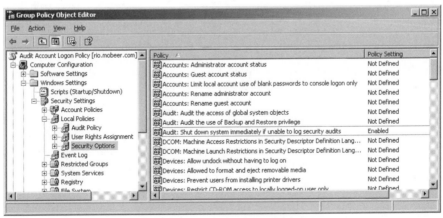

4. Close the GPO by selecting the X in the upper-right corner. Click Close in the Domain Controllers Properties dialog box.

 This policy should be effective within five minutes of closing the property pages for the domain. Users will experience these settings with their next password change.

5. Close ADUC.

Monitoring the Security Logs for Account Logon Events

1. Launch Event Viewer by selecting Start ➤ Run. In the Open field, type **EVENTVWR** and click OK.

2. In the left pane of Event Viewer, select Security.

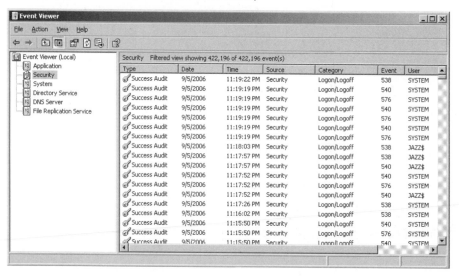

3. In the left pane of Event Viewer, right-click Security and select Properties. Select the Filter tab.

 An indication of a successful logon event is Event ID 673 – TGT Granted. An indication of a failed logon event is Event ID 675 – Failed Logon for XP or 2003 clients, or Event ID 681 – Failed Logon for non-XP or 2003 clients.

4. Clear the event types for Information, Warning, and Error, and in the Event ID field, enter the first of the account logon event IDs—673—and click Apply.

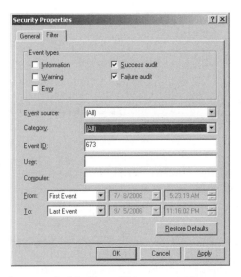

5.   Review any events that match this filter. This event indicates a successful logon.

6.   In the Event ID field, enter the event ID 675 to review failed logons.

 If there are no events that match this event ID, 675, you may perform one or two logons with an incorrect password to generate this event, and then logon successfully. Launch Event Viewer and review the security log with this filter configured.

 You must reset these manually to display all events again. Check all five event types for Information, Warning, Error, Success Audit, and Failure Audit and clear the Event ID field. Then click Apply.

7.   After resetting the filter on the security log, click OK to close the properties and close Event Viewer. You must either set the Security Log to Overwrite as needed, or you must remember to turn the log on a regular basis.

Criteria for Completion

You have completed this task when you have modified the Default Domain Controller GPO to audit success and failure of all domain account logons, configured and secured the security event log, and ensured that you will never miss an account logon event. Also, you should know how to filter and monitor these Account Logon events in Event Viewer.

Task 5.4: Securing the Default User Accounts

During the installation of a Server 2003 or XP operating system, two user accounts are created by default: the Local Administrator and the Guest account. These accounts live in the local accounts database (LAD) and remain there on XP, member servers, and stand-alone servers.

As you DCPromo a server to create a new domain and become a domain controller, the LAD is replaced with the Active Directory (AD) database on that system. All accounts in the LAD are destroyed. Two default domain accounts are created for this new domain and they live in AD. These are the Administrator for the domain, and the Guest account for the domain.

In addition to the AD database, a new LAD is created for Directory Services Restore Mode (DSRM) and for Recovery Console login. Only one account lives in this LAD. It is the Local Administrator, to be used solely for these two disaster recovery purposes.

These accounts are built automatically and named by these names—always. This makes an easy target for an attacker. These accounts must be secured to mitigate their vulnerability.

You should already have a strong password policy in place. You should also have an administrative policy that dictates that no administrator is allowed to use the true Administrator account or reset the true Administrator password.

Scenario

You are responsible for the security of your domain. You want to reduce the potential for attack on user accounts and have decided to strengthen the default user accounts for the domain, and on several of your most critical servers.

Scope of Task

Duration

This task should take 20 minutes.

Setup

You will edit the Default Domain Policy to rename the Local and Domain Administrator and Guest accounts of all systems in the domain. Using this same GPO, you will disable the local Guest account on all systems in the domain.

On the domain controller, you will reset the DSRM and Recovery Console Administrator logon password.

Caveat

Renaming the Administrator account on every system on the domain can cause services, applications, drive and printer mappings, and scheduled tasks to fail. This should be analyzed prior to changing the Administrator account.

Resetting passwords can cause the loss of data. The forced reset of the password in ADUC destroys access to all EFS content, all stored passwords in Microsoft Internet Explorer, and all encrypted e-mail by the user. If you know the old password and can change the password for a user using the Change Password utility, this loss of content is eliminated.

Always use caution when modifying any GPO, and be sure you understand the ramifications of your configuration, as well as where you have the GPO linked.

Procedure

You will implement a GPO at the domain level to rename the Local and Domain Administrator and Guest accounts on all systems in the domain, and disable the Guest account. You will create a decoy Administrator account with virtually no privileges. You will then reset the password on the Local Administrator account (used for DSRM and Recovery Console) on a domain controller to implement a standard, strong password.

Equipment Used

For this task, you need the following equipment:

- Windows Server 2003 domain controller system
- Domain Administrator access

Details

Managing the Default Users with the Default Domain Policy

1. Log on the Windows Server 2003 domain controller system as the Domain Administrator.
2. Select Start ➢ Programs ➢ Administration Tools ➢ Active Directory Users And Computers (ADUC).
3. Select the domain name. Right-click on the domain name and select Properties. Select the Group Policy tab.
4. Select the Default Domain Policy and click the Edit button.

5. Expand the GPO to view Computer Configuration ➤ Windows Settings ➤ Security Settings ➤ Local Policies ➤ Security Options.

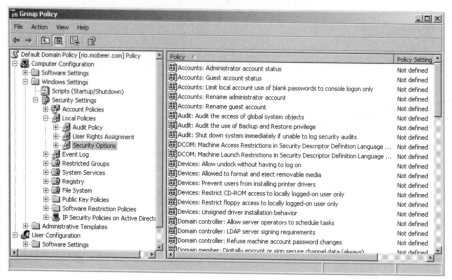

6. In the right pane, double-click Accounts and rename it to **Administrator Account**.

WARNING

Renaming the Administrator account on every system on the domain can cause services, applications, drive and printer mappings, and scheduled tasks to fail. This should be analyzed prior to changing the Administrator account. This does not rename the DSRM Administrator account on the domain controllers

7. In the Define This Policy Setting field, type the new administrator account name: **TopDog**. Click OK.

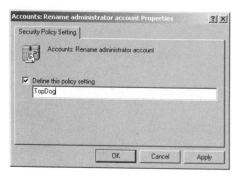

8. In the right pane, double-click Accounts and rename it to **Guest Account**.

9. In the Define This Policy Setting field, type the new Guest account name: **JoeBlow**. Click OK.

10. In the right pane, double-click Accounts and rename it to **Guest Account Status**.

11. Set the Define This Policy Setting option to Disabled. Click OK.

You may choose to disable the Administrator accounts on each local system as well. The GPO has a setting for Accounts: Administrator account status. This setting could be set to Disabled.

Disabling the Administrator account on every system on the domain can cause services, applications, drive and printer mappings, and scheduled tasks to fail. This should be analyzed prior to disabling the Administrator account.

You will not be disabling the Administrator account in this exercise.

12. Confirm your settings in the GPO.

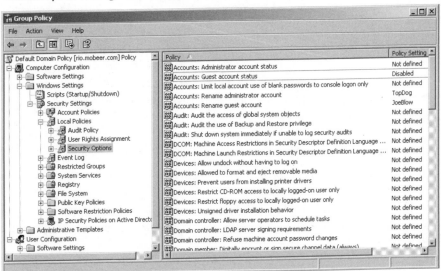

13. Close the GPO by clicking the X in the upper-right corner. Click Close in the DomainName .com Properties dialog box.

> This policy should be fully effective within 120 minutes of closing the property pages for the domain.

Creating a Decoy Domain Administrator Account

1. In ADUC, expand the domain name.

2. In the left pane, select the Users container.

3. In the right pane, select the Administrator user object.

4. Right-click on the Administrator user object and click Rename.

> You have already changed the logon name to TopDog with the Default Domain Policy. This step changes the Display Name of the account to match, and further obscures the Administrator account from the unaware attacker.

5. Type in the new name—**TopDog**—and press Enter. You will receive a warning about needing to log off immediately and logging back on with the new credentials.

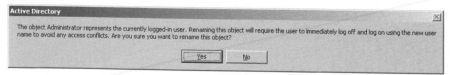

Active Directory

The object Administrator represents the currently logged-in user. Renaming this object will require the user to immediately log off and log on using the new user name to avoid any access conflicts. Are you sure you want to rename this object?

Yes   No

> Be sure you have saved all of your work and have closed all applications except ADUC before proceeding.

6. After confirming that it is safe to log off the system, click Yes.

7. Complete the Rename User dialog box by filling in the new name for the Administrator account: **TopDog**.

8. In the User Logon Name area, select the proper User Principal Name (UPN) from the drop-down list. This usually matches the user's e-mail address and can be used as a logon name. Click Next.

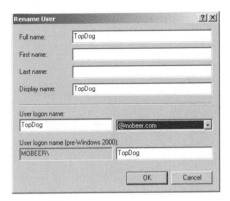

9. Close all applications. Select Start ➢ Log Off.

10. Log on to the domain with the new username, TopDog (formerly Administrator), and the appropriate password.

11. Select Start ➢ Programs ➢ Administration Tools ➢ Active Directory Users And Computers (ADUC)

12. Expand the domain. In the left pane, select the Users container.

13. Right-click on the Users container and select New ➢ User.

14. In the First Name field, type **Administrator**.

15. In the User Logon Name field, type **Administrator**.

16. In the User Logon Name area, select the proper User Principal Name (UPN) from the drop-down list. This usually matches the user's e-mail address and can be used as a logon name. Click Next.

17. Type a strong password (the stronger, the better) in the Password and Confirm Password fields.

18. Disable User Must Change Password At Next Logon, and enable the other three settings.

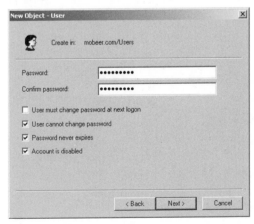

19. Click Next. Click Finish to create the decoy Administrator account.

20. Double-click on the TopDog user object. Highlight the information in the Description field. Right-click the highlight and select Cut.

21. Close the TopDog Properties dialog box.

22. Double-click the decoy Administrator user object. Right-click in the Description field and select Paste.

23. Close the decoy Administrator Properties dialog box.

 This account could be placed in groups that have restrictive Deny permissions to further reduce accesses from this account. The Deny Domain Local Group process will be covered in Task 5.5.

Resetting the DSRM Administrator Password

1. You will need to run NTDSUTIL from a command window. Close all applications. Select Start ➢ Run, and type **CMD**.

2. In the command window, at the C:\ prompt, type **NTDSUTIL** and press Enter.

3. At the NTDSUTIL prompt, type **HELP** and press Enter. Observe the response:

```
?                              - Show this help
                                 information
Authoritative restore          - Authoritatively
                                 restore the DIT database
Configurable Settings          - Manage configurable settings
Domain management              - Prepare for new domain creation
Files                          - Manage NTDS database files
Help                           - Show this help information
LDAP policies                  - Manage LDAP protocol policies
Metadata cleanup               - Clean up objects of
                                 decommissioned servers
Popups %s                      - (en/dis)able popups
                                 with "on" or "off"
Quit                           - Quit the utility
Roles                          - Manage NTDS role owner tokens
Security account management    - Manage Security
                                 Account Database -
                                 Duplicate SID Cleanup
Semantic database analysis     - Semantic Checker
```

```
Set DSRM Password                  - Reset directory
                                     service restore mode
                                     administrator account
                                     password
```

4. At the NTDSUTIL prompt, type **Set DSRM Password** and press Enter.

5. At the Reset DSRM Administrator Password prompt, type **HELP** and press Enter. Observe the response:

```
?                               - Show this help information
Help                            - Show this help information
Quit                            - Return to the prior menu
Reset Password on server %s     - Reset directory
                                  service restore mode
                                  administrator account
                                  password on specified
                                  domain controler. Use NULL
                                  for local machine.
```

 You cannot use NTDSUTIL to reset this password if the target domain controller is currently in Directory Service Restore mode.

6. To reset the DSRM Administrator password on the local domain controller, at the Reset DSRM Administrator Password prompt, type **Reset Password on Server NULL** and press Enter.

7. You will be prompted for the new DSRM Administrator password. Type the new password **Password1**, and press Enter:

```
Please type password for DS Restore Mode Administrator Account:
*********
```

8. You will be prompted to confirm the new password. Type the password **Password1**, and press Enter:

```
Please confirm new password: *********
```

You may receive a notice as shown here:

```
Because the local system doesn't support application password
validation, ntdsutil couldn't verify the password with the domain
policy. But ntdsutil will continue to set the password on DS
Restore Mode Administrator account.
```

You should see a success message:

Password has been set successfully.

> You could use this tool to reset the DSRM Administrator password on remote domain controllers in the domain by specifying the fully qualified domain name (FQDN) of each DC, as shown here: Reset Password on Server rio.mobeer.com.

9. At the Reset DSRM Administrator Password prompt, type **QUIT** and press Enter.
10. At the NTDSUTIL prompt, type **QUIT** and press Enter.
11. Close the command window by typing **EXIT** and pressing Enter.

Criteria for Completion

You have completed this task when you have modified the Default Domain GPO to rename the Administrator and Guest logon names, and have disabled the Guest accounts throughout the entire domain. You then renamed the Administrator account and created a decoy administrator account with no privileges. You then reset the DSRM.

Task 5.5: Implementing a Deny Group

It may be important to be able to lock a collection of users out of certain sensitive content. This can be accomplished by building AGDLP, and granting the NTFS Deny Full Control permission to the Domain Local Group (DLG).

The Deny permission is all powerful and overrules any collection of Allow permissions.

Scenario

You are responsible for the security of your information systems. You have a new folder with sensitive content that should not be viewed by the Widget Production Department personnel. You must implement security so that you are certain no member of the Widget Production Department will ever get access to this content

Scope of Task

Duration

This task should take 20 minutes.

Setup

You have a new folder on the domain controller that contains sensitive content. You will set the NTFS permissions on the content so that the Widget Production workers will never gain access, even accidentally.

Caveat

The Deny permission is all powerful and overrules any collection of Allow permissions. As users change jobs in an organization through promotions and transfers, their access requirements change. Being a member of a group with any Deny permissions will overrule all Allow permissions granted by adding the user into other groups.

If a user continues to receive Access Denied errors, check for membership in any Deny groups that may have been built.

Procedure

Using ADUC, you will build Deny All GG and Deny All DLG. You will then add the production workers into the Deny All GG, place the Deny All GG into the Deny All DLG, and then grant the NTFS Deny Full Control permissions to the Deny All DLG on a folder containing sensitive content.

Equipment Used

For this task, you need the following equipment:

- Windows Server 2003 domain controller system
- Domain Administrator access
- Completion of Task 5.1: Creating User Accounts

Details

Building the Deny All AGLP

1. Log on the Windows Server 2003 domain controller system as the Domain Administrator.
2. Select Start ➢ Programs ➢ Administration Tools ➢ Active Directory Users And Computers (ADUC).
3. In the left pane, expand the domain and select the Widget Production OU.
4. Right-click on the Widget Production OU and select New ➢ Group.

5. Name the new group **Deny All GG,** and select Global under Group Scope and Security under Group Type. Click OK.

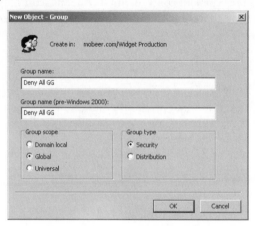

6. Right-click on the Widget Production OU and select New ➢ Group.

7. Name the new group **Deny All DLG,** and select Domain Local under Group Scope and Security under Group Type. Click OK.

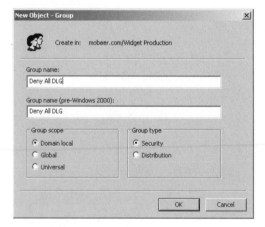

8. Now you will add the users from the Widget Production OU into the Global Group. Double-click on the Global Group named Deny All GG. On the Members tab, click Add.

9. Click Advanced.

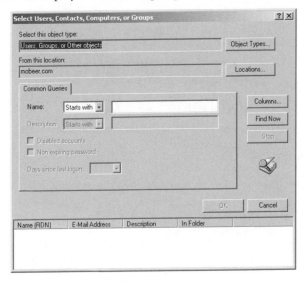

10. Click Find Now to display all users and groups in the domain.

11. Select Prod1 through Prod5. To select all five users at once, you can click on Prod1, then press and hold the Shift button on the keyboard and click on Prod5. Then click OK.

 NOTE   It doesn't matter that these accounts are disabled from the earlier exercise. They can still be managed regarding group membership.

12. Click OK a second time to add these users into the Widget Production GG.

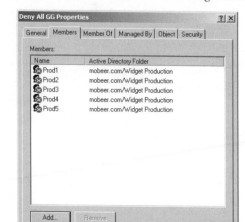

13. In the Deny All GG Properties dialog box, select the Member Of tab.

14. Add the Deny All GG into the Domain Local Group called Deny All DLG by first clicking Add.

15. Click Advanced.

16. Click Find Now to display all users and groups in the domain.

17. Select the Deny All DLG. Then click OK.

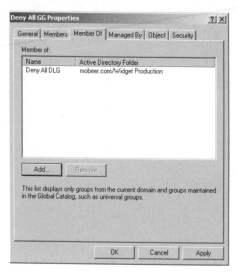

18. Click OK a second time to add the Deny All GG into the Deny All DLG.

19. Click OK to close the Deny All GG Properties dialog box.

> You have just assembled AGL of the AGDLP chain for granting permissions (Users into Deny All GG; Deny All GG into Deny All DLG).

Next you will grant NTFS Deny Full Control permissions the Deny All DLG. This will not allow any access to the content by the members of the Deny All DLG.

1. Launch Explorer by right-clicking the Start button and selecting Explore.

2. In the left pane, select the root of a drive that holds the folder STUFF.

> If the STUFF folder does not exist, create a new folder named STUFF and copy a few files into it.

3. In the right pane, right-click on the folder STUFF and select Properties. Select the Security tab.

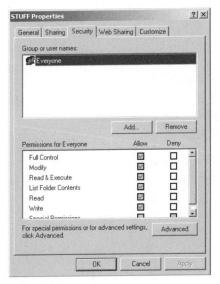

> The Security tab is used to set NTFS permissions—that is, permissions that control picking the files up off the NTFS volume.

4.   Click Add.

5.   Click Advanced.

6.   Click Find Now to display all users and groups in the domain.

7.   Select the Deny All DLG. Then click OK.

8.   Click OK a second time to add the Deny All DLG into the Access Control List for the STUFF folder.

9.   With the Deny All DLG selected in the upper pane, check the Deny Full Control permission in the lower pane. This collection of Deny All permissions denies any access to the Deny All DLG at the NTFS level for this folder.

10. Click Apply. You will receive a security warning regarding the power of the Deny permission. Review the warning and click Yes to continue.

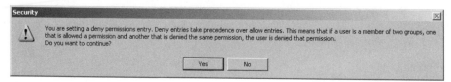

11. Click OK to close the STUFF Properties dialog box.

From this point forward, no matter what Allow permissions may be granted, through any other AGDLP chain, any member of the Deny All A-G-DL-P chain will be denied access to the content in the STUFF folder.

Criteria for Completion

You have completed this task when you have built the AGDLP and have assigned Deny Full Control permissions to the Deny All Domain Local Group on a folder with sensitive content.

Phase

6

Network Security

Network security involves the protection of data as it travels the wires of your private network, or even as it traverses the public wires of the Internet. We'll look at several techniques, including encrypting data for file transfers and implementing security on wireless networks.

The virtual private network (VPN) is one of the most common approaches to securing data as it flows over the network. There are many types of VPNs, and they vary in their strength of authentication, encryption, and integrity validation. Generally speaking, the stronger the authentication, encryption, and integrity validation, the greater the overhead is on the system, and the poorer the performance of the data transmission.

A VPN is often referred to as a tunnel, since it creates a secure tunnel through the non-secure Internet.

VPNs typically have three major components:

- An authentication mechanism (which may be one-way or mutual), such as:
  - Passwords
  - Kerberos
  - SESAME (Secure European System for Applications is a Multi-vendor Environment)
  - Digital certificates (PKI)
- An encryption algorithm (or standard), which provides confidentiality; examples include:
  - RC4
  - DES
  - 3DES
  - AES
- An integrity validation mechanism, which ensures that the data hasn't been tampered with, and can provide nonrepudiation in the strongest forms; examples include:
  - MD5
  - SHA1
  - SHA2
  - MAC
  - MIC
  - CCMP

First, you'll look at deploying VPNs on a corporate network, through the use of Group Policy Objects (GPOs), and you'll see how to take advantage of Active Directory to assist with this process. Then you'll look at building a point-to-point VPN from a VPN client to a VPN server, as you would over the Internet.

You'll also look at performing secure, remote administration and securely launching administrative tools.

The tasks in this phase map to Domains 2, 3, 4, and 5 objectives for the CompTIA Security+ exam (`http://certification.comptia.org/security/`).

Task 6.1: Deploying IPSec

Internet Protocol Security (IPSec) is currently one of the strongest VPN technologies available. In its default configuration, it can be relatively easy to set up, but is very versatile and can become quite complex. It is an open standard and can be adjusted to integrate with your existing environment. The strength of the encryption, authentication, and integrity validation can also be adjusted.

In the Microsoft implementation, currently running on Windows Server 2003 and Windows XP Professional, the default configuration uses Kerberos for authentication. This is what your Active Directory environment uses to authenticate users. It also uses three passes of the Data Encryption Standard—referred to as 3DES or triple DES—for its encryption algorithm. For integrity validation, the default settings use the Secure Hashing Algorithm, 160 bit (referred to as SHA1).

To improve performance, you can implement a single pass of DES, along with using Message Digest version 5 (MD5) for integrity validation. These are weaker but less demanding of the resources on the system, thus resulting in better system performance.

Scenario

You have several file servers that contain sensitive data. You must ensure that all communications with these servers are implemented through a VPN.

Scope of Task

Duration

This task should take 30 minutes.

Setup

You are an administrator in an Active Directory environment. You will configure a Secure Server IPSec Policy GPO on the organizational unit (OU), which holds the file servers with sensitive data. This policy will require that all communications to these servers be protected with IPSec.

You must then implement a second Client Respond IPSec Policy GPO to enable IPSec for the users. You will link this to an OU that holds the only clients authorized to access these secure servers. IPSec isn't available for users by default since it degrades the performance of the systems.

Caveat

If the IPSec policy is implemented incorrectly, the entire network infrastructure can fail. Do not implement the Secure Server IPSec policy for any systems that provide network infrastructure services, like domain controllers, DNS servers, WINS servers, or RRAS servers. These services will fail. Implement the Secure Server IPSec policy only on the select few file servers holding sensitive data. You should also expect noticeable performance degradation, due to the CPU horsepower required to perform the massive mathematical calculations inside the encryption standard.

Procedure

For this task, you will produce a Secure Server IPSec Policy GPO that is linked to a new OU called the Confidential Servers OU. You will then produce a Client Respond IPSec Policy GPO that is linked to a new OU called the Confidential Clients OU.

Equipment Used

For this task, you need the following equipment:

- Windows Server 2003 domain controller system
- Domain Administrator access

Details

Creating the OU Infrastructure

1. Log on the Windows Server 2003 domain controller system as the Domain Administrator.
2. Select Start ➤ Programs ➤ Administration Tools ➤ Active Directory Users And Computers (ADUC).
3. Expand the domain. Click on the domain name.
4. In the right pane, right-click and select New ➤ Organizational Unit.
5. Name the new OU **Confidential Servers**. This OU would be populated with the computer accounts for the file servers holding the sensitive data.

Any systems placed in this OU will require IPSec for all communications. If the system is providing any network infrastructure services, many of these services will fail. Place servers in this OU that are providing file and printer sharing services only.

6. Click on the domain name.

7. In the right pane, right-click and select New ➤ Organizational Unit.

8. Name the new OU **Confidential Clients**.

This OU would be populated with the computer accounts for the client systems that need to access the sensitive data.

Any systems placed in this OU will experience performance degradation when communicating with IPSec secure servers.

Building the Secure Server IPSec Policy GPO

1. Right-click on the Confidential Servers OU and select Properties. Select the Group Policy tab.

2. Click the New button and name the new GPO **IPSec Secure Servers Policy**.

3. Click Edit to open the IPSec Secure Server GPO.

4. Expand Computer Configuration ➤ Windows Settings ➤ Security Settings, and select IP Security Policies on Active Directory.

Notice that none of the policies are currently assigned.

5. In the right pane, right-click on Secure Server (Require Security), and select Assign.

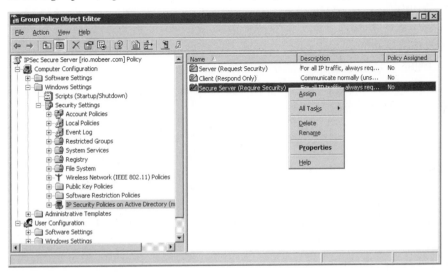

6. Confirm that the policy is now assigned.

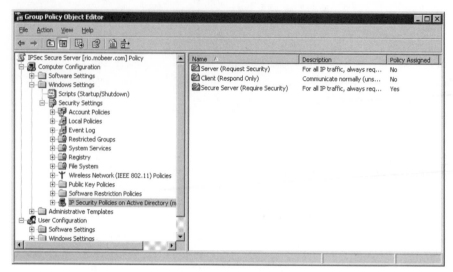

 WARNING Any Windows 2000 Server, 2000 Workstation, Server 2003, XP, or Vista system placed into this OU will require IPSec for all communications that are initiated remotely.

7. Close the IPSec Secure Server Policy GPO. Click OK to close the Confidential Servers Properties dialog box.

Building the Client Respond IPSec Policy GPO

1. Right-click on the Confidential Clients OU and select Properties. Select the Group Policy tab.

2. Click the New button and name the new GPO **IPSec Client Respond Policy**.

3. Click Edit to open the IPSec Client Respond GPO.

4. Expand Computer Configuration ➢ Windows Settings ➢ Security Settings, and select IP Security Policies on Active Directory.

 NOTE Notice that none of the policies are currently assigned.

5. In the right pane, right-click on Client (Respond Only), and select Assign.

6. Confirm that the policy is now assigned.

WARNING Any Windows 2000 Server, 2000 Workstation, Server 2003, XP or Vista system placed into this OU will implement IPSec for all communications that are initiated locally, to IPSec Servers.

7. Close the IPSec Client Respond Policy GPO. Click OK to close the Confidential Clients Properties dialog box.

Criteria for Completion

You have completed this task when you have created the OU for the servers and another one for the clients. You must also have created and assigned the Secure Server IPSec Policy on the servers OU and the Client Respond IPSec Policy on the Clients OU.

Task 6.2: Configuring the VPN Server

As more and more employees telecommute to the office, VPN technology has become increasingly important. A VPN server at the office allows for secure communications between the worker at home connecting to the office LAN over the public wires of the Internet.

There are many vendors of VPN server software and appliances, offering a wide variety of strengths of authentication, encryption, and integrity validation. Any Microsoft server-class operating system has the capability to be configured as a VPN server, securely connecting the telecommuter to the corporate LAN, as if they were directly connected to the Ethernet cabling inside the office.

The weaker—but often considered acceptable strength—VPN implements Point-to-Point Tunneling Protocol (PPTP), which is based on the RC4 encryption algorithm. This is only available for Microsoft clients (from Windows 95 and up), and uses standard Microsoft authentication schemes (NTLM or NTLMv2).

The next step up in VPN strength is IPSec, which implements 3DES (or DES) for encryption and SHA1 (or MD5) for integrity validation. This is only available for Microsoft clients (from Windows 2000 and up), and uses standard Microsoft authentication schemes (Kerberos), but can be strengthened to use digital certificates for authentication.

The third and strongest VPN from Microsoft is the combination of Layer 2 Tunneling Protocol (L2TP) with IPSec. L2TP provides strong, mutual authentication, based on digital certificates on the VPN client and server computers. This authentication scheme is so strong that a sender cannot deny sending the message. This is called *nonrepudiation*. L2TP also provides strong integrity validation using Message Integrity Check (MIC). Interestingly, L2TP does not provide data encryption. This is why you typically add IPSec that does provide data encryption for confidentiality.

Remember that, generally speaking, the stronger the security (authentication, encryption, and integrity validation), the poorer the performance on both the VPN server and the VPN client. The mathematical calculations implemented by the encryption and hashing algorithms, and the increased complexity of authentication, all take their toll on the speed of the connection and data flow.

> At the time of this writing, Microsoft had not yet released the stronger Advanced Encryption Algorithm (AES) implementation of IPSec. AES is currently considered "un-crackable." If you're interested in the nitty-gritty of how AES works, see ""Keep Your Data Secure with the New Advanced Encryption Standard," at http://msdn.microsoft.com/msdnmag/issues/03/11/AES/.

Scenario

You are the administrator of a Microsoft Windows Active Directory environment and have workers who telecommute. You must configure a system to securely provide resources to these workers who connect over the Internet.

You will build the VPN client and test the configuration in Task 6.3, "Configuring the VPN Client."

Scope of Task

Duration

This task should take 20 minutes.

Setup

You will initialize and configure the VPN server. On Windows Server 2003, the VPN is configured in the Routing and Remote Access Services (RRAS) server.

Caveat

VPN servers are often connected to public networks, like the Internet. In other words, these systems are exposed to the most hostile of environments and are subject to frequent attacks. Because of this public exposure, it is not uncommon that these systems become compromised. These systems should be hardened and dedicated-purpose servers. Don't run anything more on these systems than is absolutely required.

Procedure

For this task, you will initialize and configure the RRAS server on a Windows Server 2003 server. You will configure the ports for inbound VPN connections.

You will also configure a user account with the privilege to connect to the server using the RRAS service. VPN technology is an extension of dial-in services, originally utilizing slow, analog modems over telephone lines. Users require the privilege to dial in to connect to the VPN server. No user account is granted the dial-in privilege by default.

Equipment Used

For this task, you need the following equipment:

- Windows Server 2003 system
- Access to Active Directory Users And Computers (ADUC)
- Administrator access

Details

Initializing the VPN Services in RRAS

1. Log on the Windows Server 2003 system as the Administrator.
2. Select Start ➢ Programs ➢ Administration Tools ➢ Routing And Remote Access.
3. If this is the first time you've used RRAS, the service will be stopped.

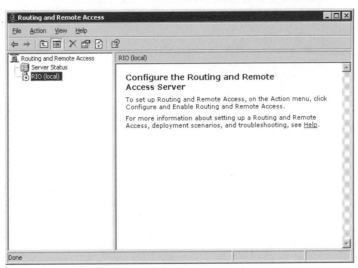

4. In the left pane, select the *server_name* (local). Right-click and select Configure And Enable Routing And Remote Access. Click Next in the RRAS Setup Wizard.

5. Select Custom Configuration, and click Next.

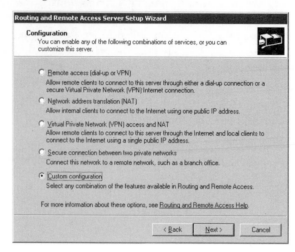

6. In the Custom Configuration dialog box, select VPN Access and click Next, and then click Finish.

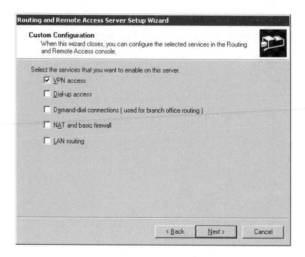

7. You will be prompted to start the RRAS Service. Click Yes.

8. Expand *server_name*(local) as necessary. Select Ports.

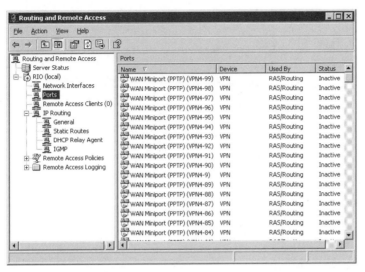

9. Right-click on Ports and select Properties. Notice that by default, there are 128 PPTP ports enabled and 128 L2TP ports enabled. For performance and security reasons, you should reduce these numbers to something closer to the number of concurrent VPN connections you are expected to support.

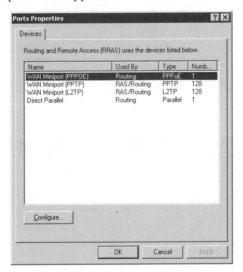

10. Select WAN Miniport (PPTP) and click Configure to open the Configure Device dialog box.

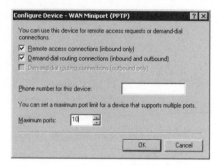

11. Reduce the Maximum Ports value to 10 and click OK. You will receive a warning message about possibly disconnecting active sessions. Click Yes to continue.

12. Select WAN Miniport (L2TP) and click Configure.

13. Reduce the Maximum Ports value to 10 and click OK. You will receive a warning message about possibly disconnecting active sessions. Click Yes to continue.

14. Minimize the RRAS console.

You will be returning to this console in the following task, "Configuring a VPN Client."

Granting the Dial-in Privilege to Users

1. Select Start ➤ Programs ➤ Administration Tools ➤ Active Directory Users and Computers (ADUC).

2. Expand the domain. Select the Users container.

3. In the right pane, select the Administrator account. Right-click the Administrator account and select Properties.

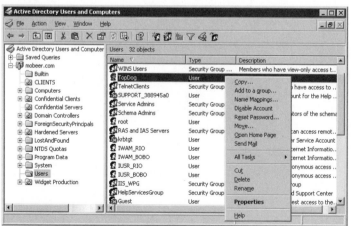

You will remember that in Task 5.4 you renamed the Administrator account, and created a useless account named Administrator to increase security for default accounts. The account shown in the graphic named TopDog is the administrator for the domain. You would select (multiple-select with Shift-click or Ctrl-click) the accounts that require VPN access and grant the dial-in privilege, as necessary.

In production, it is generally not advisable to install the RRAS/VPN service on a domain controller. Domain controllers are the foundation for the security of the Active Directory environment and remote connectivity is typically not enabled for these systems. In your configuration, if the VPN server is configured on a domain controller, additional privilege must be granted to any nonadministrator VPN users. Nonadministrator users are not allowed to log on to a domain controller by default. Nonadministrator users would need to be granted the right to log on locally to the domain controller/VPN server.

4. Select the Dial-in tab of the user account Properties dialog box. Select Allow Access in the Remote Access Permission (Dial-in Or VPN) section.

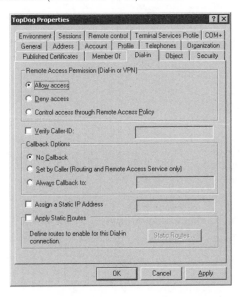

5. Click OK to close the user Properties dialog box. Close ADUC.

Criteria for Completion

You have completed this task when you have initialized and configured RRAS for ten PPTP ports and ten L2TP ports. You must have then granted the dial-in privilege to the appropriate VPN user accounts in ADUC.

Task 6.3: Configuring the VPN Client

In Task 6.2, you initialized and configured the VPN server. The server would be connected to the corporate LAN, behind a firewall. The firewall, actually the Network Address Translation (NAT) server component of the firewall, would be configured to forward all inbound VPN connections to the internal VPN server.

No server service is useful until it has clients. That goes for VPN servers as well.

Scenario

You are the administrator of a Microsoft Windows Active Directory environment and have workers that telecommute. You must configure the client systems to securely access resources over the Internet.

This task requires the completion of Task 6.2, "Configuring the VPN Server."

Scope of Task

Duration

This task should take 20 minutes.

Setup

You will configure the client side of the VPN.

Caveat

The encryption process demands large amounts of CPU clock cycles. This will cause noticeable degradation in the performance of both the VPN server and the VPN client systems.

Procedure

For this task, you will configure the VPN client to connect to the VPN server you configured in Task 6.2. You will then confirm the connection on the VPN server.

Equipment Used

For this task, you need the following equipment:

- Windows XP Professional system
- Administrator access
- Connectivity to the VPN server configured in Task 6.2

Details

Configuring the VPN Client

1. Log on the Windows XP Professional system as the Administrator.
2. Select Start ➤ Programs ➤ Accessories ➤ Communications ➤ New Connection Wizard.
3. Click Next on the first page of the New Connection Wizard.
4. Select Connect To The Network At My Workplace. Notice the reference to the VPN in the description. Click Next.

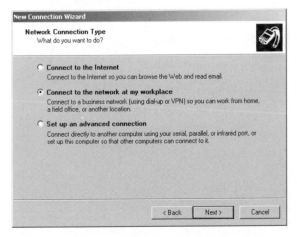

5. In the Network Connection screen, select Virtual Private Network Connection, and click Next.

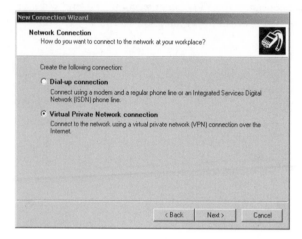

6. In the Connection Name screen, type the description **VPN** for your VPN connection. Click Next.

7. In the VPN Server Selection screen, type the name or IP address for your VPN server. Click Next.

8. In the Connection Availability screen, select My Use Only as the Create This Connection For option. Click Next.

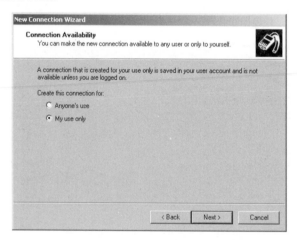

9. In the Completing The New Connection Wizard screen, select the check box to add a shortcut to your desktop and click Finish to complete the wizard.

10. Launch the VPN connection from the desktop icon. Select Properties and then select the Networking tab.

11. From the Type Of VPN drop-down in the Networking tab, select PPTP VPN. Click OK to close the Properties dialog box.

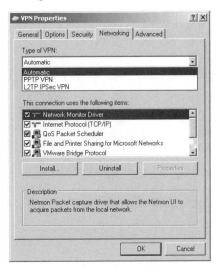

Connecting the VPN Client to the VPN Server

1. In the Connect VPN dialog box, type in the name of the account you granted dial-in permissions to in Task 6.2.

2. Type the password for this account.

3. Select the option Save This Username And Password For The Following Users Me Only.

4. Click Connect. You should see a dialog box that details the process of the authentication and then the registration of your computer on the (remote) network.

5. You are now connected to the VPN server. All communications between this client system and the VPN server system are encrypted.

Confirming the VPN Connection

1. Log on to the VPN server as the Administrator.

2. If it's not already running, launch RRAS by selecting Start ➤ Programs ➤ Administration Tools ➤ Routing And Remote Access.

3. Expand *server_name*(local) as necessary. Select Ports.

4. In the right pane, click on the column title Status, once or twice, to see the active connection on the PPTP port.

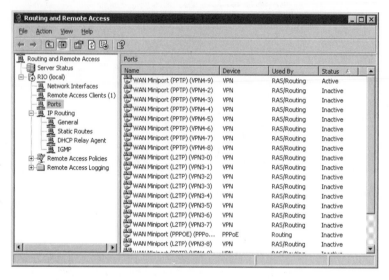

5. In the left pane, notice that there is currently one Remote Access Client. Select Remote Access Clients in the left pane.

6. You should see your inbound VPN connection in the right pane. Right-click on the VPN client connection in the right pane and select Disconnect

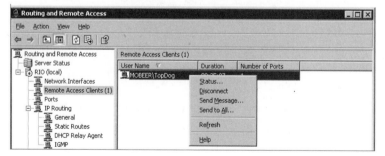

Notice that you can disconnect this VPN client, or send the client a message.

Criteria for Completion

You have completed this task when you have configured a VPN client and successfully connected to the VPN server, then confirmed the connection by viewing the Ports and Remote Access Clients properties of the RRAS/VPN server.

Task 6.4: Implementing Secure Remote Administration

It has become routine practice to perform administrative tasks from the comfort of your own office, rather than sitting in the cold, cluttered, noisy server room. This is done by utilizing remote administration tools, one of the most prevalent being the Remote Desktop Protocol (RDP).

RDP is an extension of Terminal Services (TS). It allows for a maximum of two inbound connections for administrative purposes. Terminal Services limits the number of inbound connections by the number of client access licenses you purchase and activate.

RDP uses the same port as TS, port 3389, and is automatically encrypted using 128-bit RC4. This can be further strengthened by implementing the newer RDP over SSL. RDP over SSL still uses port 3389 and requires a digital certificate on the TS server. For even stronger security, you can implement mutual authentication by requiring a digital certificate on the TS client as well.

RDP has been available as long ago as Windows NT 4, and can be used on both server and client operating systems.

Scenario

You are the administrator of a Microsoft Windows environment and need to perform administrative tasks on remote XP Professional computers.

Scope of Task

Duration

This task should take 30 minutes.

Setup

Remote Desktop must be enabled on the target, remote system. This system will be the RDP server.

There are several considerations regarding the status and configuration of the user account that will be performing the remote administration. The client system must be configured correctly to implement the RDP connection to the RDP server.

Caveat

RDP access to a system is a fine thing for an administrator who doesn't have physical access to a system, or who prefers to work in the comfort of their own office instead of the server room. It is also a fine thing for an attacker. This is his remote doorway into your systems. Allowing RDP connections to any system increases the vulnerability of those systems and should be carefully considered prior to implementation.

Procedure

You must configure the target XP Professional system to allow for remote administration.

Once enabled, members of the Local Administrators group (or Domain Administrators group if the system is a domain member) already have Remote Administration access. If the remote administration account is not an administrator, their account must be added to the local Remote Desktop Users Group.

In addition, every remote administration user account must have a password (the password cannot be blank) in order for RDP to allow the connection.

Finally, you must configure the RDP client to make the connection to the target RDP Server.

Equipment Used

For this task, you need the following equipment:

- Windows XP Professional system

- Windows XP Professional or Server 2003 system (target system)

- Administrator access

Details

Configuring the RDP Server

1. Log on to the Windows XP Professional or Server 2003 target system as the Administrator. This system will be the RDP server.

2. Right-click on My Computer and select Properties. (This can be located in the Control Panel as well by selecting the System applet.)

3. Select the Remote tab.

4. In the Remote Desktop section, enable the Allow Users To Connect Remotely To This Computer check box.

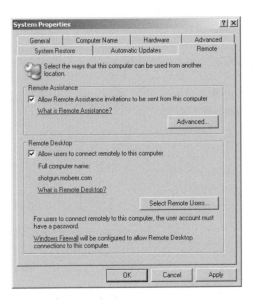

 Notice the statement regarding the password requirement for remote administration users.

5. Click the Select Remote Users button. The resulting dialog box is where you would add nonadministrator user accounts to enable them for remote administration purposes on this target RDP server.

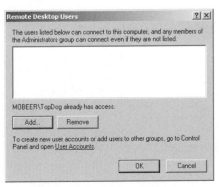

> Notice the statement regarding members of the Administrators group already having access through RDP. Since you will be using an Administrator account to perform the remote administration, you do not need to add any accounts to this dialog box.

6. In the Remote Desktop Users dialog box, click Cancel. Click OK to close the System Properties dialog box.

Configuring the RDP Client

1. Log on the Windows XP Professional system you will use for remote administration as the Administrator. This system is not the target system and will be the RDP client.

2. Select Start ➤ Programs ➤ Accessories ➤ Communications ➤ Remote Desktop Connection.

3. Select the Display tab. This is where you configure the display quality.

> Increasing the display quality could degrade the performance of the RDP connection. Decreasing the number of colors typically provides the greatest improvement on the performance of the RDP connection.

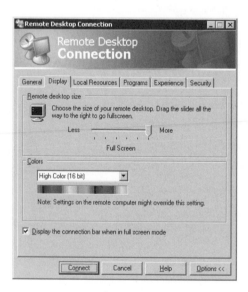

4. Select the Local Resources tab. This is where you connect your local resources (sound, keyboard, and local devices) to the remote system inside the RDP session.

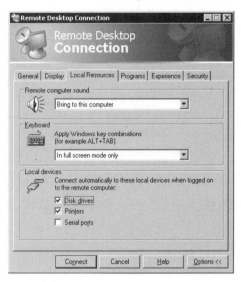

5. Enable the Disk Drives check box in the Local Devices section of the Local Resources tab.

 WARNING You should only connect your local drives to the remote system if you trust the remote system. This connection could provide access for the transfer of viruses or other malware between the two systems.

 NOTE The Programs tab is used to configure an application to launch automatically when the RDP connection is initialized. This tab could be used to launch administrative tools, like the backup utility, on the remote system, for example.

6.   Select the Experience tab. From the drop-down list, select the appropriate connection type that exists between the RDP client and the RDP server.

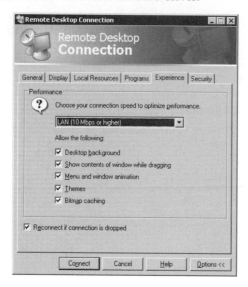

 Selecting a connection type that exceeds the actual connection performance may degrade the performance of the RDP session.

7.   Select the Security tab. This is where you would configure the SSL component if you had implemented this correctly on the RDP server. Since this was not configured in this task, select No Authentication in the Authentication drop-down list.

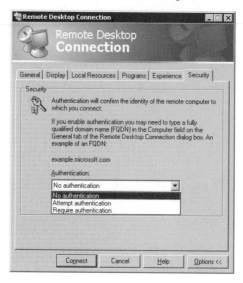

Implementing authentication would require a digital certificate on the RDP server, and could be strengthened further by implementing a digital certificate on the RDP client as well.

8. Select the General tab.

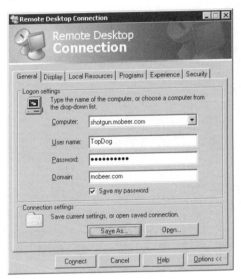

Complete this tab as follows:

- Computer: Type the name of the RDP server.
- User Name: Type the name of the administrative account you plan to use for the RDP session.
- Password: Type the password for the administrative account you plan to use for the RDP session.
- Domain: Type the domain name that the RDP server and client are members of. If they are not members of a domain, leave this field blank.
- Enable the Save My Password check box.

9. Click the Save As button to record your settings. Save the RDP client configuration to the desktop and assign it the name of the *RDP_Server*.rdp.

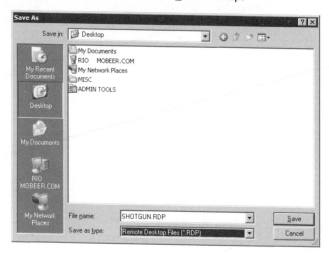

Launching the RDP Connection

1. On the General tab of the Remote Desktop Connection dialog box, click Connect.

2. You should receive a warning regarding the risks associated with connecting your local disk drives to the remote system. Click OK to clear the warning message.

3. You should now be presented with a session on the remote system, the RDP server. You are logged on locally to this system and are functioning as if you were sitting at the local console of the remote system.

4. You can use the controls at the top of the display to window or minimize the RDP session.

> **NOTE** From here you can now run any applications and/or administrative utilities on the remote system.

5. Click the Start button and select to disconnect the RDP client.

6. Confirm the disconnection to close the RDP session.

Criteria for Completion

You have completed this task when you have configured the RDP server and the desired user account for the remote administration. You must also have configured the RDP client and initiated, then terminated the RDP session.

Task 6.5: Secure Administration Using Run As

A fundamental concept behind most operating systems is that a single user should have only a single user account, and that all functions that user is required to perform should be accomplished from that single user account. This is true for all users, except the administrators of the network.

Administrators of the network should have two user accounts: one user account with Administrator privileges, and one user account with nonadministrator privileges.

> The highest levels of administrators, which should be a rare few individuals, would have a third account; access to the Administrator account for the domain. This is the default, built-in Administrator account that cannot be locked out on domain controllers and that cannot be deleted. This account should only be utilized in extreme emergencies where an administrator (a user account that has been added to the Domain Administrators global group in a domain, or the local Administrators group in a workgroup) account is unavailable or doesn't have sufficient privileges to accomplish a given task.

The nonadministrator account is the one that you should use to log on to any system, every time. This is your daily use account. This account cannot accomplish administrative tasks.

In order for you to perform your administrative functions, while logged in as the nonadministrator, you right-click on the desired administrative tool and select Run As from the menu. This prompts you for credentials. You enter your Administrator credentials, which launches the administrative utility with the elevated, Administrator privilege.

This procedure keeps the desktop and all processes running at a nonadministrator level of privilege, and only invokes the Administrator privilege when it is required to perform administrative tasks.

The Run As function relies on the Secondary Logon service. This service must be running on the system where the second set of credentials will be utilized. If the Run As function fails, confirm that this service is running. If the Secondary Logon service is running and the Run As attempt fails, it is usually a good idea to stop and restart the service (this is referred to as "bouncing" a service).

> You can find more information on the Run As function at http://www.microsoft .com/resources/documentation/windows/xp/all/proddocs/en-us/runas .mspx?mfr=true.

Scenario

You are the administrator of a Microsoft Windows environment and need to perform daily administrative tasks as securely as possible.

Scope of Task

Duration

This task should take 30 minutes.

Setup

There is no setup for this particular task.

Caveat

By logging in as a nonadministrator user and using the Run As function, you are securing all of the desktop processes to a standard user level of privilege. This limits the potential extent of compromise if an attacker is able to hack into your system through these processes.

However, any applications you launch with elevated privilege may be the compromised process. The processes launched with elevated privileges should be terminated as soon as the administrative task is complete to minimize the potential exposure to an attacker. In other words, don't launch the tool with elevated privileges and leave it running overnight, or even for the day. Kill the process as soon as possible, and launch it a second time if and when it is needed.

Procedure

You must create a nonadministrator user account, intended for routine, daily use. You will then confirm that the secondary logon service is available and responsive.

You will log on as the nonadministrator account and attempt to launch an administrative tool to confirm the Access Denied response to the nonadministrator user. Then you'll launch the administrative tool using the Run As function, inputting Administrator-level credentials. This time the administrative tool will launch, with the elevated privilege of the administrator credentials you've provided.

Finally, you'll explore the Run As function from the command line. Command-line tools are useful when scripting administrative functions. This command line can be written in a batch file, for repeat use or to be launched after hours in a scheduled task.

Equipment Used

For this task, you need the following equipment:

- Windows XP Professional system
- Administrator access

Details

Creating the Nonadministrator User

1. Log on the Windows XP Professional system as the Administrator.

2. Right-click on My Computer and select Manage. Or you may select Start ➤ Programs ➤ Administrative Tools ➤ Computer Management to open the same console.

3. Expand Local Users And Groups. In the left pane, select the Users folder.

4. Right-click on the Users folder and select New User.

5. Complete the New User dialog box as follows:

    - User Name: BoBo

    - Full Name: BoBo

    - Description: Nonadministrative User

    - Enter a password twice.

    - Clear the User Must Change Password At Next Logon check box.

    - Enable the Password Never Expires check box.

6. Click Create to create the user account. Click Close to close the New User dialog box.

Confirming the Secondary Logon Service

1. In the Computer Management console, expand Services And Applications.

2. In the left pane, select Services. In the right pane, scroll down to view the Secondary Logon service.

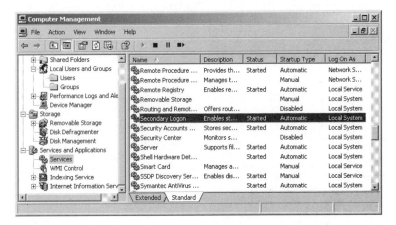

Notice this service is configured to start automatically and is currently started.

3. Right-click on the Secondary Logon service and select Restart.

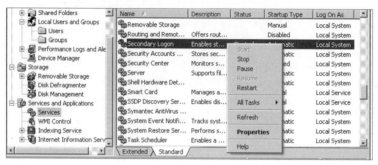

As we mentioned earlier, this is called *bouncing* the service, and it confirms that the service is alive and should be responsive.

A Service Control dialog box opens that shows the progress of the restart process.

4. Close the Computer Management console. Log off as Administrator.

Administrative Activities When Logged On As a Nonadministrator User

1. Log on the Windows XP Professional system as BoBo, the nonadministrator user.

2. From the Start button, select Control Panel.

3. In the left pane, select Switch To Classic View.

4. Double-click the System applet. In the System Properties dialog box, select the Hardware tab. Click the Device Manager button.

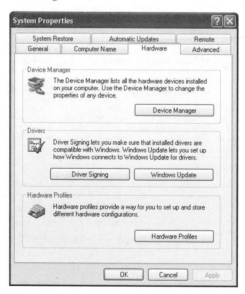

5. You should receive a Device Manager warning message regarding insufficient security privileges.

This is evidence of the use of the nonadministrator user account.

6. In Device Manager, expand the Display Adapters. Right-click on the adapter and select Properties. Select the Driver tab.

Notice that other than viewing information about the display adapter driver, you cannot make any configuration changes.

7. Click Cancel to close the Display Adapter Properties dialog box. Click the X in the upper-right corner to close Device Manager. Click Cancel to close the System Properties dialog box.

8. In Control Panel, press the Shift button on the keyboard while you right-click on the System applet. Select Run As from the menu.

9. You should see a Run As credentials dialog box.

10. Click the radio button for The Following User.

11. Enter the correct Administrator username and password. Click OK.

12. In the System Properties dialog box, select the Hardware tab. Click the Device Manager button.

13. In Device Manager, expand the Display Adapters. Right-click on the adapter and select Properties. Select the Driver tab.

 Notice that you can now make any configuration changes desired. This is evidence of your elevated privilege level from your secondary logon using Administrator credentials.

14. Click Cancel to close the Display Adapter Properties dialog box. Click the X in the upper-right corner to close Device Manager. Click Cancel to close the System Properties dialog box. Close the Control Panel.

Using the Command-Line RunAs

1. Still logged in as BoBo, from the Start button select Run. Type **CMD** and click OK.

2. In the command window, type **runas /?**.

3. View the resulting help information on the RunAs command.

4. At the command prompt, enter **defrag.exe c:** to launch `Defrag.exe`.

5. You should receive a message stating the following:

`You must have Administrator privileges to defragment a volume.`

6. At the command prompt, enter **runas /user:TopDog "defrag.exe c:"** to launch `Defrag.exe` with the RunAs function.

On this system, the Administrator account has been renamed to TopDog.

 The double quotes are necessary around defrag c:, due to the space used in the command between defrag and c:

7. You should get prompted for the password for the administrator. Type the password and press the Enter button.

8. This should launch a command-line version of Defrag.exe.

Criteria for Completion

You have completed this task when you have utilized the RunAs function to launch applications with elevated privileges, in both the graphical user interface (GUI) and from the command line.

Task 6.6: Configuring a Packet Filter

Packet filters are a fundamental component of every router and firewall, and are built into virtually every operating system. They primarily operate at Layer 3 of the Open Systems Interconnection (OSI) model, but have functionality at both Layer 3 and Layer 4. They are fast, easy to configure, and strong.

The downside of packet filters is that they are not very intelligent. They either allow an IP/port combination, or they block them. They are either wired open or wired closed.

Most contemporary firewalls combine the packet filter (called a generation 1 firewall) with a proxy service (called a generation 2 firewall), and a stateful inspection engine (called a generation 3 firewall).

Scenario

You are the administrator of a Microsoft Windows environment and have been experiencing unexpected and undesired traffic from a remote network. You also suspect that your server has been being probed in an attempt to execute a specific exploit. You must stop these activities from affecting your network and your systems.

Scope of Task

Duration

This task should take 20 minutes.

Setup

The configuration of packet filters, in this case, will be performed on a Windows Server 2003 system that is also performing a routing function in your network. You will utilize the Routing And Remote Access Service (RRAS) server to implement the packet filter.

Caveat

Implementing a packet filter to block undesirable traffic will also block desirable traffic that matches the filter specifications.

Also, attacks come from many different locations, target many different systems on your network, and can be implemented using any number of ports and/or protocols. The packet filter is one of your tools to secure your environment, but it is certainly not going to be the answer to all risks. You must implement many layers of security in addition to packet filters.

Procedure

You have noticed unsolicited, unexpected, and undesired traffic on your network that is coming from a network whose IP address range is 192.168.10.0. You want to stop all of this traffic.

You have also noticed many failed Telnet logon attempts on your server, and you need to block this inbound traffic as well.

You will implement two packet filters to eliminate this traffic from your network.

Equipment Used

For this task, you need the following equipment:

- Windows Server 2003 system running RRAS
- Administrator access

Details

Configuring the Packet Filter in RRAS

1. Log on the Windows Server 2003 system as the Administrator.
2. From the Start button, select Programs ➤ Administrative Tools ➤ Routing And Remote Access.
3. Expand *server_name*(Local). Expand IP Routing and select General.
4. In the right pane, select your Local Area Network Interface.

In this graphic, this interface has been renamed with the IP address bound to the interface: 192.168.222.200.

5. Right-click on the Local Area Network Interface and select Properties.

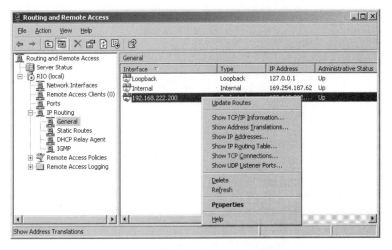

6. In the Properties dialog box, click the Inbound Filters button on the General tab.

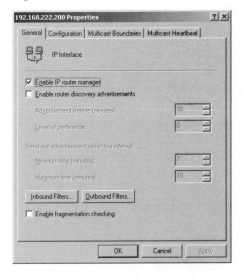

7. In the Inbound Filters dialog box, click New to add a new packet filter.

8. Your first objective is to block all traffic coming from the network 192.168.10.0.

9. Select the Source Network check box, and fill in the IP address **192.168.10.0**. Fill in the Subnet Mask value of **255.255.255.0**. Leave the Protocol option set to Any.

10. Click OK to close the Add IP Filter dialog box.

 This packet filter will drop all packets from the IP address range of 192.168.10.0 through 192.168.10.255, going to any destination and using any port or protocol.

11. Your next objective is to block any inbound packets aiming at Telnet, which uses TCP port 23.

12. In the Inbound Filters dialog box, click New to add a new packet filter.

13. Select the Destination check box, and fill in the IP address of this system: **192.168.222.200**. Fill in the Subnet Mask value of **255.255.255.255**. Select TCP from the Protocol drop-down list. Leave the Source Port option blank. Type **23** in the Destination Port field.

In this packet filter, the subnet mask of 255.255.255.255 means any packet whose destination is this one system. It identifies a single machine on the network.

14. Click OK to close the Add IP Filter dialog box.

 This packet filter will drop all packets from any IP address, going to this server and using TCP port 23, the port used by Telnet.

15. In the Inbound Filters dialog box, carefully read the filter actions. They can be confusing at first.

- Receive All Packets Except Those That Meet The Criteria Below allows all traffic except the traffic type you need to block.

- Drop All Packets Except Those That Meet The Criteria Below would drop all traffic, allowing only the undesired traffic that you've identified. In this case, this is the opposite of what you want.

Select Receive All Packets Except Those That Meet The Criteria Below.

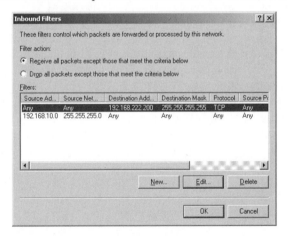

16. Click OK to close the Inbound Filters dialog box.
17. Click OK to close the Interface Properties dialog box.

WARNING   These filters will disallow traffic that you may desire. You may want to delete these two packet filters when you have successfully completed Task 6.6 to restore your system to its normal operating state.

Criteria for Completion

You have completed this task when you have implemented the two identified packet filters.

Task 6.7: Implementing 802.11 Wireless Security

Wireless networks are becoming more prevalent every day. They are inexpensive, easy to set up, and easy to relocate. They can also be one of the most vulnerable forms of network communications today.

In January of 2006, during a wireless security course being held in Washington D.C., a survey of the local access points showed that approximately 30 percent of wireless networks are nonsecured, with no user or access point (AP) authentication and no encryption for the data being transmitted. Further, that survey also showed that approximately 15 percent of wireless APs remain with the default settings, including the default administrative logon credentials.

Not only can an attacker connect to the network and read all data transmitted, but he can also log on to the AP as the administrator and reconfigure the system to lock the legitimate users out of their own networks.

Wireless network specifications were originally defined in IEEE's 802.11 standard. There are now a series of 802.11x standards, and various implementations of wireless networks now occupy several more 802 standards. The original 802.11 standard contained several security measures, including:

- Disable the Service Set Identifier (SSID) broadcast
- MAC address filtering
- Wired Equivalent Privacy (WEP) authentication
- WEP data encryption

The AP administrator should immediately change the SSID to something nondescriptive and nonattractive, change the administrative username (if possible) and password, and disable DHCP, if possible.

Security in 802.11 was found to be seriously flawed in several areas. 802.11i was developed to correct the shortcomings of security in 802.11. The WiFi Alliance also improved security for wireless networks with WiFi Protected Access (WPA, WPA2) for home network use, called

Personal, and for business network use, called Enterprise. WPA uses an acceptable encryption algorithm that is strong and easier on the devices performing the encryption. WPA2 uses a significantly stronger encryption algorithm that is considered uncrackable, but the performance of your devices may suffer with the heavy work load.

Scenario

You are the administrator of a Microsoft Windows environment and must implement a wireless network. Since you probably don't have resources to implement a business class system on your home network, you will be implementing WPA-Personal that uses a Pre-Shared Key (PSK).

Scope of Task

Duration

This task should take 30 minutes.

Setup

You will need to configure WPA – Personal with a PSK on your wireless AP. Then, you will need to configure the same settings on your (compatible) wireless client device (wireless network interface card).

In the wireless networking arena, technology and manufacturers are leading the standards. Unfortunately, many wireless devices are incompatible with many other wireless devices.

Prior to performing this task, you might want to check for more current firmware updates and driver updates for your wireless devices. Such updates may improve compatibility issues.

Caveat

Wireless networks are inherently vulnerable to attack. If you fail to complete securing the wireless network, disable the access point's radio or remove power from the device. Failure to secure the wireless network could expose your systems and information.

Procedure

You will first configure the wireless AP with several security features. Then you will configure the wireless client with a compatible configuration. You will then have the wireless client authenticate and associate with the AP.

Equipment Used

For this task, you need the following equipment:

- Windows XP Professional system, with Service Pack 2 installed
- Administrator access on the XP Professional system

- 802.11i-compliant wireless Network Interface Card (NIC), the wireless client, including 802.11a, 802.11b, or 802.11g radio (compatible with the radio in the wireless AP. For example, if your AP is 802.11b compliant, your client NIC must also be 802.11b compliant. Plus both the AP and the client NIC must be 802.11i compliant to support the advanced WPA security settings.)

- 802.11i-compliant Wireless AP, including 802.11a, 802.11b, or 802.11g radio (compatible with the radio in the wireless client Network Interface Card)

- Administrator access on Wireless AP

In this task, we will be referring to dialog boxes, navigation, and procedures for configuring the NetGear WGT624 Wireless Access Point. Your dialog boxes, navigation, and procedures may be different. However, if the device you are using is 802.11i-compliant, these same settings will be available on the configuration settings of the AP. Follow the specific instructions for your AP.

It is assumed that your Wireless AP is connected to your network via a wired, Ethernet connection. It is also assumed that the wired interface is configured with a static IP address compatible with your wired network. It is further assumed that the Channel and Country options have been configured correctly.

Details

Securing the Wireless Access Point

1. Log on the Windows XP Professional system as the Administrator.

2. Launch Internet Explorer. In the address bar, type the IP address of the access point and press the Enter key.

3. You should be prompted for the administrative username and password for the AP. Type in the correct administrative username and password for your AP.

This administrative username and password should be supplied in the man-ufacturers documentation for the AP device.

Notice that this username and password might be sent in clear text. This could be "sniffed" by an attacker. You should only authenticate as the AP's Admin-istrator the AP over the wired LAN, and when connected electrically close to the AP. If this is a new AP, you will use the default username and password that should be referenced in your device documentation. You should change this default information at the first opportunity.

4. You should be presented with the web-based administrative interface for the AP. If this is a new AP with the default username and password, locate the configuration area to change the administrative username and password. Change it now.

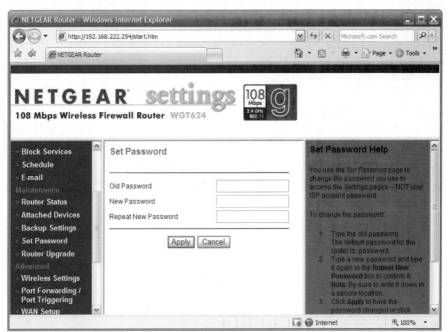

5. Once you have secured the administrative account on the AP, locate the configuration area to check for a firmware update. Perform the firmware update as necessary, carefully following the instructions provided by the manufacturer of the AP.

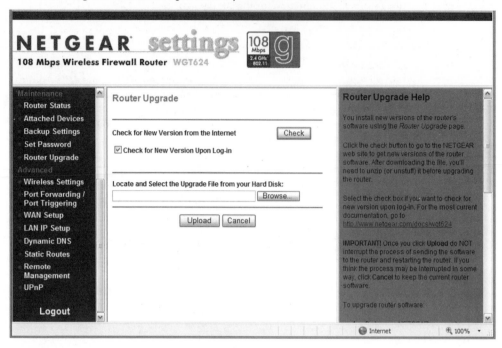

 Each of these steps may require you to click Apply, or may require an AP reboot. If so, apply the changes or reboot and log back into the AP as necessary.

6. In the AP configuration console, locate the configuration area to change the SSID. Change the SSID to something nondescriptive and nonattractive. The SSID in the graphic has been changed to WAP.

 You will need to know this SSID information later.

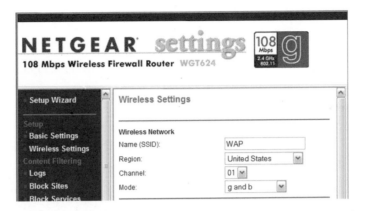

7. In the AP configuration console, locate the configuration area to disable the SSID broadcasts (these may be called announcements, beacons, or something similar). Select to disable the SSID broadcasts.

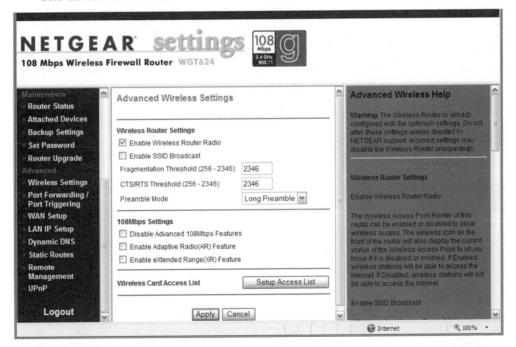

If you have a limited list of known, wireless client devices, you can configure MAC address filtering. If you must support unknown devices (like in a lobby or conference room), you should not implement MAC address filtering. Skip Steps 8–10.

Only the devices configured on the list will be able to associate with the AP.

8. In the AP configuration console, locate the configuration area to enable MAC address filtering. Select to enable MAC address filtering.

9. To add devices to the MAC address filtering list, enter the device name and MAC address, and click Add.

The MAC address is 12 hexadecimal (0–9 and A–F) characters. It may need to be entered without any spaces, or with one blank space between pairs, with dashes between pairs, or with a colon between pairs, depending on the manufacturer.

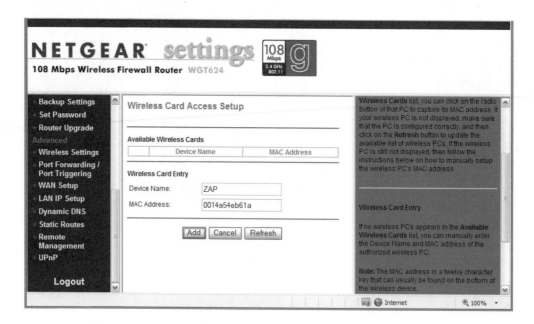

10. Once you have completed the MAC Address Filter List, click Apply to implement the filter.

11. In the AP configuration console, locate the area to configure security options.

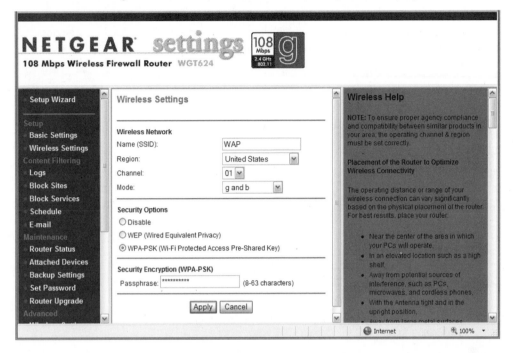

12. Select the configuration for WPA – Personal (this may be called WPA – PSK, WPA – SOHO, or WPA – Home).

13. Enter a passphrase. This is a strong password and should contain at least 8 characters (20 is considered strong for a passphrase), and should contain a mix of uppercase, lowercase, numeric, and symbol characters.

 You will need to know this passphrase information later.

14. Apply your changes, as required by your AP, and log off the AP administrative console.

How to Find the MAC Address

The MAC address may be referred to as the physical, MAC, hardware, burned-in, or Ethernet address. The MAC address is often printed on wireless devices. It can also be obtained once the device is installed on an XP Pro system by executing the command **IPCONFIG /ALL** at a command prompt:

```
D:\AA>IPCONFIG /ALL
Ethernet adapter INTERNAL ABG WIRELESS:
        Description . . . : Broadcom 802.11a/b/g WLAN
        Physical Address. . : 00-14-A5-4E-B6-1A


Ethernet adapter LAN:
        Description: Realtek RTL8139/810x
                        Family Fast Ethernet NIC
        Physical Address. . : 00-0F-B0-F8-7A-AE
```

Configuring the Wireless Client

1. While logged in to your XP Professional system, select Start ➤ Settings ➤ Control Panel ➤ Network Connections. Right-click on your installed, wireless NIC and select View Available Wireless Networks.

 If you receive a message regarding the Wireless Zero Configuration (WZC) service, you may need to configure and start the WZC service. Right-click on My Computer and select Manage. Expand Services And Applications, then select Services. Locate the Wireless Zero Configuration service. Configure it for automatic startup and start the service.

 Some wireless client device manufacturers implement driver sets that conflict with Microsoft WZC. If this is the case with your device, again, the dialog boxes, navigation, and procedure to configure WPA – PSK may be different, but the settings should all be available and the configuration settings should be the same on your third-party device configuration dialog boxes.

2. In the Choose A Wireless Network dialog box, in the left pane select Change Advanced Settings.

3. On the Wireless Networks tab, add a preferred network.

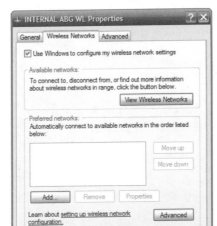

4. On the Association tab do the following:

- Enter the SSID: WAP

This is case sensitive. Type it in exactly as you did on the AP.

- Select WPA-PSK from the Network Authentication drop-down list.
- Select TKIP from the Data Encryption drop-down list.
- Enter the passphrase you selected while configuring the AP in the Network Key field, and enter it again in the Confirm Network Key field.

WPA – PSK may be called WPA – Personal, WPA – SoHo, or WPA – Home on your device.

The passphrase is case sensitive. Type it in exactly as you did on the AP.

5. On the Connections tab, confirm that the Connect When This Network Is In Range option is enabled. Click OK to close the Wireless Network Properties dialog box.

6. On the Wireless Networks tab, click Advanced.

7. On the Advanced tab, select Access Point (Infrastructure) Networks Only, and ensure the Automatically Connect To Non-preferred Networks option is cleared. Click Close to close the Advanced dialog box.

8. Click OK to close the Interface Properties dialog box.

9. You should see a notice that you are now connected to WAP.

10. If you are not connected, in the Control Panel select Network Connections. Right-click on your installed, wireless NIC and select View Available Wireless Networks.

11. Select WAP and then click the Connect button at the bottom of the dialog box.

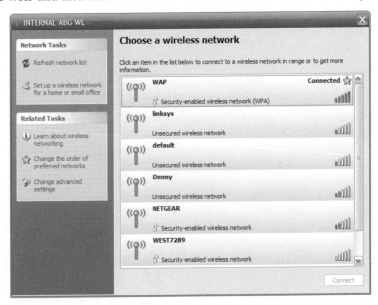

Notice in the previous graphic that only half of the APs are secured (50 percent), and one-third (33 percent) are set to their default settings

12. The true test is when you disable your wired interface and can browse the network using the wireless interface only.

This assumes the AP is correctly configured to connect to the network.

Criteria for Completion

You have completed this task when you have successfully connected to your AP using WPA – PSK.

Phase

7

Securing Internet Activity

The Internet is truly a great thing. It makes a huge amount of information instantly available. It also provides connectivity to near and distant sites and facilitates things like web browsing, e-mail, and instant messaging. However, it is not without its dangers. It's the source of most viruses and worms that organizations are faced with. Melissa, Code Red, Nimda, I Love You, and SQL Slammer are examples of viruses that were spread via the Internet. Internet users are also faced with all types of scams, phishing schemes, and malware that seek to lure them in or infect their computer.

For the security professional, this means configuring Internet access, securing e-mail, and verifying the authenticity of the people we deal with through the Internet. This is accomplished by means of certificates. These are all important parts of the security professional's daily duties.

 The tasks in this phase map to domains 1 and 2 objectives in the CompTIA Security+ exam (http://certification.comptia.org/security/).

Task 7.1: Configuring Internet Access

Internet access is an integral part of business and the workplace. While configuring a client for Internet access may not be the most exciting part of the day, it is a common task of the IT professional.

The Internet can be accessed through several different methods.

Modem   This connection method allows you to connect a single computer to the Internet.

LAN   This connection method allows you to connect multiple computers to the Internet.

Internet Connection Sharing (ICS)   This connection allows all the computers in the network to share the Internet connection of one computer.

 ICS will be discussed in a later task.

The most common way to establish a connection by modem or LAN is by using the Internet Connection Wizard.

Scenario

You have been asked to configure Internet access on a number of LAN-based computers.

Scope of Task

Duration

This task should take about 10 minutes.

Setup

For this task, you'll need a Windows computer, access to the Administrator account, and an Internet connection.

Caveat

While almost every employee would love to have Internet access, just remember the principle of least privilege. Employees should only have the access and privilege they need to perform their duties. This technique builds greater security as it limits users access and rights in the network.

Procedure

In this task, you will configure basic Internet access.

Equipment Used

For this task, you will need the following:

- A Windows XP computer
- Administrator access
- An Internet connection

Details

This task will walk you through the steps required to configure basic Internet access through a LAN connection.

To configure Internet access with the Internet Connection Wizard, follow these steps:

1. From the Windows desktop, right-click on the Internet Explorer icon and choose Properties.

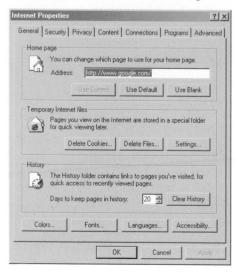

2. Click on the Connections tab, and click the Setup button. This will start the Internet Connection Wizard.

3. Here, you can chose to set up the Internet connectivity via modem or LAN. Choose the option to configure manually via LAN. Click Next.

4. On the next screen, choose the option I Connect Through A Local Area Network (LAN) to connect via LAN. Click Next.

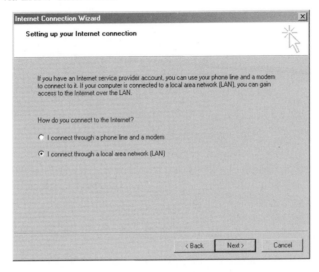

5. On the Local Area Network Internet Configuration screen, make sure all the boxes are unchecked and click Next.

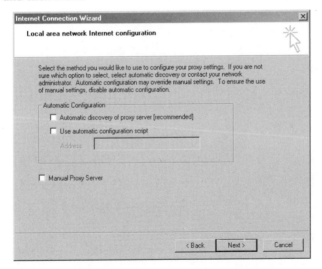

6.   On the Set Up Your Internet Mail Account screen, choose to not set up an e-mail account at this time.

7. Click Finish to complete the wizard.

Criteria for Completion

You have completed this task when you have configured a networked computer for Internet access using the connection wizard.

Task 7.2: Using Internet Explorer Security Zones

Internet Explorer uses a simple concept to provide security when surfing the Internet: security zones. Security zones allow users to set levels of security based on the trust level of the site. With a fully trusted site, you will probably want to let all types of web content execute. With untrusted sites, you may want to block active content or prompt the user before the content is allowed to execute.

Scenario

Your manager has been reading up on the different ways that computers can become infected with malicious code. His main concern is the web access that most of the company's end users have. He has asked you to come up with a simple way to control active web content and block this activity to all but a few trusted sites.

Scope of Task

Duration

This task should take about 10 minutes.

Setup

For this task, you need a Windows computer, access to the Administrator account, and an Internet connection.

Caveat

While increasing security can better secure a computer, it also can reduce usability and add a layer of complexity to users attempting to view active web content.

Procedure

In this task, you will learn configure Internet Explorer security zones.

Equipment Used

For this task, you will need the following:

- A Windows XP computer
- Access to the Administrator account
- An Internet connection

Details

This task will show you how to configure Internet Explorer security zones to reduce the threat of Internet-based malicious code. Zones have flexibility in allowing various levels of security.

To configure Internet Explorer security zones, follow these steps:

1. Open Internet Explorer. Then choose Tools ➢ Internet Options.

2. Click the Security tab. You will notice four icons at the top of the page:

   Internet This includes all websites that are not contained in any of the following categories.

   Local Intranet These are websites that your organization manages and are internal.

   Trusted Sites These are trusted websites that must be specified by address.

   Restricted Sites These are untrusted sites that have strict security setting applies.

   These categories allow websites to be segregated. As an example, web sites located within your company would be given a higher level of trust than those outside the organization.

3. On the Security tab, select the Internet globe icon. This will allow you to configure the settings for this category of websites. Four settings are available:

   High This is the highest setting. Many websites will not display content at this setting.

   Medium Notice that this is the default setting as Microsoft feels that it offers a good balance between usability and security.

   Medium-Low This setting offers little security as most content will run without prompting. However, it does block unsigned ActiveX controls from being downloaded.

   Low There is no real protection at this level and should be used only for sites you fully trust.

WARNING Even on a High security setting, it may still be possible for a user to download content from a site and run it locally. To do so would bypass security controls and allow the malware to execute.

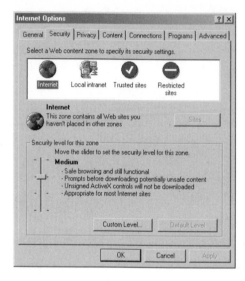

4. Click the Custom Level button at the bottom of the page. This will allow you to make specific changes to the profile.

5. In the Security Settings dialog box, change Run Components Not Signed With Authenticode to Disable. Next, change Run Components Signed With Authenticode to Prompt. Click OK to save these changes and complete the changes needed for the Internet zone.

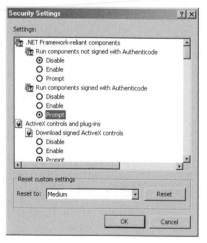

6. Choose the Local Intranet icon at the top of the page, then click the Sites button.

7. Verify that the Local Intranet settings are checked for:

   - Include All Local (Intranet) Sites Not Listed In Other Zones

   - Include All Sites That Bypass The Proxy Server

   - Include All Network Paths (UNCs)

   After verifying these options are checked, close the Local Intranet window.

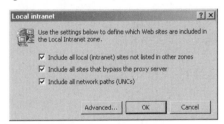

Network paths or Universal Naming Convention (UNC) paths are treated as local sites. These usually take the form of \\company_server\share\ schedule.htm) and are used for network files that are included in the Local Intranet zone.

8. Select the Trusted Sites icon and click the Sites button. The Trusted Sites window is where you can add or remove websites that you trust and that have a low level of security applied.

9. Add www.thesolutionfirm.com to the list of trusted sites and then close the Trusted sites window.

10. Select the Restricted Sites icon and click the Sites button. This will allow you to add sites that could potentially damage or harm the computer.

11. With the Restricted Sites window open, add www.thewhitehouse.com to the list of restricted sites.

12. Once this site has been added to the Restricted Sites window, you may click OK and then close the Internet Options dialog box.

Criteria for Completion

You have completed this task when you have used Internet Explorer Security Zones to add a site to the trusted list and blocked access to a restricted site.

Task 7.3: Configuring IE for Secure Use of Cookies

Cookies have a legitimate purpose. They help maintain state in the stateless world of HTTP. Cookies maintain information as you move from page to page. As an example, if you go to your airline website to book a flight, you will be presented with several questions, such as the date and destination. Cookies help keep track of this information and store it for your browser to use.

Cookies can also be used by advertisers to track your movement, target you with specific ads, and even monitor how many times you go to a specific site. That is why cookie management is such an important issue.

Scenario

You have been tasked with setting up several user computers and have been asked to configure the systems so that they block third-party cookies.

Scope of Task

Duration

This task should take about 10 minutes.

Setup

For this task, you need a Windows computer, access to the Administrator account, and an Internet connection.

Caveat

There is a real balance when dealing with cookies. Blocking none can allow the user's privacy to be violated, whereas blocking all cookies can cause the user to be endlessly prompted to accept cookies as they move from web page to web page. Blocking all cookies can even make some sites inaccessible, so as with most security options, a balance is preferable.

Procedure

In this task, you will learn how to block third-party cookies in Internet Explorer.

Equipment Used

For this task, you will need the following:

- A Windows XP computer
- Access to the Administrator account
- An Internet connection

Details

This task will teach you how to block third-party cookies. First-party cookies come from the site itself, while third-party cookies come from the providers of advertising banners or other graphics that make up a specific web page. These cookies are not used by the site you are visiting and can be used for advertising or track your movement. Restricting these will increase security.

To block third-party cookies, follow these steps:

1. Cookies are managed in the Tools ➢ Internet Options dialog box in Internet Explorer. After opening the Internet Options dialog box, choose the Privacy tab.

2. On the Privacy tab, click the Advanced button. These settings will allow you to customize the handling of cookies. In the Advanced Privacy Settings dialog box, select the Override Automatic Cookie Handling check box.

3. Once you select that option, settings for first-party and third-party cookies will be available. You will want to choose to allow all first-party cookies and to block all third-party cookies. Session cookies should be allowed.

4. Once these changes have been completed, you should save the settings by clicking OK and then closing the Internet Options dialog box.

To override the handling of individual websites, click the Edit button on the bottom of the Privacy tab. The resulting dialog box allows you to block or allow all cookies from a specific site.

Criteria for Completion

You have completed this task when you have configured Internet Explorer to allow all first-party cookies and block all third-party cookies.

Task 7.4: Using Internet Connection Sharing

When is a computer more than just a computer? When you make it into a router. That's what Internet Connection Sharing (ICS) can do. ICS allows you to use one computer to route the Internet to one or more secondary computers.

Without the Internet, some may consider the network a boring place. The typical network without Internet access consists of one or more computers connected by means of a hub or switch. With ICS, the network will be configured with the ICS computer bridging the connection between the hub and Internet. Its role will be to act as the gateway, provide Network Address Translation (NAT), and dial-on demand if needed.

NAT translates client internal network IP addresses into the appropriate address on the NAT-enabled gateway device and protects internal client IP addresses by making them invisible to Internet hosts.

Scenario

You have been asked to set up a branch office that is short on funds. They have asked if you can use an existing computer to route Internet traffic to three other computers in this small office.

Scope of Task

Duration

This task should take about 30 minutes.

Setup

For this task, you need two Windows computers. The primary computer will need two NIC cards and the secondary Windows computer will need one NIC card. You will also need access to the Administrator account on each system and an Internet connection.

Caveat

While ICS does bypass the need for a router, it places priority on the system providing access. This computer must be running for other computers in the network to have Internet access.

Procedure

In this task, you will learn how to install and configure ICS.

Equipment Used

For this task, you will need the following:

- Two Windows XP computers
- Access to the Administrator accounts
- An Internet connection
- Three NICs

Details

This task will show you how to install and configure ICS. This alternative method allows you to share Internet access when a router is not available.

Configuring the ICS Server

1. The first step in this process is to set up the system that will be running ICS. It will be referred to as the ICS server. Before starting any software configuration, you will need to install two NICs into this computer.

 While only one Ethernet card is required for modem-based ICS sharing, a high-speed, Ethernet-based Internet connection such as Digital Subscriber Line (DSL) or a cable modem requires the ICS server to have two Ethernet cards installed.

2. Once the NICs are installed, select Start ➤ Settings ➤ Control Panel ➤ Network And Dial-up Connections. At least two connections should be listed.

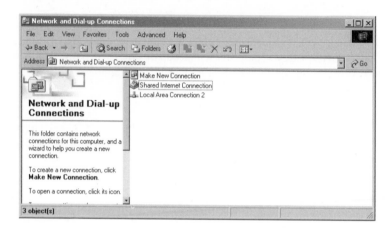

 WARNING If you don't see at least two entries in the Network And Dial-up Connections dialog box, your network adaptors are not properly configured. Verify that the NIC hardware and software has been properly installed.

3. To configure ICS, right-click on the entry that corresponds to your Internet connection and select Properties. Select the Networking tab. Verify that the following items have been checked:

    - Internet Protocol
    - File And Print Sharing For Microsoft Networks
    - Client For Microsoft Networks

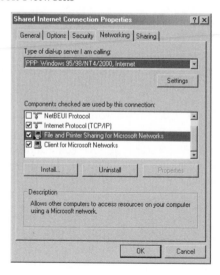

If one or more of the required protocols are not present, you can add them by choosing Install.

4. With the required protocols configured, click the Sharing tab, select the Enable Internet Connection Sharing For This Connection check box, and click OK.

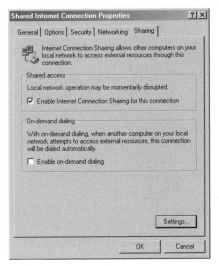

If a modem is being used on-demand, dialing can be implemented. This service automatically activates the modem when a computer on the LAN attempts to access external resources.

Configuring ICS Clients

1. Clients using ICS do not need any special software installed. They simply have to be configured to recognize the proper gateway to access external resources. On the client systems that we'll be using the ICS server to access the Internet, select Start ➤ Settings ➤ Control Panel ➤ Network And Dial-up Connections to start the configuration.

2. At least one network connection should be listed for your local area connection. Right-click on the network connection and choose Properties.

3. You should see several protocols and services installed. One of these should be Internet Protocol TCP/IP. Highlight the Internet Protocol services and select properties.

4. In the Internet Protocol (TCP/IP) Properties dialog box, there are two settings:

    ▪   Obtain An IP Address Automatically

    ▪   Use The Following IP Address

    Choose the first option, Obtain An IP Address Automatically. Also, make sure Obtain DNS Server Address Automatically is highlighted.

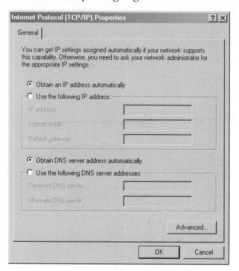

5. Click the Advanced button and make sure the various lists in the IP Settings, DNS, and WINS tabs are all empty. Click OK and then click OK again. This will complete the ICS configuration on the client computer and you should now have access.

6. You can check this access by opening a command prompt and pinging www.google.com. Then open Internet Explorer and browse to www.google.com.

If you cannot connect from an open command prompt type IPCONFIG /all and verify your IP address, subnet mask, and default gateway are correct.

Criteria for Completion

You have completed this task when you have configured one system with ICS and configured a second to use the ICS connection to access the Internet.

Task 7.5: Securing E-mail

Everyone loves e-mail. It's a fast, convenient way to communicate and send information. It is also a direct path to your computer for an attacker. If an attacker can get you to open an attachment or run an attached executable, you may be in real trouble. The Melissa virus affected 20 percent of all computers in the United States. The I Love You virus caused $15 billion worth of damage worldwide, and SQL Slammer infected more than 500,000 computers. These numbers should drive home the importance of securing e-mail. This is the focus of this task.

E-mail security starts outside of the Outlook application. Windows systems have a nasty habit of turning off file extensions. This means that if you get an attachment titled `MyVacationPhoto.jpg`, it may really be `MyVacationPhoto.jpg.exe` and you may never even know since file extensions were turned off.

Scenario

Last week, several computers in your network became infected with a new computer virus. Management is now very concerned about any vulnerability in the e-mail system. The organization uses Microsoft Outlook and is most worried about what might slip by antivirus software. They would like you to harden the application.

Scope of Task

Duration

This task should take about 30 minutes.

Setup

For this task, you need a Windows computer, access to the Administrator account, and the Microsoft Outlook application.

Caveat

Securing e-mail takes more than just technical expertise. End users must be trained to think before opening attachments and be taught good e-mail practices.

Procedure

In this task, you will modify Windows to display file extensions, adjust Outlook for maximum security when handling graphics, and adjust the security zones.

Equipment Used

For this task, you will need the following:

- A Windows XP computer
- Access to the Administrator account
- Microsoft Outlook installed

Details

This task will focus on securing e-mail. It is an easy point of attack. If an attacker can get someone to run his attachment or code, he can take control of the user's system. This task will focus on specific ways that Outlook can be hardened and made more secure for the end user.

Displaying File Extensions

1. Double-click the My Computer icon located on the Desktop.
2. Select Tools ≻ Folder Options to open the Folder Options dialog box.

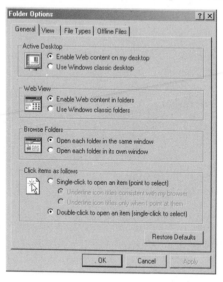

3. Select the View tab.

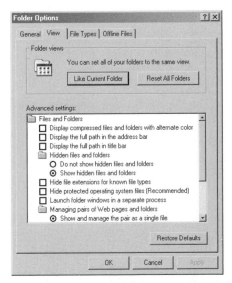

4. On the View tab, uncheck Hide File Extensions For Known File Types. This will allow you to see file extensions and make more informed decisions when dealing with attachments. Click OK.

5. Close the My Computer window.

Configuring Outlook Security for Graphics

1. There are a number of settings that can be configured to increase the security of Outlook. The best place to start is to properly configure Outlook's security preferences. Open Outlook and choose Tools ➢ Options to open the Options dialog box.

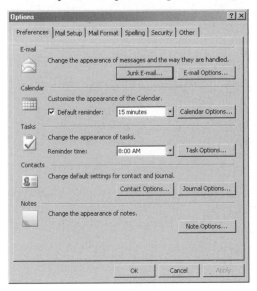

2.   Select the Security tab and click the Change Automatic Download Settings button.

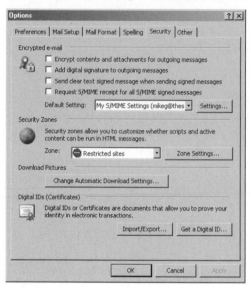

3.   The resulting dialog box will let you control how Outlook downloads and handles pictures. Blocking graphics can help protect your privacy. Malicious individuals can use graphics requests to verify your identity and detect if they have connected with a valid e-mail account. Make sure that the Don't Download Pictures and Warn Me Before Downloading Content check boxes have been selected.

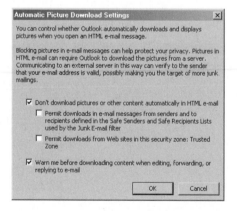

4.   Click OK to close the Automatic Picture Download Settings dialog box.

Adjusting Security Zones

1. On the Security tab, you will see the Security Zones area. This feature can be used to control the activity of content, such as scripts, Java, and ActiveX, that can cause problems. Click the Zone Settings button to open the Security dialog box.

2. Click the Custom Level button. This will open the Security Settings Dialog Box. Scroll down to Script ActiveX Controls Marked Safe For Scripting and change the setting from Enable to Prompt. Then click OK. This will return you to the Security Dialog Box.

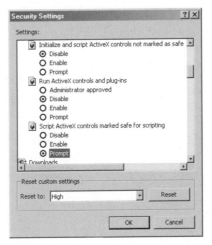

3. On the Security dialog box select the Internet icon and choose Custom Level. This will open the Security Settings dialog box.

4. In the Security Settings, you will want to make several changes to increase security. Make the following changes:

    -   Run Components Not Signed With Authenticode: Prompt

    -   Font Download: Prompt

    -   User Authentication: Prompt For User Name And Password

5. After making these changes, click OK, then click OK again. At the Security tab choose OK to save your changes and exit the configuration.

Criteria for Completion

You have completed this task when you've modified Windows to display file extensions, adjusted Outlook for maximum security when handling graphics, and adjusted the security zones.

Task 7.6: Spam Management

Spam is simply unsolicited e-mail. Some surveys show that as much as 80 percent of the mail that circulates the Internet is spam. Spammers go to great lengths to get this mail into the recipient's inbox. One major task for the security professional is to decrease spam and filter as much as possible.

One easy way to reduce the amount of spam you must deal with is to increase Outlook's junk mail settings to a higher level. There are five options for dealing with junk mail:

Safe Senders List   Allows you to receive messages from e-mail addresses in your address book and contact list.

Safe Recipients List   A list of mailing lists or other subscription domain names and e-mail addresses that you belong to and want to receive messages from.

Blocked Senders List   A list of domain names and e-mail addresses that you want to be blocked.

Blocked Encodings List   A list that allows you to block a language encoding or character you do not want to receive.

Blocked Top-Level Domains List   A list that allows you to block top-level domain names.

Scenario

You have been asked to configure the Windows systems to reduce spam.

Scope of Task

Duration

This task should take about 15 minutes.

Setup

For this task, you'll need a Windows computer, access to the Administrator account, and an Internet connection.

Caveat

Spammers typically stay at the front of the technology curve. This means that stopping spam is hard work as each time a defensive technique is implemented, spammers find new techniques to bypass those defenses.

Procedure

In this task, you will learn how to reduce the amount of spam that an end user must deal with.

Equipment Used

For this task, you will need the following:

- A Windows XP computer
- Access to the Administrator account
- Microsoft Outlook
- An Internet connection

Details

This task will teach you how to lock down Microsoft Outlook to more effectively handle spam and how to install the Outlook spam filter.

Tweaking Outlook to Reduce Spam

1. To configure Outlook to filter a greater amount of spam, select Actions ➤ Junk E-mail ➤ Junk E-mail Options. Outlook provides its users with four levels of junk mail protection:

   No Automatic Filtering   Doesn't filter mail but does send blocked sender e-mails to the junk mail folder.

   Low   Only the most obvious junk mail is moved to the junk mail folder.

   High   Most junk mail is detected but so can some legitimate e-mail.

   Safe Lists   Filters mail so that you only receive e-mail from individuals who are on a safe sender's list.

   Choose the High setting.

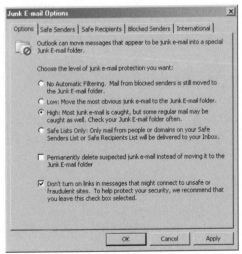

2. Select the International tab and click on the Blocked Top-Level Domain List button. The resulting dialog box will allow you to block e-mail from specific countries.

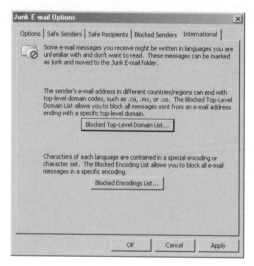

3. In the Blocked Top-Level Domain List dialog box, select the following countries to block e-mail from: China, South Korea, Russia, and Brazil.

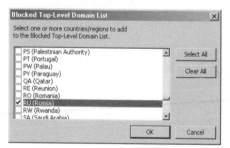

Surveys have shown the top five spam-producing countries are China, South Korea, Russia, Brazil, and the United States.

If your company has a legitimate need to communicate with individuals within one of these countries you would not want to block that particular country.

4. Click OK to close the Blocked Top-Level Domain List dialog box. Then, close the Junk E-mail Options dialog box.

Installing Outlook Spam Filter

1. Go to `http://www.outlook-spam-filter.com/spam-blocker-download.shtml` and download the Office spam filter. Once the program has been downloaded, install it and accept the default install settings.

2. After the installation, the spam filter will add a set of tools to the Outlook menu bar. These settings include Mark As Good, Mark As Spam, and Settings. The program can be used for 30 days as a trial application.

3. Click the Settings option. In the resulting dialog box, select the Advanced tab. Under Treat Messages As Spam, select If Message's Character Set Is Different From English.

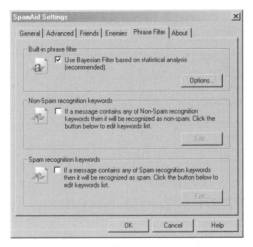

4. Select the Phrase Filter tab, and then click the Spam Recognition Keywords button. The resulting dialog box will allow you to block messages based on keywords. (Several good spam keywords lists can be found on the Internet. One is at `http://wiki.wordpress.org/SpamWords`.) Use the Spam Recognition Keywords List dialog box to add to your keywords list. As an example you may want to add lottery. To do so choose the Add button, enter the word lottery and select the OK button.

5. Once you have added all the words in the list, you can close the Spam Recognition Keywords List dialog box and save your Outlook spam filter settings.

Criteria for Completion

You have completed this task when you have configured Outlook's junk e-mail settings and installed the spam filter.

Task 7.7: Installing and Using a Digital Certificate

The Internet makes it possible to do business with people from around the world, but this brings up the issue of trust. How do you establish trust with someone you have never seen? The answer is digital certificates. Certificates give users the ability to have confidence in the identity of whom they deal with and can also aid in protecting the confidentiality of information.

Scenario

Management has become worried about spoofing and the lack of ability to determine true identity during electronic transactions. They have asked for your advice.

Scope of Task

Duration

This task should take about 20 minutes.

Setup

For this task, you'll need a Windows computer, access to the Administrator account, and an Internet connection.

Caveat

While digital certificates are very secure, they can be compromised if private key information is not guarded or if an attacker can get someone to accept a fake certificate.

Procedure

In this task, you will learn how to install and use a digital certificate.

Equipment Used

For this task, you will need the following:

- A Windows computer
- Access to the Administrator account
- Microsoft Outlook
- An Internet connection

Details

This task will show you how to get a certificate, install it into Microsoft Outlook, and use it to add digital signatures to e-mails.

Installing a Digital Certificate

1. The first step in this task is to obtain a digital certificate. These can be obtained from many different vendors, including VeriSign, Comodo, and GeoTrust. In this task, you will be downloading the certificate from Comodo. They provide certificates for free as long as they are for noncommercial use.

2. Go to www.comodogroup.com/products/certificate_services/index.html to get your free digital certificate. You will need to fill out a short form. Details on how to download the certificate will be sent to your e-mail address.

3. Open your e-mail from Comodo and follow the link to the certificate download to install the certificate in your computer.

4. To use the certificate, first open Outlook.

5. Select Tools ➤ Options.

6. In the Options dialog box, choose the Security tab. Then chose the Settings button. This will open the Change Security Settings dialog box.

7. Once at the Change Security Settings dialog box enter a name for your security setting in the Security Settings Name field.

8. Ensure S/MIME is selected from the Cryptography Format drop-down.

9. Check Default Security Setting For This Secure Message Format.

10. In the Certificates And Algorithms section, click the Choose button for the Signing Certificate field.

11. In the Select Certificate dialog box, select your secure e-mail certificate.

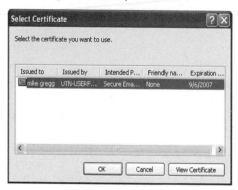

12. View your certificate by clicking the View Certificate button. The Certificate dialog box displays four tabs, which provide more detail about your certificate. Click on each tab to learn more about the certificate. After examining the options, click OK to return to the

Select Certificate dialog box and click OK again to select the certificate and return to the Change Security Settings dialog box.

13. While in the Change Security Settings dialog box, make sure Send These Certificates With Signed Messages is selected.

14. Click OK to return to the Options dialog box and then click OK to return to Outlook.

Using a Digital Certificate

1. With Outlook open, create a new message to send to an associate. You are free to fill out this message as you see fit. You may simply want to tell a friend you are now using a digital certificate for e-mail so that your friend will be certain that the mail is really from you.

2. After creating the message, click the Options button at the top of the Message window.

3. In the Options dialog box, click the Security Settings button. This will open the Security Properties dialog box. Now, select Add Digital Signature To This Message. Then click Ok.

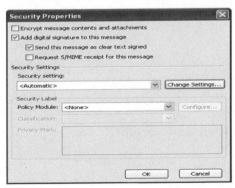

4. You may now close the Message Options dialog box. You may now send your signed e-mail.

 Remember, the task has demonstrated the process to sign e-mails to verify proof of identity. To encrypt e-mails, you will need to have someone sign his e-mail and send you his public key.

Criteria for Completion

You have completed this task when you have created and installed a digital certificate.

Task 7.8: Certificate Backup and Management

Installing the right certificate on a single computer is only half the battle. As a security expert, you face more challenges because many users have more than one system. They may want their certificates installed on their laptops too.

Scenario

Your company is deploying laptops to the sales force and would like you to set up these laptops to use the existing digital certificates for the employees. Management would also like you to clear out any other certificates on the system and make a backup copy.

Scope of Task

Duration

This task should take about 15 minutes.

Setup

For this task, you'll need a Windows computer, access to the Administrator account, and an Internet connection. You will also need to have completed Task 7.7.

Caveat

Certificates can be misused if stolen or acquired by attackers.

Procedure

In this task, you will work with digital certificates.

Equipment Used

For this task, you must have:

- Two Windows XP computers
- Access to the Administrator account
- An Internet connection

Details

This task will show you how to make a backup copy of a digital certificate and how to clear out existing certificates to eliminate any that may have been accepted by accident.

Backing Up an E-mail Certificate

1. Start Internet Explorer and select Tools ➢ Internet Options. In the Internet Options dialog box, select the Content tab and click the Certificates button.

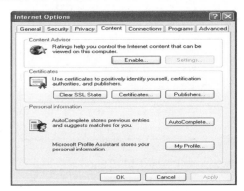

2. In the Certificates dialog box, on the Personal tab, click on the certificate you created in the previous task and click Export.

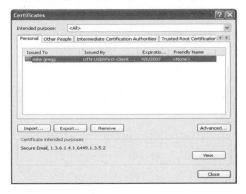

3. The Certificate Export Wizard launches. Select Yes, Export The Private Key, then click Next.

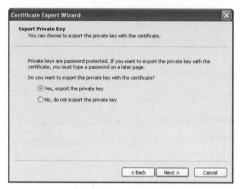

4. On the next wizard screen, select the options Include All Certificates In The Certification Path If Possible and Enable Strong Protection.

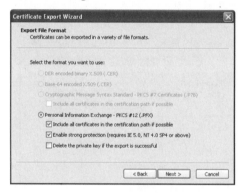

5. As the wizard continues, you will be asked to choose a password.

 Make sure you will be able to remember the password later or you will not be able to access the exported certificate.

6. Select the save location—for example, a floppy or USB thumb drive—and give the file a name such as the *YourName*-Cert. Leave the Type field set to Personal Information Exchange (*.pfx).

7. Once finished, the file and associated private key is saved as a .pfx file.

Installing an E-mail Certificate

Now that you have saved the certificate to a floppy or USB thumb drive, it is time to install it on a second system.

 In real life, this would most likely be a laptop.

1. Start Internet Explorer and select Tools ➢ Internet Options. In the Internet Options dialog box, select the Content tab and click the Certificates button.

2. Click the Import button.

3. The Certificate Import Wizard starts. Click Next.

4. Browse to select the saved certificate and then click Next. The saved location will be the floppy or USB drive you saved the certificate to.

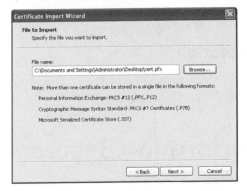

5. Enter the password you created for the certificate.

6. Allow Windows to automatically select certificate placement.

7. Click Finish and you have successfully imported a certificate.

Checking for Certificate Revocation

Certificates are only valid for a fixed period of time. Even during this period, things can happen that might cause a certificate authority or the owner of the certificate to revoke it. Therefore, it is a good idea to check that certificates are valid before use. Internet Explorer has the ability to automatically check for certificate revocation.

1. Start Internet Explorer and select Tools ➢ Internet Options. In the Internet Options dialog box, select the Advanced tab.

2. Scroll down to the Security section and check the Check For Publisher's Certificate Revocation and Check For Server Certificate Revocation.

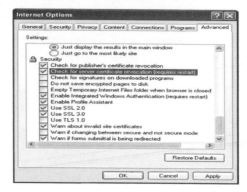

3. Apply these changes and close the Internet Options dialog box. You have now configured Internet Explorer to check for invalid certificates before use.

Criteria for Completion

You have completed this task when you have backed up a certificate, installed a certificate into a second system, and changed Internet Explorer's settings to check for revoked certificates.

Task 7.9: Performing Secure File Exchange

Identifying the individuals you communicate with via the Internet is just one of the tasks that a security professional is faced with. Many times, you are going to want to send or receive files from these individuals. This needs to be done in a secure way to protect the confidentiality and integrity of the information.

Scenario

Individuals in your company need to send and receive files to a branch that is opening in India. Management has tasked you with coming up with a way to do this securely.

Scope of Task

Duration

This task should take about 30 minutes.

Setup

For this task, you need two Windows XP computers, access to the Administrator account, and an Internet connection.

Caveat

Although there are secure methods to send and receive information, attackers may still attempt to analyze the flow and amount of encrypted traffic that moves between two parties. If the flow of information increases, they may infer that a significant event is about to occur.

Procedure

In this task, you will learn how to implement a secure alternative to File Transfer Protocol (FTP).

Equipment Used

For this task, you must have:

- Two Windows XP computers
- Access to the Administrator account
- An Internet connection

Details

This task will teach you how to set up a Secure FTP (SFTP) server and use it to send and receive files securely.

Setting Up a SFTP Server

1. This task will involve using the VShell SFTP server software from http://www.VanDyke .com. The program can be downloaded as a 30-day trial by going to their site and choosing the Download option.

2. During the install, accept the default settings and continue with the setup, and allow the system to reboot as needed once the installation is complete.

3. After the reboot, VShell will automatically load the VShell dialog box.

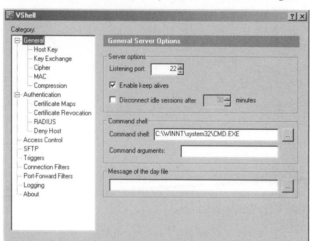

4. Look first at the Access Control category. VShell uses your existing Windows user accounts and privileges; there is no need to set up another user list. If you were running this on a production server, you could simply use the list of users already built-in.

5. In the VShell dialog box, click the Access Control category on the left side. This will open the Access Control dialog box. In the Name area, you will want to add at least one user. Chose the Add button and then enter a username. For this example, we created the user Jerry to test the account.

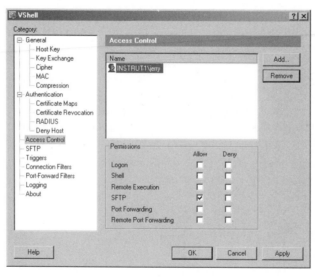

6. You will want to make sure that Allow is checked next to the SFTP option and that all other options are left blank.

7. Select the SFTP category on the left side of the dialog box.

8. Select the folders that you want your users to have access to. It's a good idea to limit users to a selected subfolder.

9. Use Windows Explorer to browse to the C:\ drive and create a folder named **SFTP**.

10. Return to the VShell program and click the Add button under the SFTP Options category.

11. In the SFTP Root Path dialog box, in the SFTP Root field add the SFTP folder you created in the last step. Name it **root** in the Alias field. Then, click OK.

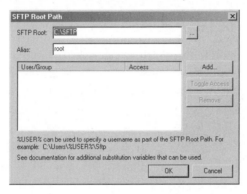

12. Click the OK button to save your configuration.

13. You have now completed the setup of your SFTP server.

Setting Up a SFTP Client

Now that you have setup a SFTP server, you will want to check it out to see how it works. To do so, you will need an SFTP client. For this task, you will use WinSCP. It is a free SFTP client that can be downloaded from

1. Download the WinSCP client by first going to `http://winscp.net/eng/index.php`.

2. To execute the program, simply open it; no installation is necessary.

3. Once WinSCP is open, enter the IP address of the server on which you have installed VShell. You will also need to enter the username and password of the account that had SFTP enabled.

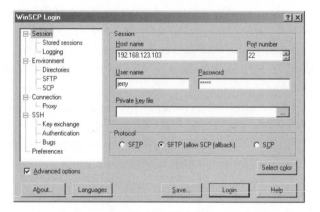

4. WinSCP will now connect to the VShell, which is the SFTP server. Upon connection, it will open the folder you have configured as the default folder.

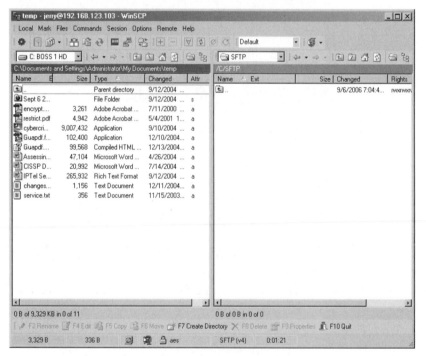

5. You can now upload or download files as you like from this folder as no restrictions have been established.

6. The real value of SFTP over FTP is that the communication channel is secure and items like username and passwords are not passed in clear text. To see this yourself download a copy of Ethereal. It is available at http://www.ethereal.com/download.html.

Once installed, it can be used to capture encrypted and unencrypted traffic. If you were to capture SFTP traffic you would see the information above the TCP level is actually encrypted.

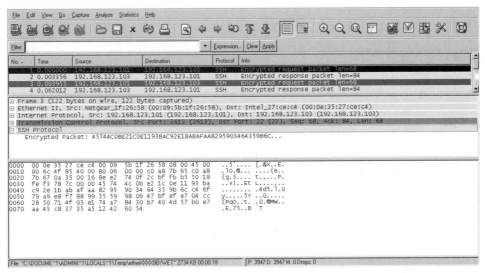

Criteria for Completion

You have completed this task when you have set up an SFTP server, connected to it with an SFTP client, and verified its operation.

Task 7.10: Validating Downloads and Checking the Hash

There is more to security than moving files over an encrypted channel. You also need to have a means of verifying the integrity of the files and information transmitted. This is the purpose of a *hash*. Hashes are used to check authentication and message integrity.

Scenario

You organization will soon start posting code and applications on its SFTP site for its partners in India. You have been asked to develop a method to verify the integrity of these files and prove they remain intact.

Scope of Task

Duration

This task should take about 10 minutes.

Setup

For this task, you'll need a Windows computer, access to the Administrator account, and an Internet connection. You must also have completed Task 7.9.

Caveat

Hashing algorithms only verify integrity and authentication. They cannot provide confidentiality or protect information from changes. They only have the ability to detect change.

Procedure

In this task, you will learn how to use the md5sum application.

Equipment Used

For this task, you must have:

- A Windows XP computer
- Access to the Administrator account
- An Internet connection

Details

This task will show you how hashing algorithms are used to ensure integrity and prove that a program remains unchanged.

Using Hashing Algorithms

1. Download the Windows version of md5sum from http://etree.org/md5com.html. It is a command-line program that you should install in the root of the C:\ drive.

The MD5 hashing algorithm is based on RFC 1321. It has been used as the basis to create md5sum and several similar programs. md5sum is one of the most widely used checksum algorithms today. It was created by Ron Rivest and published in 1992. It is available for both Unix and Windows platforms.

2. After saving md5sum to the C:\ drive, create a text file there named `demo.txt`. Add a line of text to the file such as **Hello World!**.

3. Open a command prompt and change to the C directory.

4. Run **md5sum demo.txt** from the command-line prompt. Your output should appear similar to this:

   ```
   C:\>md5sum demo.txt
   3579c8da7f1e0ad94656e76c886e5125 *demo.txt
   ```

5. Notice the string of numbers; that is the MD5 hashed value. If you record this value, you can use it to compare later and detect whether any changes to the file have been made.

6. To better understand how hashing works, you should now change the filename to **demo2.txt**.

7. With the filename changed, rerun md5sum and compare the results to those you got earlier:

   ```
   C:\>md5sum demo2.txt
   3579c8da7f1e0ad94656e76c886e5125 *demo2.txt
   ```

8. Notice how the two values are the same. This demonstrates that hashing algorithms do not care about filenames.

9. Edit the demo2.txt file and change the text inside to **It's a cold cruel World!**.

10. Run **md5sum demo2.txt** from the command-line prompt. Your output should appear similar to this:

    ```
    C:\>md5sum demo2.txt
    863433c5ba2f0c83c23810fa48ad6459 *demo2.txt
    ```

11. As you can see, the MD5 value has changed. Hashing sums are changed when the contents of a file are changed. They are unaffected by changes in the file date and filename.

Comparing the Hash of a Known File

1. In Task 7.9, you downloaded the WinSCP program. Go to the folder to which it was installed and run md5sum against the `WINSCPsetup.exe` file.

   ```
   C:\>WINSCP\md5sum WINSCPsetup.exe
   3bb053732844b7cac6a856ac06dab642 *WINSCPsetup.exe
   ```

2. Now, go to the WinSCP web page at `http://sourceforge.net/project/` `shownotes.php?group_id=85589&release_id=425996` and observe the listed md5sum that is posted.

3. Notice that these two values match. This verifies that the file you downloaded and installed is in fact intact and remains unchanged. This same feature could be used on your own SFTP site to capture the integrity of files and assure users that the files are correct and unchanged.

Tripwire is another well-known file-integrity program. It can perform hashing on files, folders, and even complete drives to track changes or violations in integrity.

Criteria for Completion

You have completed this task when you have created a text file, verified its integrity, and downloaded a second file and compared its md5sum to one posted on the creator's website.

Phase

8

Security Testing

Security testing is a key component of the security professional's duties. Attackers are becoming more sophisticated every day; therefore, security professionals are required to scan systems and networks to look for vulnerabilities. These tools can examine internal or external systems. Some of these tools are free, while others require you to pay an annual subscription.

Security testing tools are not perfect. Any given tool can produce false positives or negatives, or simply wreak havoc on your network if not used correctly. You need to plan on using these tools at the appropriate time and will also need a remediation plan to address how discovered problems will be addressed. What makes these tools so useful is their ability to probe entire networks and find potential problems. Then you can examine your network and identify whether security updates or system patches are missing. It's much better that you find and fix potential problems before an attacker does. By securing these systems, your company can protect itself against the financial losses associated with system downtime, theft of intellectual property, denial-of-service (DoS) attacks, and negative publicity.

The tasks in this phase map to domains 2, 3, and 5 objectives in the CompTIA Security+ exam (http://certification.comptia.org/security/).

Task 8.1: Penetration Testing with Nessus

Nessus was developed in 1998 and has grown to be the world's most well-known security scanner. Its primary purpose is to alert the user to security holes and vulnerabilities in scanned systems. It can be used to scan Windows, Linux, or other operating systems. It uses a client-server technology so that Nessus servers can be placed throughout the network and then be contacted when they are needed by Nessus clients to perform scans. Nessus is an open source product which means it is free to use with paying a license fee.

Scenario

Your employer has asked that you scan the organization's systems for vulnerabilities and known exploits. The employer does not want you to run any test that might compromise the system by damaging it or by taking it offline.

Scope of Task

Duration

This task should take about 25 minutes.

Setup

For this task, you will need two or more network computers, access to the Administrator account, and an Internet connection.

Caveat

Vulnerability scanners can cause problems and have been known to crash systems or make systems hang. You will need to closely examine what types of scanner plug-ins are available to help minimize the possibility that this could happen.

Procedure

In this task, you will learn how to install and run Nessus.

Equipment Used

For this task, you will need two or more computers. One Windows XP system will be used to perform the scan while one or more systems will be scanned. You will need Internet access to download the Nessus application.

Details

This task will show you how to install and run Nessus. This program will allow you to scan networked systems for known vulnerabilities and security holes.

Be sure to scan only your own systems or those that you have been given written permission to scan. System owners can become rather upset when individuals scan their systems without permission, since this activity is commonly performed by hackers before they launch an attack.

1. Once you have accessed your Windows computer and logged in as Administrator, open your browser and go to http://www.nessus.org/download/.

    For this task, you will be using the Windows version of Nessus. Once the download is completed, you will be prompted to begin the installation.

2. During the installation, you will be prompted to accept the licensing agreement. You must accept this agreement to complete the installation. Continue with the setup and accept all the other default settings to complete the installation. Once the installation is completed, Nessus will prompt you to update the plug-ins. Click OK to install all plug-ins.

Plug-ins are written to address specific vulnerabilities.

3. Once installed, Nessus will have placed a shortcut on the desktop. Double-click on this shortcut to open the Nessus application. Click Start Scan Task.

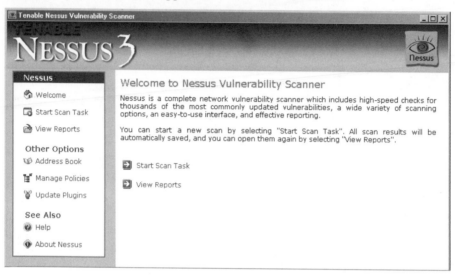

4. Before the scan can begin, you will need to specify what systems are to be scanned. You may enter single system or enter a range of systems to be scanned. For this task choose your entire network range. I have chosen the 192.168.123.1–254 range.

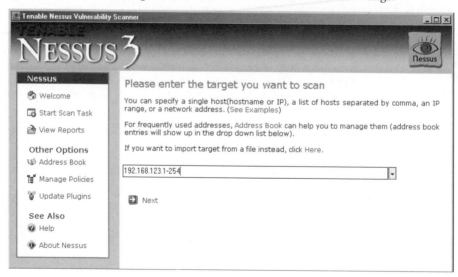

5. Nessus uses plug-ins to scan for specific vulnerabilities. Each plug-in performs a specific security check. For this task, you should choose Enable All But Dangerous Plugins With Default Settings. This is the recommended setting and will ensure that no systems are crashed or brought down during the test.

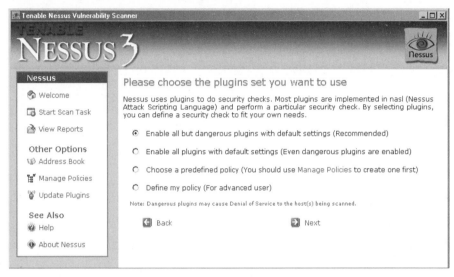

6. Next, choose a Nessus server. As mentioned earlier, a Nessus client can connect to many different Nessus servers. This gives you the ability to place Nessus servers on many different network nodes. For this task, choose Scan From The Localhost.

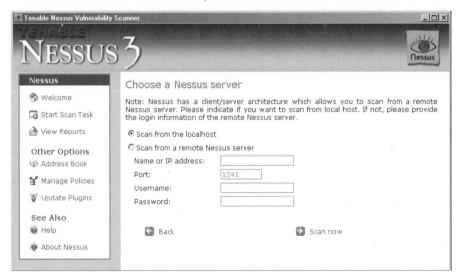

7. Once the Nessus server has been chosen, you may begin the scan. Nessus will provide the user with a status screen while the scan is being performed.

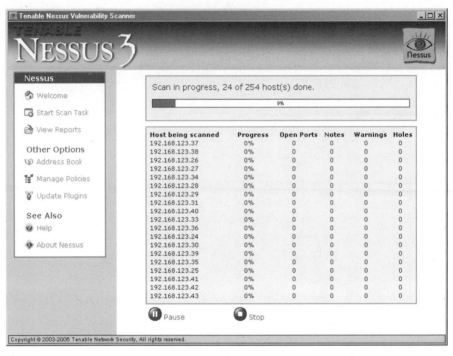

8. Once Nessus completes its scan, you will be presented with a detailed report of its findings. The report lists each system that was scanned and provides specific details on all vulnerabilities that were found. You will need to scroll down the list to get a more in-depth listing of what was found during the scan.

Although Nessus is a great tool for performing automated vulnerability scanning, its results can sometimes provide false positives. If you are unsure of the results you can double check the results by running a second scan, use an alternate tool, or even perform a manual inspection of the computer.

9. Nessus provides a lot of detail about the vulnerabilities it found and makes it easy to use the information to patch or harden the system. An example follows:

```
Type - Warning
Port - 7/tcp
Issue and Fix - Warning echo 7/tcp). The 'echo' port is open.
  This port is not of any use nowadays, and may be a source of
  problems, since it can be used along with other ports to
  perform a denial-of-service. You should really disable this
  service.
Risk factor: Low
Solution: comment out 'echo' in /etc/inetd.conf
CVE: CVE-1999-0103
Nessus ID: 10061
```

Information provided by Nessus includes:

Type   Details the magnitude of concern.

Port   Port and protocol of finding.

Issue   Details of what was found.

Risk Factor   Severity of the risk ranked as low, medium, or high.

Solution   Provides information on how to eliminate the problem.

CVE   The Common Vulnerabilities and Exposures (CVE) is a listing that provides common names for publicly known information security vulnerabilities.

Nessus ID   The ID number that specifies the plug-in number used to discover the vulnerability.

Criteria for Completion

You have completed this task when you have downloaded, installed, and run Nessus to perform a vulnerability scan.

Task 8.2: Penetration Testing with Retina

Now that you have experienced a good example of an open source vulnerability scanner, it is also appropriate that you see how one of the top-rated commercial scanners, Retina, works. It is fast and has the ability to scan an entire Class C network in less than 15 minutes. Most functions can be run from a nonadministrator account.

Scenario

You have been asked by your manager to evaluate Retina's vulnerability scanner.

Scope of Task

Duration

This task should take about 15 minutes.

Setup

For this task, you will need two or more network computers and an Internet connection to download the program.

Caveat

Vulnerability scanners can cause intrusion detection systems (IDSs) to signal an attack. Make sure that you have permission to run a vulnerability scan on any network that you do not own.

Procedure

In this task, you will learn how to install and run Retina.

Equipment Used

For this task, you will need two or more computers. You will need an administrator account with Internet access to download Retina and install it. One Windows XP system will be used to perform the scan while one or more systems will be scanned.

Details

This task will show you how to install and run Retina. This program will allow you to scan networked systems for known vulnerabilities and security holes.

Scanning systems can sometimes cause problems or crashes; therefore, you may want to run such tests during nonpeak production times.

1. Once you have accessed your Windows computer and logged in as Administrator, open your browser and go to `http://www.eEye.com/html/products/retina/download.htm?id=060830.091338.953315`.

   You can download the trial version of Retina from this location. Once you've downloaded the program, execute it from the folder to which you saved it. This will start the installation process.

2. During the installation, you will be prompted to accept the licensing agreement and the program will need to reboot the system to complete the setup. After rebooting, the installation will complete and Retina will start.

3. Upon startup, Retina will launch a wizard that will ask you several questions and guide you through the scanning process. You will want to cancel out of the wizard and go directly to the Retina interface so that you can explore its features. You will see four tabs across the top of the screen that describe Retina's capabilities: Discovery, Audit, Remediate, and Report.

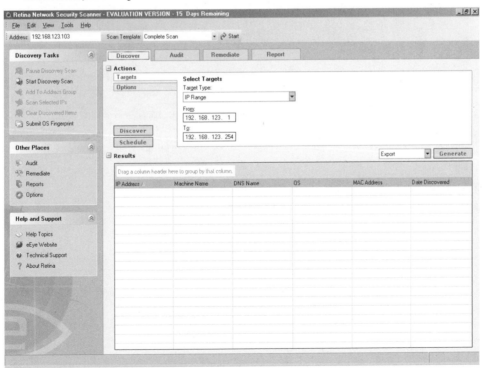

4. On the Discovery tab, enter the range of addresses for your local network. After doing so, select Options and ensure that all network discovery options are highlighted.

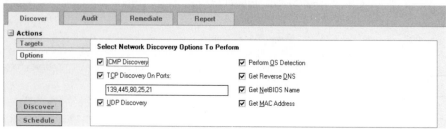

5. Start the scan by choosing Discover. After a few minutes Retina should finish the scanning of your network. You will be provided with a list of discovered systems, their IP address, and the operating system version they are running.

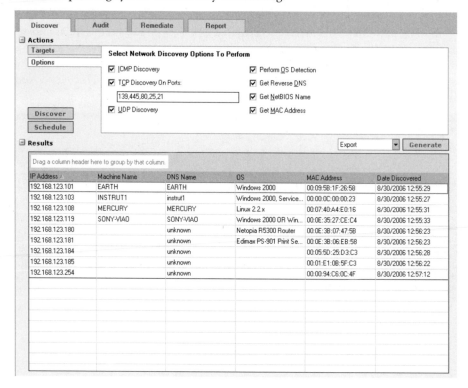

6. Next, choose the Audit tab. The Audit tab is used to detail the scan results from each scanned system. Once the scanning process is started as described in the previous step Retina will look for and examine open ports once they are discovered. At the completion of the audit, it gives a complete listing of security vulnerabilities found.

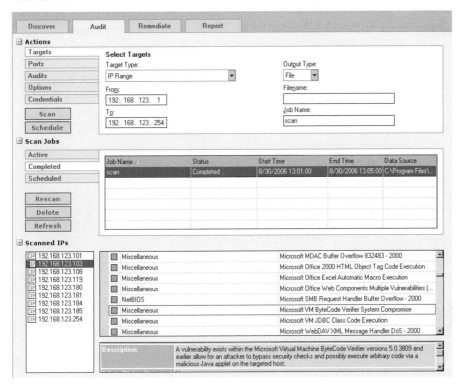

7. Next, choose the Remediate tab. The Remediate tab is used to generate a remediation report. To generate, click once on the Generate button and allow the program a few seconds to generate the report.

The easy part of vulnerability analysis is finding problems. The hardest work is in the process of assigning individuals the task of plugging each vulnerability that was discovered.

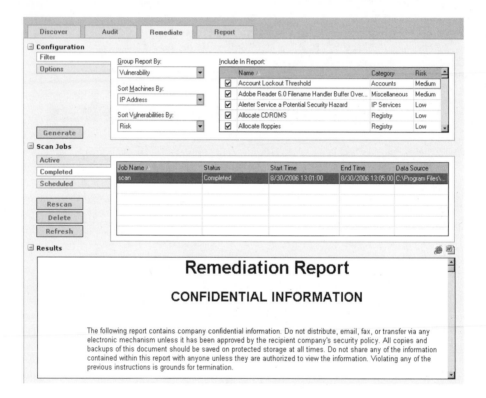

8. The final tab is the Report tab. This tab is used to generate the final report. Several options are available that allow you to simply summarize the findings or format the findings as an executive report. For this task, choose Executive from the Report Type drop-down and include all test results.

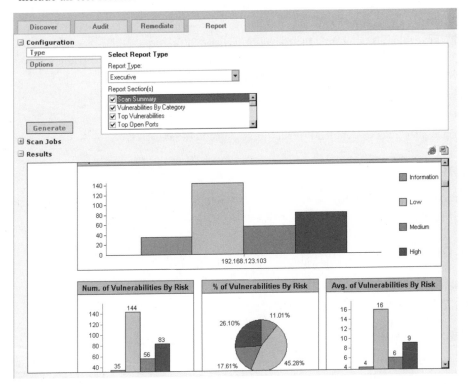

Criteria for Completion

You have completed this task when you have downloaded Retina, installed it on a Windows system, and used it to perform a vulnerability scan on one or more systems.

Task 8.3: Performing Assessments with Microsoft Baseline Security Analyzer

Microsoft Baseline Security Analyzer (MBSA) is a free tool provided by Microsoft to help security professionals determine their level of security. It provides guidance as to how to improve the overall security of Microsoft systems. MBSA can also detect missing security patches and flag potential problems. Its strengths include the following:

- It is free.
- It provides an easy-to-read, browser-based report.
- It provides links to detailed information of specific weaknesses.

Scenario

You need to examine several network servers to investigate their overall security level and make sure they are secure enough to withstand an attack.

Scope of Task

Duration

This task should take about 15 minutes.

Setup

For this task, you will need a Windows computer, access to the Administrator account, and an Internet connection.

Caveat

MSBA may clash with some of the other common security workarounds and it may not properly detect some of Windows updated information.

Procedure

In this task, you will learn how to install and run MBSA.

Equipment Used

For this task, you will need the following:

- A Windows XP computer
- Access to the Administrator account
- An Internet connection

Details

This task will show you how to install and run MBSA. This program will scan a system for security vulnerabilities and common misconfigurations.

1. Once you have accessed your Windows computer and logged in as Administrator, open your browser and go to `http://www.microsoft.com/technet/security/tools/mbsa2/default.mspx`.

    You can download the program from this page. Once the program has completed downloading, execute it from the folder to which it was saved. This will start the installation process.

2. Once the installation is completed, you may start MBSA from the shortcut on the desktop or from the Start menu. The program will give you three options:

    -   Scan One Computer
    -   Scan More Than One Computer
    -   View Existing Reports

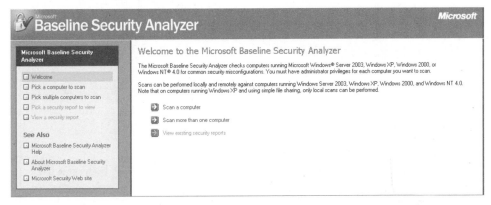

For this task, choose Scan More Than One Computer. This will allow you to put in a range of IP addresses and check a range of computers at once.

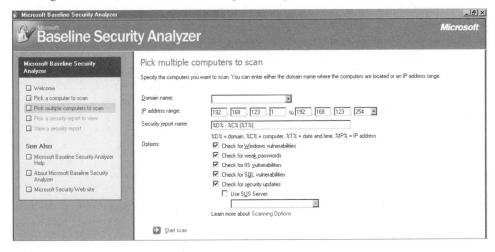

3. Once the scan is completed, you will be taken to the View Security Report screen. This page will describe the findings for each system that was scanned. The report is broken down into five areas:

    Security Update Scan Results   Details which security scans are missing.

    Windows Scan Results   Lists Windows vulnerabilities that were discovered.

    Additional System Information   List details, such as open shares and services.

    Internet Information Services Scan   Lists information about IIS such as version and patch level.

    Desktop Application Scan   Lists details about vulnerable applications.

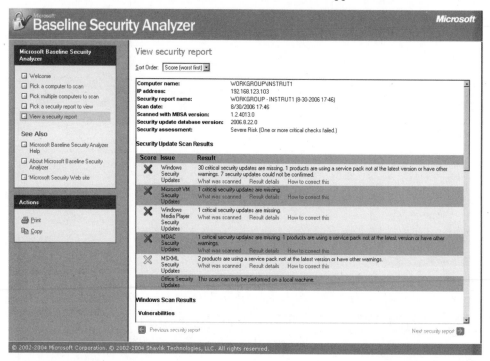

4. Each problem found lists of what was scanned, the scan results, and instructions on how to correct the problem. Choosing How To Correct The Problem provides details on the specific security concern and more information on solving the problem.

Service Packs and Security Updates

Issue

To ensure that the most recent security updates are applied, you need to install all of the latest service packs and individual updates on your system.

Solution

The scan report identifies which service packs and security updates are missing on your computer. Users can click the link in the security report to view the Microsoft security bulletin or download page, which includes the install location for the security update. The Windows Update Web site also has the latest service pack and security update releases available for you to download for the Microsoft® Windows® operating system and its components.

In order to obtain and install the latest updates and to effectively use the MBSA results, please observe these guidelines:

- Register with the Microsoft Security Notification Service to ensure you are notified when new security bulletins become available.

- When updating your computer, remember that changes in configuration may require additional use of Windows Update or MBSA to check the new configuration for compliance. This is particularly true when installing applications, or adding new optional components such as Internet Information Services (IIS) which may install programs that have not been updated with the latest fixes.

- By clicking on **Result Details** in the report you will be able to identify the update as being under one of the following 3 headings:

    Security updates confirmed as missing are marked with a red X

    These updates require immediate installation to ensure the strongest security of your computer.

    Products using a service pack not at the latest version or have other warnings are marked with a yellow X

    Service packs: If the description for an item is "The latest service pack for this product is not installed.", you should obtain and install the latest service pack by using Windows Update or the Microsoft Download Center prior to installing other updates. When using the download center, simply enter the name of the service pack at the Keywords prompt, and follow the instructions on the page.

    Updates: Other items in this page will typically have a newer than expected file version and are usually of strong security. Because the installed file(s) having a greater than expected version may have been provided directly from Product Support Services or from an update or product that was not security related, these items may require additional confirmation to ensure the specific security fix has been included. Addressing such items is an ongoing aspect of the release process for Microsoft, and allows MBSA to become updated automatically with understanding of the newer file versions.

    Security updates that the tool cannot confirm as installed on the scanned computer are marked with a blue asterisk

    These updates cannot be detected with adequate precision due to the complexity of the updates or platform configurations. You should refer to the bulletin

Criteria for Completion

You have completed this task when you have downloaded and installed MSBA on a Windows system, and scanned one or more systems for vulnerabilities.

Task 8.4: Performing Security Assessments with HFNetChk

Patch management is never an easy task, especially if you are in charge of a large number of systems. It can seem like a never-ending task. Virulent code, such as Code Red, Nimda, Nachi, SoBig, and Blaster, are all exploited systems that have not been properly patched.

The first step to the patch-management process is to develop a complete network inventory. The next step is to implement a change control policy; after all, an inventory list doesn't do any good if you can't track and control changes to your network. You are now ready to begin monitoring for new vulnerabilities and patches that are available for everything you have identified as being part of your inventory. This is where HFNetChk comes in. This tool will allow you verify what systems are up-to-date and make patch management a painless process.

 You learned how to apply patches in Phase 2, "Hardening Systems."

Scenario

The organization for which you work has grown very quickly. The firm has now expanded to three locations. You need to find a way to quickly check systems and verify whether they are patched or need to be updated. Therefore, you have decided to investigate the HFNetChk software tool.

Scope of Task

Duration

This task should take about 10 minutes.

Setup

For this task, you will need a Windows computer, access to the Administrator account, and an Internet connection.

Caveat

While patch-management programs can vastly reduce your workload, you should always test them on a nonproduction system before deploying them into a production environment.

Procedure

In this task, you will learn how to install and run HFNetChk.

Equipment Used

For this task, you will need the following:

- A Windows XP computer
- Access to the Administrator account
- An Internet connection

Details

This task will show you how to install and run HFNetChk. This program will provide you with the information for those patches installed on the scanned computer.

1. Once you have accessed your Windows computer and logged in as Administrator, open your browser and go to: `http://www.download.com/HFNetChk-exe/3000-2653_4-10173801.html`.

Once the program has completed downloading, execute it from the folder to which it was saved. This will start the installation process. The default location to which it is saved is `C:\Program Files\Shavlik Technologies\HFNetChk`.

2. Once it's installed, open a command prompt and change directories to `C:\Program Files\Shavlik Technologies\HFNetChk`.

From this folder execute HFNetChk from the command line. This is done by typing in the HFNetChk command and pressing Enter.

3. After running the tool, it will provide you with a listing that details what patches have not been installed on the scanned system. An example of the results is as follows:

```
C:\>hfnetchk
Shavlik Technologies Network Security Hotfix Checker 3.86
Shavlik Technologies, LLC
info@shavlik.com (www.shavlik.com), 651-426-6624
All Rights Reserved
================================================================
Scan performed Wed Aug 30 19:14:41 2006
Shavlik Technologies Network Security Hotfix Checker, 3.86
Using XML data version = 1.1.3.2043  Last modified on 8/24/2006.
Scanning Client
--------------------------
Client (192.168.123.101)
--------------------------
        * WINDOWS 2000 SP4
        Patch NOT Installed     MS02-050     Q329115
        Patch NOT Installed     MS03-011     Q816093
        Patch NOT Installed     MS03-023     Q823559
        Patch NOT Installed     MS03-034     Q824105
        Patch NOT Installed     MS03-041     Q823182
        Patch NOT Installed     MS03-042     Q826232
        Patch NOT Installed     MS03-043     Q828035
```

```
* INTERNET EXPLORER 6 SP1
Patch NOT Installed       MS06-023        Q917344
Patch NOT Installed       MS06-042        Q918899


* WINDOWS MEDIA PLAYER 7.1 GOLD
Patch NOT Installed       MS03-040        Q828026
Patch NOT Installed       MS06-024        Q917734


* MDAC 2.7 SP1
Patch NOT Installed       MS06-014        Q911562


* SQL SERVER 2000 SP3 ( MICROSOFTBCM )
Warning
The latest service pack for this product is not
installed.
Currently SQL Server 2000 SP3.


Information
        All necessary hotfixes have been applied.
```

Criteria for Completion

You have completed this task when you have downloaded HFNetChk, installed it on a Windows system, and scanned to verify the system is current with all patches and security updates.

Task 8.5: Performing Internet Vulnerability Profiling

Internet vulnerability profiling is reviewing what others can see when scanning your systems from the Internet. Before an attacker can launch an attack, they must know what ports are services are open and what potential services are tied to those ports. Once this has been determined, the attacker can begin to research known vulnerabilities for the applications found.

For the security professional, this means that it is important to know what outsiders and those on the Internet can access or determine about your network.

Scenario

The organization for which you work has grown quickly. Your manager asked you to run a quick, low-cost test from several of the organization's systems to determine what attackers can see about these systems from the Internet. He has asked you to get this information together before his 4:00 staff meeting.

Scope of Task

Duration

This task should take about 10 minutes.

Setup

For this task, you will need a Windows computer, access to the Administrator account, and an Internet connection.

Caveat

Scanning activities can trip intrusion detection systems and should therefore only be conducted with the knowledge of network administrators.

Procedure

In this task, you will learn how to use Shields Up, an Internet vulnerability profiling tool.

Equipment Used

For this task, you will need the following:

- A Windows XP computer
- Access to the Administrator account
- An Internet connection

Details

This task will run Shield Up. It will be used to scan your Internet connection from the Internet side and see what ports are open on your computer. It will also probe your computer to see if it responds to various requests, such as ICMP echo requests or pings.

Running Shields Up

1. Once you have accessed your Windows computer and logged in as Administrator, open your browser and go to https://www.grc.com/x/ne.dll?bh0bkyd2.

   This will take you to the start page of Shields Up. This is an Internet-based tool that will scan your Internet connection and report its security status. You will want to read the warnings carefully before proceeding.

2. Click the Proceed button to continue and select All Scan Ports. This option will allow the Shields Up application to scan all ports on the requested system and determine what services are opened and closed.

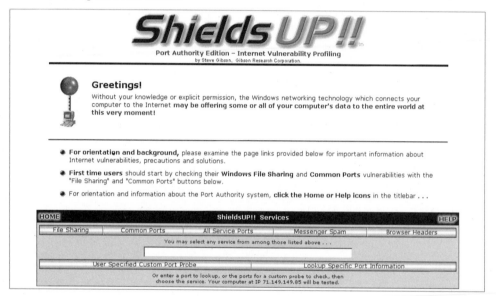

3. After a few minutes the scan will finish. You can then view the scan results in HTML or text. A text version of the report is shown here:

   ```
   ----------------------------------------------------------------

   GRC Port Authority Report created on UTC: 2006-09-10 at 18:28:36

   Results from scan of ports: 0-1055
   ```

```
   0 Ports Open
   2 Ports Closed
1054 Ports Stealth
---------------------
1056 Ports Tested

NO PORTS were found to be OPEN.

Ports found to be CLOSED were: 68, 113

Other than what is listed above, all ports are STEALTH.

TruStealth: FAILED - NOT all tested ports were STEALTH,
               - NO unsolicited packets were received,
               - A PING REPLY (ICMP Echo) WAS RECEIVED.

------------------------------------------------------------
```

4. You will want to look over these results closely. Any open ports should be examined to understand why they are open and what the potential security risks are if these ports remain open. Common open ports that should be examined closely include 21, 25, 53, 80, 110, 135, 139, and 445.

 To learn more about ports, check out http://www.iana.org/assignments/ port-numbers.

Scanning for Messenger Spam

1. Shields Up can also be used to scan for Messenger spam. Remember that the Microsoft Windows Messenger Service on Windows systems used by administrators to send messages to users on the network is on by default. Shields Up can be used to verify the service is disabled spam.

2. Return to https://www.grc.com/x/ne.dll?bh0bkyd2 and choose the Messenger Spam option from the menu.

3. On the Messenger Spam page, choose Spam Me With This Note. This will send several UDP packets to port 135 in an attempt to spam the Messenger service. If you receive a message, the Messenger Service is open.

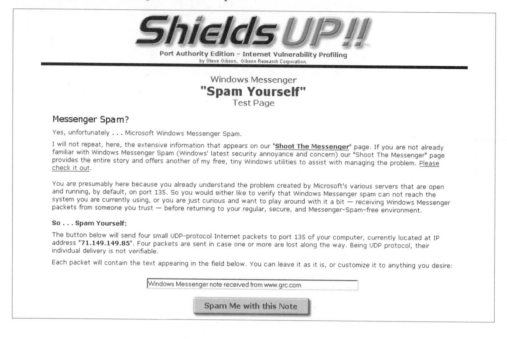

 The Messenger Service can be disabled in the Services menu of Administrative Tools.

Examining Browser Headers

1. Our final system evaluation of Shields Up will be to use the tool to examine browser leakage. Return to `https://www.grc.com/x/ne.dll?bh0bkyd2`. This time choose Browser Headers.

2. Remember that browser header information is transferred each time your browser makes a request to a web server. While much of this information may be harmless, more advanced types of information can sometimes be displayed.

3. Once you click on the Browser Header option, the test will be executed rather quickly and the screen will return its findings.

```
------------------------------------------------------------------
Accept:
    text/xml,application/xml,application/xhtml+xml,text/html;q=0.9
    ,text/plain;q=0.8,image/png,*/*;q=0.5
Accept-Language: en-us,en;q=0.5
Connection: keep-alive
Host: www.grc.com
Referer: https://www.grc.com/x/ne.dll?rh1dkyd2
User-Agent: Mozilla/5.0 (Windows; U; Windows NT 5.0; en-US;
    rv:1.7.12) Gecko/20050915 Firefox/1.0.7
Cookie: temp=3uwye4rty5cfh; perm=1u5hcenz41ecd
Content-Length: 32
Content-Type: application/x-www-form-urlencoded
Accept-Charset: ISO-8859-1,utf-8;q=0.7,*;q=0.7
Keep-Alive: 300
FirstParty: https://www.grc.com
ThirdParty: https://www.grctech.com
Secure: https://www.grc.com
Nonsecure: http://www.grc.com
Session: tp50n5rvhm2we
------------------------------------------------------------------
```

While no critical information was exposed in this example, you can see that the version of the operating system—NT 5 or Windows 2000—was uncovered.

4. Look closely through your results to see what type of information was reveled.

> One way to hide browser information while browsing is to use a proxy service. An example of one can be found at `http://www.the-cloak.com/anonymous-surfing-home.html`.

Criteria for Completion

You have completed this task when you have run Shields Up to examine open ports, scanned for Messenger spam, and examined what information your browser leaks to other Internet clients.

Phase

9

Investigating Incidents

Well, it's happened. Somehow, in spite of all your hard work, researching technology and devices, planning, budgeting and managing, implementation and training, a security breach has occurred.

What now? How should you proceed? What should you be doing first? What should you do after that? You know that over the next few weeks or months that the big shots will study every move you've made, and that they'll find some level of fault with every step you took.

In the midst of the chaos of the incident, as the lead on the Computer Emergency Response Team (CERT), you must rise to the role of leader in response to the incident. This means you must have a plan. The plan must be rehearsed. You must have a team. That team must be trained. The training must be repeated, and the process must be updated using the latest tools and technologies. The team must be ready to react in a moment's notice, 24/7. Not to mention the legalistic mumbo-jumbo you'll have to deal with.

You have auditing and intrusion detection systems (IDSs) in place. Your plan is in place. Your team is trained, rehearsed, and ready to go. Both you and they know what to do, and how to do it. Your team knows how to investigate the telltale clues that were left behind by the attacker. They know how to identify, protect, collect, document, store, analyze, transport, and present the evidence to reach conclusions about how the incident occurred. This may be done for "lessons learned," so you'll know how to strengthen your system against this type of attack. This may be done for evidence preparation for prosecution, to put the attacker behind bars.

Investigating computer-related incidents is a highly evolved and refined process, and even more, a highly refined science. Your initial job is to stop the bleeding and stabilize the patient. In this case, that means you don't allow the attack to continue, and you quickly assess the rest of the system to see if this is an isolated incident or if there is a wider attack under way. After that, you begin your detective work. You identify and protect anything that may be evidence. Then you collect and document the evidence. You review the output from your sensors, your IDS, your audit logs, and the memory dump from the attacked system. You examine the system to try to uncover fingerprints left by the attacker, fingerprints that may lead you to the attackers' exposure and prosecution.

You'll be exploring some of these techniques in this phase. The tasks presented in this phase may not make you a forensic investigator, but they lead to that path.

The tasks in this phase map to Domain 1, 3, and 5 objectives for the CompTIA Security+ exam (http://certification.comptia.org/security/).

Task 9.1: Configuring an Audit Policy for Object Access

Auditing is an integral component of security for any system or network. Auditing is the tracking and recording of events in a log. What events? Well, that's up to you. An audit policy can be set on individual systems, or configured for groups of systems, or for every system in the enterprise.

If you don't have auditing turned on before the event, you won't have any information recorded about the event. This must be set up in advance. You will place a more elaborate audit policy on systems that are more exposed, on your most critical infrastructure systems, and on systems that hold your most sensitive information assets.

When you implement an audit policy, you should also configure the Security log in Event Viewer, to increase its size and to avoid overwriting the existing log data. This should be part of the process as you develop your monitoring plan for the Audit log.

Scenario

You are an administrator in an Active Directory environment. You need to record all accesses to sensitive content on one of your systems. You are concerned about actual and attempted access to a folder on a system that contains sensitive documents.

Scope of Task

Duration

This task should take 30 minutes.

Setup

This audit policy should apply to authenticated users and should include Read, Modify, Create, and Delete accesses to the file and folder content.

The audited events will be written to the Security log in the Event Viewer application, on the server holding the sensitive content.

Caveat

Auditing can easily overwhelm a system, a network, and your administrators. Thousands of events can occur on a system every hour. The system can become so busy recording all of the event details that resources available to service actual client requests become limited. If you are using a collection and analysis application, these thousands of events—for numerous systems—must be sent over the network to the central database for storage and analysis. None of this activity does you any good, unless a responsible human is involved to interpret the output, and react if and as necessary. The monitoring of event logs can consume most, if not all, of an administrator's time.

Auditing should only be configured if you intend to regularly review and use the information that will be generated from the audit policy.

Procedure

For this task, you will then build a new Auditing GPO for object access and link it to the organizational unit (OU) that contains the system that holds the sensitive content. To complete the object access auditing, you must configure auditing in the System Access Control List (SACL) on the system that holds the sensitive content for the folder where the critical data is stored.

Equipment Used

For this task, you need the following:

- Windows Server 2003 domain controller system
- Windows XP Professional system, which is a member of the domain
  - This is the system that holds the sensitive data
- Domain Administrator access
- Completion of Tasks 4.8 and 6.1

Details

Configuring an Auditing GPO for Object Access

1. Log on the Windows Server 2003 domain controller system as the Domain Administrator.
2. Select Start ➤ Programs ➤ Administration Tools ➤ Active Directory Users And Computers (ADUC).
3. In the left pane, expand the domain. Click on the OU named Confidential Servers that you created in Task 6.1.
4. In the left pane, right-click on the OU named Confidential Servers and select Properties.
5. Select the Group Policy tab.

 In Task 6.1, this OU was configured with an IPSec policy to require encrypted communications. You will first disable this policy to avoid any potential conflicts with this task. If you have already disabled or deleted this GPO, skip to Step 8.

6. Double-click on the IPSec Secure Servers Policy in the area under Disabled. You should receive a Confirm Disable warning message.

7. Click Yes to confirm that you intend to disable the IPSec GPO.

8. On the Group Policy tab, click New to create a new GPO.

9. Name the new GPO Object **Access Audit Policy**.

10. On the Group Policy tab, click Edit.

11. In the left pane, expand Computer Configuration Settings | Security Settings | Local Policies, and select Audit Policy.

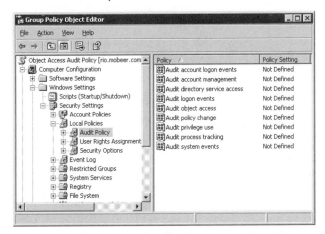

12. In the right pane, double-click on Audit Object Access to open its properties dialog box.

13. Under Define These Policy Settings, enable the Success and Failure checkboxes.

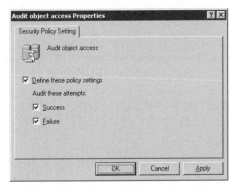

14. Click OK to close the Audit Object Access Properties dialog box.

15. Confirm that Success and Failure are enabled for the Audit Object Access policy.

16. Next you'll configure the Security log properties, where the audited events get recorded. In the Group Policy dialog box, in the left pane select Event Log.

17. In the right pane, double-click the Maximum Security Log Size Policy.

18. Enable the Define This Policy Setting checkbox, and set the log size to 500032 Kilobytes (500MB). Click OK.

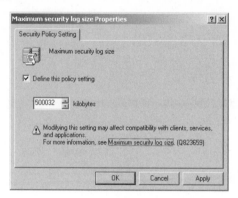

 Log file sizes must be in increments of 64KB. Each event logged adds approximately 500 bytes to the log file size. Each file access can trigger the logging of 4–12 events. If you conservatively assume 12 events logged per file access and 1,000 accesses each day, you get 180MB per month added to the Security log each month for object access in this folder. In this example, you should schedule to turn Security log at least once each month. To turn the log, save the log as a file to a secure location, and then clear all events on that log in Event Viewer.

 There are many other events that get written to the Security log and increase its size. Measure, evaluate, and determine the correct file size for the Security log in your environment. Adjust this file size as necessary over time.

19. In the right pane, double-click the Prevent Local Guests Group From Accessing Security Log Policy.

20. Select the Define This Policy Setting checkbox, and select the Enabled option. Click OK.

21. In the right pane, double-click the Retention method for Security Log Policy.

22. Check the Define This Policy Setting checkbox, and select Do Not Overwrite Events (Clear Log Manually). Click OK.

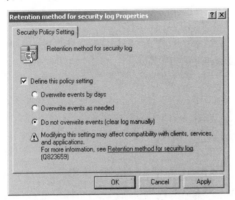

23. You will get a Confirm Setting Change warning regarding another policy setting that can shut down this system if the log file fills and cannot be written to because of the Do Not Overwrite setting you just defined. You will not be implementing that additional policy. Click Yes to confirm your Do Not Overwrite setting.

24. Confirm your settings in the Event Log section of the Audit Policy GPO.

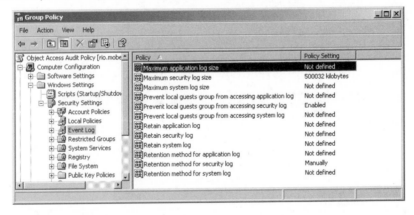

25. Close the GPO to save it. Click Close to close the Confidential Servers Properties dialog box.

Moving the Resource Server into the Proper OU

1. In ADUC, locate the system that holds the sensitive data that you need to implement auditing on. The default location for all non–domain controller systems is the Computers container.

> In this task, you are using an XP Professional system as the resource server. In the graphic, the resource server is an XP Professional system named SHOTGUN.

2. Right-click on the resource server and select Move.

3. In the Move dialog box, select the Confidential Servers OU, and click OK. This places the resource server into the Confidential Servers OU, making it subject to the new Auditing policy.

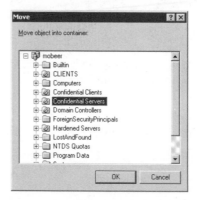

4. Confirm that your resource server is now located in the Confidential Servers OU.

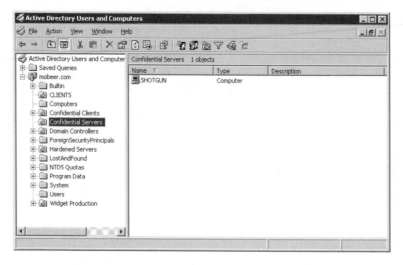

5. Close ADUC.

Refresh the Group Policies on the XP Professional System

1. Log on the Windows XP Professional system as the Domain Administrator.

2. Select Start ➤ Run.

3. In the Open field, type **gpupdate /force** and click OK.

> This opens a command window that says Refreshing Policy, and may take a few moments to complete. This reapplies all GPOs that affect the XP Professional system, right now. Since we relocated the XP Professional system into a new OU with different GPOs, you want to be certain that the Auditing GPO is currently applied to, and effective on, this system right away. The GPO would have automatically refreshed within two hours by default.

Configuring Auditing for Object Access on the Resource Server

1. On the Windows XP Professional system, launch the Explorer application.

2. In the left pane, expand the folders as necessary to locate the folder named STUFF.

3. Select the STUFF folder.

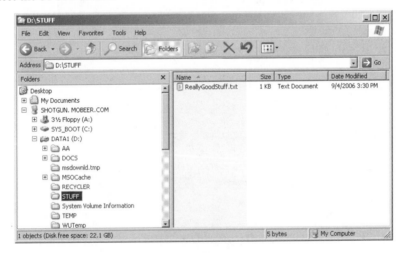

> In Task 4.8, you created a folder named STUFF on an XP Professional system, and placed some sensitive content in it. If that folder and content is still available, use it. If not, create a new folder named STUFF and place a new text document into it.

4. Right-click on the STUFF folder and select Properties.

5. On the Security tab, click Advanced. Select the Auditing tab of the Advanced Security Settings For STUFF dialog box.

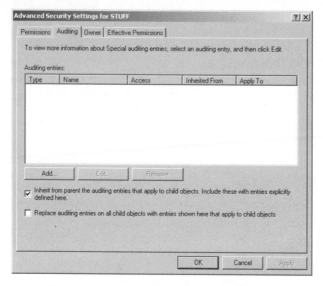

6. Click Add to build the System Access Control List (SACL) to implement auditing on this folder.

7. In the Select User, Computer, Or Group dialog box, click Advanced.

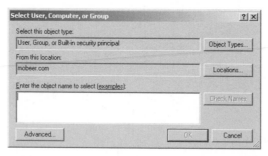

8. Click the Find Now button to display a list of users, computers, and groups in the domain.

9. Select Authenticated Users from the resulting Name (FQDN) list. Click OK to accept Authenticated Users.

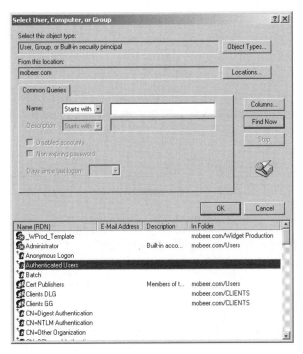

10. In the Select User, Computer, Or Group dialog box, click OK to close the dialog box.

11. In the resulting Auditing Entry For STUFF dialog box, select Successful and Failed for the following access types:

   - List Folder/Execute File

   - Create Files/Write Data

   - Create Folders/Append Data

   - Delete Subfolders And Files

   - Delete

With the Auditing GPO linked to the OU that contains this system, these settings will audit successful and attempted access for all authenticated users. Access types being audited include Read, Modify (Write), Create, and Delete accesses to the file and folder content. These auditing attributes will now be inherited by all newly created content in the STUFF folder by default.

12. Confirm your settings, and click OK to close the Auditing Entry For STUFF dialog box.

13. In the Advanced Security Settings For STUFF dialog box, enable the Replace Auditing Entries On All Child Objects With Entries Shown Here That Apply To Child Objects checkbox.

With this setting enabled, these auditing attributes will now be inherited by all existing and newly created content in the STUFF folder.

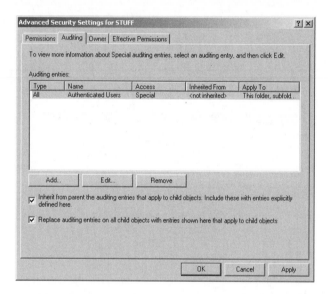

14. Click OK to close the Advanced Security Settings for STUFF dialog box.

You may see a progress dialog box that monitors the writing of the new SACL attributes to all existing content in the STUFF folder. This could take quite a while if the folder contains numerous files and folders.

If this folder is accessed a lot, the auditing processes can consume massive resources on this system and degrade system performance severely. Auditing should only be configured if you intend to regularly review and use the information that will be generated from the audit policy.

Criteria for Completion

You have completed this task when you have built a new Auditing GPO that is linked to the Confidential Servers OU. Then, on the server (XP Professional system in this case) holding the sensitive content, you should have configured the SACL on the sensitive content folder.

Task 9.2: Reviewing the Audit Logs

Once you have completed the implementation of an audit policy, you must implement a standard monitoring routine. This is often a huge challenge. Audit logs are recorded in the Security log in Event Viewer and can record thousands of events each day, or even each hour. You may have many systems to monitor, and this easily becomes an overwhelming task. Many organizations acquire third-party software to retrieve, analyze, and report on audited events for a network environment. These software tools are essential in many cases, and can cost just a little—or a lot.

Securing your audit logs is a major concern as well. The employee agreement for all network administrators should include a requirement that every log must be saved to a specified archive location, and failure to properly save a log (clear the log without saving it) should be grounds for termination. Highly restrictive permissions should be placed on these log files to allow only a rare few, highly trusted administrators access to this content. In many industries, regulatory compliance laws require the retention of these logs for many years. You should know what these requirements are for your organization.

Scenario

You are an administrator in an Active Directory environment. You are concerned about actual and attempted access to a folder on a system that contains sensitive documents. You have implemented an Object Access audit policy to log these accesses, including Read, Modify, Create, and Delete accesses to the file and folder content for authenticated users.

You must now establish a routine to identify unauthorized access attempts to determine if and when this attack occurs.

Scope of Task

Duration

This task should take 30 minutes.

Setup

You implemented an audit policy on authenticated users that tracks Read, Modify, Create, and Delete accesses to the file and folder content in the STUFF folder.

The audited events are being written to the Security log in the Event Viewer application, on the server holding the sensitive content.

Caveat

Auditing can easily overwhelm a system, a network, and your administrators. Thousands of events can occur on a system every hour. The system can become so busy recording all of the event details that limited resources available to service actual client requests become limited. If you are using a collection and analysis application, these thousands of events—for numerous systems—must be sent over the network to the central database for storage and analysis. None of this activity does you any good, unless a responsible human is involved to interpret the output, and react if and as necessary. The monitoring of event logs can consume most, if not all, of an administrator's time.

Auditing should only be configured if you intend to use the information that will be generated from the audit policy.

Procedure

For this task, you will create a new user in the domain. You will then configure permissions on the STUFF folder to deny access to the new user. You will create some content in the STUFF folder as the Administrator, who has sufficient permissions to create content.

Next you will log on to the system as the new user and attempt to access the STUFF folder. Of course, you should receive Access Denied errors. This should trigger Failed Access events in the Security log.

Finally, you will log on as Administrator and open Event Viewer. You will see many events in the log. You will build a filter to view successful accesses, and another filter to view only failed accesses to the STUFF content.

Equipment Used

For this task, you need the following:

- Windows Server 2003 domain controller system
- Windows XP Professional system, a member of the domain
  - The system that holds the sensitive data from Task 9.1
- Domain Administrator access
- Completion of Task 9.1

Details

Creating a New User Account

1. Log on the Windows Server 2003 domain controller system as the Domain Administrator.

2. Select Start ➤ Programs ➤ Administration Tools ➤ Active Directory Users And Computers (ADUC).

3. In the left pane, expand the domain. Click on the container named Users.

4. In the left pane, right-click on the container named Users and select New ➤ User.

5. Type the name **BoBo2** in the First Name and User Logon Name fields. Click Next.

6. Enter the password **Password1** in both the Password and Confirm Password fields. Clear the User Must Change Password At Next Logon checkbox and enable the Password Never Expires checkbox. Click Next.

7. Click Finish to confirm the creation of the new user BoBo2.

8. Log off the Windows Server 2003 domain controller system.

Configuring Permissions on the XP Professional System

1. Log on the Windows XP Professional system as the Domain Administrator.

2. Launch Windows Explorer.

3. In the left pane, expand the folders as necessary to locate the folder named STUFF.

4. Select the STUFF folder.

 In Task 9.1, you configured a folder named STUFF with an audit policy for Object Access, Success, and Failure.

5. Right-click on the STUFF folder and select Properties.

6. On the Security tab, click Add to configure deny permissions for BoBo2.

7. In the Select Users, Computers, Or Groups dialog box, click Advanced.

8. Click Find Now to display domain users, computers, and groups.

9. Select BoBo2 from the Name (FQDN) list. Click OK.

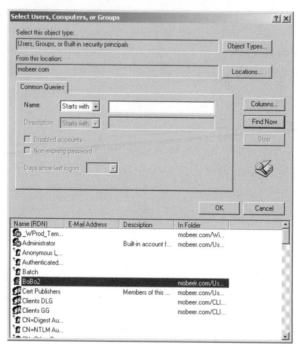

10. Click OK in the Select Users, Computers, Or Groups dialog box to add BoBo2 to the Discretionary Access Control List (DACL) for the STUFF folder.

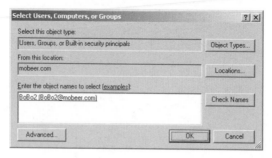

11. On the Security tab of the STUFF Properties dialog box, with BoBo2 selected in the top pane enable the Deny checkbox for Full Control in the bottom pane. This denies all access to BoBo2 for any content in the STUFF folder.

If you have completed Task 5.5 on this system, you could have placed BoBo2 into the Deny All GG to accomplish the same level of restrictive permissions.

12. Click OK to close the STUFF Properties dialog box.

Triggering the Audit Policy on the STUFF folder for Audit Success

1. While logged in to the Windows XP Professional system as the Domain Administrator, in Windows Explorer in the right pane of the STUFF folder, right-click on white space and select New ➢ Folder. Name the folder **AdminStuff**.

2. Double-click on the AdminStuff folder. In the right pane, right-click on white space and select New ➢ Text Document. Name the document **AdminStuff.txt**.

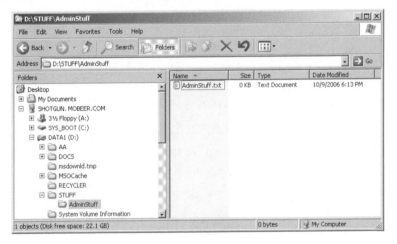

3. Edit the contents of AdminStuff.txt with the Notepad application. Save the changes and exit Notepad.

4. Create two more documents: AdminStuff2.txt and AdminStuffDel.txt. Edit and save these documents.

5. Delete AdminStuffDel.txt.

6. Close the Explorer application and log off the XP Professional system.

Triggering the Audit Policy on the STUFF folder for Audit Failure

1. Log on the Windows XP Professional system as BoBo2, with the password Password1.

2. Launch Windows Explorer.

3. In the left pane, expand the folders as necessary to locate the folder named STUFF.

4. Select the STUFF folder. You should receive an Access Denied error.

5. Click OK to clear the Access Denied error.

6. Select other folders on the system, and try to select the STUFF folder again. You should receive an Access Denied error again.

7. Click OK to clear the Access Denied error.

8. Log off the XP Professional system as BoBo2.

Reviewing the Security Log (Audit Log) on the XP Professional System

1. Log on the Windows XP Professional system as the Domain Administrator.

2. Select Start ➢ Run. Type **Eventvwr** in the Open field and click OK to launch the Event Viewer application.

3. In the left pane, select the Security log. Notice that in the example there are already 914 events in this newly configured log.

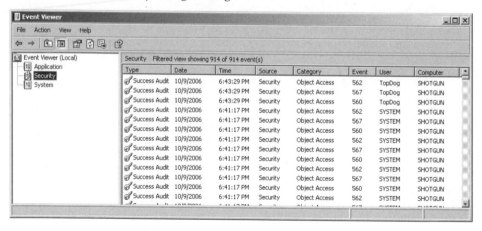

Your system will show a different number and different types of events.

You'll notice that the object access Event IDs are 560, 562, and 567. By correlating the timestamps, you should also notice that these three Event IDs represent a single access event, like a read or a write or a delete. This could take some time to review and interpret, especially after logging events for a month.

4. In the left pane, right-click on the Security log and select Properties. Select the Filter tab.

5. First, disable the Information, Warning, Error, and Failure Audit checkboxes. In the User field, enter the user name **TopDog**, the administrator for the domain.

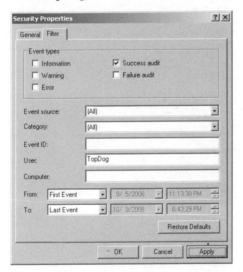

6. Click OK to apply the filter and view the filtered Security log.

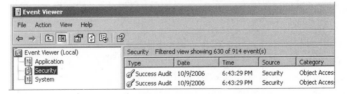

Notice that this filter still only knocks down the number of events by about one-third in the example. Your results may be different.

7. In the left pane, right-click on the Security log and select Properties. Select the Filter tab. This time add the Event ID of 560.

8. Double-click on the top event. In the graphic, notice the upper portion. This shows a Success Audit, Object Access for the user TopDog, and TopDog was accessing the object from the computer named SHOTGUN. (In this case, TopDog was logged on locally to the resource server.) Your events should look similar, but with different times and names.

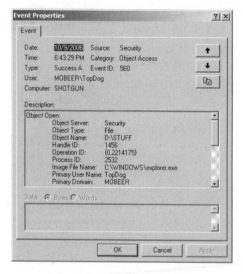

9. Notice the Description field. It shows that the object was accessed by the `explorer.exe` application, and the user accessed the `D:\STUFF` folder.

10. As you scroll down, you will see that the access type was listing the contents of the STUFF directory.

11. Select the down arrow in the upper-right corner of the Event Properties dialog box to scroll down the list of 560 events for TopDog. Review the details of several of these events. Locate the DELETE event where you deleted the `AdminStuffDel.txt` file.

12. In the left pane, right-click on the Security log and select Properties. Select the Filter tab. This time change the Event ID to 567. Click OK to apply the filter.

13. Double-click on the top event. Select the down arrow in the upper-right corner of the Event Properties dialog box to scroll down the list of 567 events for TopDog. Review the details of several of these events. Locate a WriteData event where you saved one of the `AdminStuff.txt` files.

Notice the time selection, and the From and To filters. These would help you isolate for a specific time period.

14. In the left pane, right-click on the Security log and select Properties. Select the Filter tab. This time disable Success Audit, enable Failure Audit, change the Event ID to 560, and clear the User field.

15. Click OK to apply the filter.

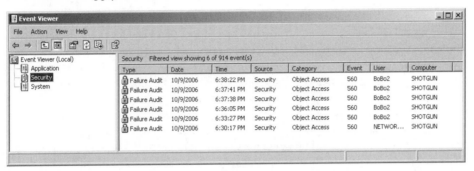

16. Double-click on the top event. Select the down arrow in the upper-right corner of the Event Properties dialog box to scroll down the list of 560 Failure Audit events. Review the details of several of these events.

These would be indications of users who were trying to access content that they should not be accessing. Fortunately, permissions stopped their access, but perhaps it might be a good idea to pose a question or two to their supervisor, or to them (BoBo2 in this case) directly, just to let them know that you know. Repeated incidents could be cause for reprimand, or even termination. Document these incidents and warnings to the users.

17. In the left pane, right-click on the Security log and select Properties. Select the Filter tab. This time, enable all settings: Information, Earning, Error, Success Audit, and Failure Audit, and clear all of the fields below by clicking the Restore Defaults button.

Failure to reset the filter could easily cause misinterpretation of the event logs by hiding critical events. Be sure this filter gets reset to its original default.

18. Close Event Viewer.

Criteria for Completion

You have completed this task when you have generated some audit events, both success and failure. You must have then interrogated the Security log in the Event Viewer application and applied several filters to isolate the types of events you were looking for, and then reset the Security Log filter to its original default settings.

Task 9.3: Forcing a Memory Dump

The memory dump takes the contents of physical random access memory (RAM) and writes it to a file on the hard drive, to serve as a persistent copy for later analysis. Memory dumps may be useful for two main purposes: debugging problematic applications (not our issue here) and investigating an attack incident. As a record of what was going on in RAM, it can reveal to the trained analyst many details of the interactions among applications and between applications and the operating system. Many forms of *exploit software*, the type of code used in viruses, worms, Trojans, and so forth, implement code that interacts with applications and the operating system in an atypical manner. This software attempts to interact in ways that it should not. Understanding the method of attack, or the attack vector, is essential in developing the proper defense against this form of attack.

Most forensic investigation guidelines declare that this memory dump is an essential component of a post-incident investigation. (This seems to contradict the other golden rule of incident investigation: to pull the plug on the system, and go down "dirty" to avoid altering the contents of the hard drive(s). But this book isn't here to debate forensic investigation issues. At this point, it is important to know how to accomplish the task.)

The more sophisticated forensic investigators have tools and techniques to gather this information without violating the integrity of the hard drives, but these tools can be quite expensive and the procedures require specialized training and rehearsal.

Scenario

You are operating a system and you suspect that you might have a virus. You observe several unexpected systemic activities that concern you, and you hope to gather information to identify what might be going on in the system.

Scope of Task

Duration

This task should take 20 minutes.

Setup

The function of forcing the memory dump is not built into the operating system by default. This capability must be added by editing the Registry and rebooting the system. This means that you must have this capability in place on each system where you desire the forced memory dump prior to needing to utilize this feature.

Caveat

In Task 9.3, you will be editing the Registry. This is always dangerous. This is like performing brain surgery on a live and awake patient.

The forced memory dump performs an abnormal shutdown, an "abend," or abnormal end (termination). It is a "dirty" shutdown and it does not properly close files and applications. This can corrupt many types of critical files that are being accessed by the system, and can lose any data files you have open. If your hardware includes any type of write or disk caching, shutting the system down dirty can cause serious problems. You may not want to perform this task to avoid this.

If you elect to proceed, you should have backups of your data, and you should generate a system restore point prior to editing the Registry and before performing the forced memory dump, just in case.

 To review the manual creation of a system restore point, see Task 10.3.

Procedure

First you'll configure the memory dump in system properties, to get the desired amount of information and specify the location of the output file.

You must then perform an edit in the Registry, and reboot the system to have the change mounted by the operating system. After the reboot, you'll launch an application or two—nothing too important or volatile, though.

Then you'll push the magic buttons. Boom! Bluescreen! This is followed by a reboot.

After the reboot completes, you'll open and examine the contents of the dump file. There may not be much to see by the untrained eye. Much of the file contains machine language code that is unreadable by humans. There are a series of analytical tools that experts use to extract the most detail out of these files. This investigative procedure almost always includes sending this memory dump file to one of these types of individuals for the hard-core analysis.

Recognize that this Registry edit and reboot must be configured on your systems prior to an attack. If the attack has occurred before these settings are in place, this technique cannot be used to capture the contents of RAM.

Equipment Used

For this task, you need the following:

- Windows XP Professional system
- A member of the domain
- Administrator access

Details

Configuring the Minidump

1. Log on the Windows XP Professional system as the Administrator.
2. Right-click on My Computer and select Properties.

System Properties are also available by choosing the System applet in Control Panel.

3. Click the Advanced tab.

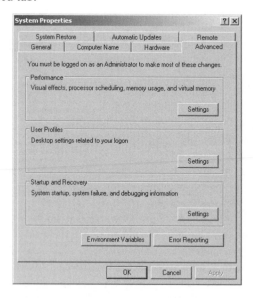

4.   In the Startup And Recovery section, click the Settings button.

5.   In the System Failure section, observe that the three checkboxes are enabled. If you needed to, you could disable any one of these three configuration parameters. Clearing the Automatically Restart checkbox leaves the bluescreen on the display until a manual power down is initiated.

6.   Clear the Automatically Restart checkbox.

7.   In the subsection Write Debugging Information, select the drop-down list to view the three choices:

Small Memory Dump (64 KB)   This is called the minidump.

Kernel Memory Dump   This represents the larger amount of content, with no user data and just the OS.

Complete Memory Dump   This represents the largest amount of information, historically too much to send via the Internet, but that is changing more and more.

8.   Alternately select the three different dump types and observe the dialog box. Select the Small Memory Dump (64 KB) for this exercise.

9.   In the Small Dump Directory field, notice the location where the dump file will be written. %SystemRoot% means the WINDOWS directory (or whatever else you may have called it during installation of the system). The \Minidump indicates that, upon triggering, the system

will build a folder if it doesn't already exist and store the minidump files in it. You could relocate this to any local, writable disk in case this drive is too full, or if you are fighting a hardware/driver issue that is supporting the spindle holding the boot partition. Leave this at its default setting of %SystemRoot%\Minidump.

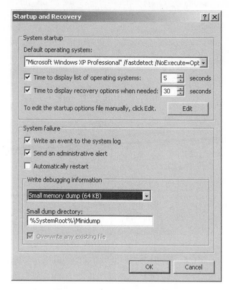

10. Click OK to close the Startup And Recovery dialog box.

11. Click OK to close the System Properties dialog box.

Implementing the Registry Edit (the "Reg Hack")

1. Still logged on the Windows XP Professional system as the Administrator, select Start ➢ Run. In the Open field, type **regedit** and click OK to launch the Registry editing tool.

2. In the Registry Editor, in the left pane, expand the folders to the following location: HKEY_LOCAL_MACHINE | System | CurrentControlSet | Services | i8042prt and select the Parameters folder.

WARNING   Editing the Registry is a potentially dangerous action. You should always manually trigger a system restore point and perform a backup of all data on the system. Follow the instructions precisely. Double-check (and then triple-check) your entries. Treat all entries as if they are case sensitive.

3. In the right pane, right-click the white space and select New ➢ DWORD Value.

4. Name the new DWORD value **CrashOnCtrlScroll** and press Enter.

5. Right-click on the new CrashOnCtrlScroll DWORD value and select Modify.

6. In the Edit DWORD Value dialog box, first select Decimal in the Base section, and then in the Value Data field, type the number **1**.

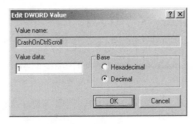

7. Click OK to close the Edit DWORD Value dialog box.

8. Confirm your settings carefully. Close the Registry Editor application.

 If you wish to disable the system from being able to perform the manually triggered memory dump, all you have to do is delete the DWORD Value CrashOnCtrlScroll from the Registry, and restart the system.

9. Close all applications and restart the system.

Triggering the Memory Dump

1. Log on the Windows XP Professional system as the Administrator.

2. Launch Notepad, Calculator, and Paint, and minimize all three.

3. Press and hold the Ctrl key and press the Scroll Lock button twice. You should get a bluescreen.

```
A problem has been detected and windows has been shut down to prevent damage
to your computer.

The end-user manually generated the crashdump.

If this is the first time you've seen this stop error screen,
restart your computer. If this screen appears again, follow
these steps:

Check to make sure any new hardware or software is properly installed.
If this is a new installation, ask your hardware or software manufacturer
for any windows updates you might need.

If problems continue, disable or remove any newly installed hardware
or software. Disable BIOS memory options such as caching or shadowing.
If you need to use Safe Mode to remove or disable components, restart
your computer, press F8 to select Advanced Startup Options, and then
select Safe Mode.

Technical information:

*** STOP: 0x000000E2 (0x00000000,0x00000000,0x00000000,0x00000000)


Beginning dump of physical memory
Physical memory dump complete.
Contact your system administrator or technical support group for further
assistance.
```

4. Review the bluescreen message.

5. Power down the system.

Reviewing the Memory Dump

1. Power up the system and log on the Windows XP Professional system as the Administrator.

2. As the desktop stabilizes, you should receive a Microsoft Windows error message. Review the message.

3. Click on the Click Here hyperlink to review the event information related to the bluescreen.

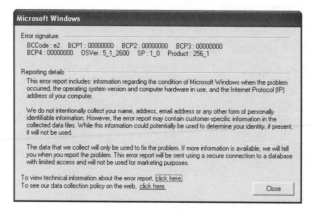

4. Select the Click Here hyperlink to view technical information about the error report.

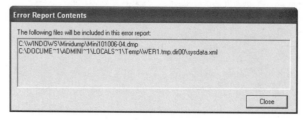

5. Notice that Microsoft wants two files:

   - The memory dump named `Mini101006-04.dmp` (the numbers represent a date code, followed by a sequential number)

   - `sysdata.xml`, which is a file that logs system details and all hardware devices and drivers that were loaded at the time of the system crash

> You might want to locate and copy this file to the desktop for later review. It contains an excellent summary of details. Notice the path to the file in the dialog box. The parent folder name will begin with WER (Windows Error Report), but the number(s) behind it will vary. The extension should be .dir00.

6. Click Close to exit the Error Report Contents dialog box. Click Close to exit the Error Signature dialog box. Click the Don't Send button to close the Windows Error Reporting dialog box without sending crash information to Microsoft. You triggered the crash, not a real application or operating system problem.

7. Launch Windows Explorer. In the left pane, expand the folders as necessary to locate the `WINDOWS\Minidump` folder.

8. If there is more than one file in the `Minidump` folder, locate the file with today's date and the timestamp that matched the most recent bluescreen.

9. Right-click on the correct `Minidump` file and select Open.

10. Enable the Select The Program From A List option and click OK.

11. In the Programs list, select Notepad and click OK.

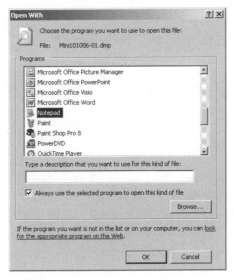

12. Adjust the window size of Notepad as desired. Select Format ➢ Word Wrap.

13. Scroll through the memory dump. Notice the reference to PageDump. The memory dump gets written first to the pagefile, and then on reboot, it gets written to the minidump file, Mini101006-04.dmp file in this case.

14. Notice the reference to .SYS, .DLL, and possibly some .EXE files. You may also see some BIOS and hardware device information.

15. Scroll to the top of the file and click in the very first space. From the menu, select Edit ➢ Find. Type **KDBG** in the Find What field, and click Find Next. KDBG refers to the Kernel Debugger, a tool used to diagnose kernel-related processes.

16. Scroll back to the top of the file and click in the very first space. From the menu, select Edit ➢ Find. Type **TRGD** in the Find What field, and click Find Next. TRGD refers to the Triage Data (it may also be referred to as Triggered Data). Triage implies sorting, based on an evaluation and categorization, into three levels of severity to be able to address the most critical issues first. This TRGD tag indicates the end of the memory dump, but the file may continue with system-related information.

17. Your conclusion regarding the memory dump is probably that it is cryptic and largely unreadable. If you did have to extract worthy information from this file, you would solicit the services of a worthy forensic investigator, or contact Microsoft for additional analytical assistance. The good news is that you now know how to create the file for further analysis.

18. Close Notepad.

Criteria for Completion

You have completed this task when you have configured the system to be able to force a memory dump, and then performed and reviewed the memory dump.

Task 9.4: Capturing Packets with the Packet Analyzer: Ethereal

Ethereal is a free, commonly used packet analyzer. Packet analyzers—also called network analyzers, protocol analyzers, or sniffers— monitor the network and record the packets (frames, actually) on the network that it sees Packet analyzers are useful for analyzing traffic patterns, identifying rogue protocols and nodes on the network, and troubleshooting many types of network- or protocol-related problems.

A *rogue* protocol is a protocol that should not be present on your network. If your network only uses TCP/IP for a transport protocol, there should be no TP4 or IPX/SPX frames on the network. We are using the word *node* to represent a system or device that communicates on the network.

There is a problem with sniffers these days, as most networks use switches, which is essentially a multiport bridge that isolates each node from all other nodes, unless there is specific traffic destined for the node. This is called *nonpromiscuous mode*. Your sniffer can only see and record (capture) traffic destined for your node. This traffic would include frames sent by your node; frames sent to your node; broadcast frames, which go to every node; and multicast frames that your node has registered to receive. This occurs because the switch learns your Media Access Control (MAC) address, and makes forwarding decisions based on a frame's destination MAC address.

In the past, networks all ran on hubs that shared a common backplane. In other words, each node could see all the traffic that existed on the hub, or on multiple, daisy-chained hubs, up until the segment hit a bridge or router. You could monitor (eavesdrop on) dialogs, network conversations between two nodes that did not include your node. This is called *promiscuous mode*. It can be useful for analytical purposes, but it can also be dangerous, since you are more likely to get infected with all sorts of malware, and if the sniffer is in the hands of an attacker, he may be accessing data he is not authorized to see—a compromise of the confidentiality of your information assets.

For administrative purposes, many of the industrial-class switches can implement promiscuous mode, through a diagnostic (or spanning) port that connects directly to the backplane, or a diagnostic mode that can be toggled on or off for a specified port by a system administrator.

Attackers can also cause this to happen. One approach is to flood the switch with so many frames that, instead of dropping frames, the switch connects all ports and acts as a hub. It's faster and easier to not think about each frame and just send each frame to all ports. Another approach is to report to the switch that your node is every node. You're telling the switch to "Send me every frame." A good switch will detect this attack, and disallow this from happening.

Scenario

You have recently become responsible for several segments on your corporate network. You want to understand more of the nature of the traffic on these segments. You are looking for traffic flow patterns, and you always have your eye open for rogue nodes and protocols on the network.

Scope of Task

Duration

This task should take 45 minutes.

Setup

You will need to download Ethereal v0.99.0 or later. Ethereal was first written for the Unix/Linux) family of operating systems. Because of this, it is open source licensing, and free for you to use. It was ported over to run on the Microsoft platform. Older versions of Ethereal required that an additional component be installed first, called WinPcap (currently at v3.1), but this is now a component of the installation executable.

Caveat

Downloading and installing software from the Internet is always risky. Be sure your system is fully patched, and that you are running recently updated antivirus and antispyware applications. Scan these downloaded files before you install them. Scan your system after installing them and before using them.

Procedure

You will first download and install Ethereal. You will then initiate a scan and surf the Internet for a while. Then you will stop and save your capture. You will then review the scan.

Equipment Used

For this task, you need the following:

- Windows XP Professional system
- Administrator access
- Internet access

Details

Downloading Ethereal

1. Log on the Windows XP Professional system as the Administrator.
2. Launch Internet Explorer and browse to http://www.ethereal.com/.
3. In the upper-left corner, click Download.
4. On the Ethereal Download page, select to download the Windows Official Release (at the time of writing, the current version is v0.99.0).

On this same page, toward the bottom, you can pursue downloading sample captures. These can provide massive insight as to how specific protocols and network functions occur. If you have many hours to burn but learn, download a handful of these and spend the day just being the geek that you are.

5. On the File Download – Security Warning Dialog screen, select to save the file. Save the file to your desktop using the default name, `ethereal-setup-0.99.0.exe`.

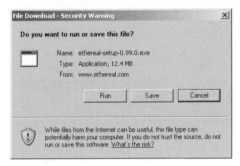

Installing Ethereal

1. Upon completion of the file download, double-click the executable that should be located on your desktop.

2. In the Open File – Security Warning dialog box, click Run to execute the installation application for Ethereal.

3. The installation application confirms that the package has not been corrupted.

4. In the Ethereal Setup Wizard's Welcome screen, click Next.

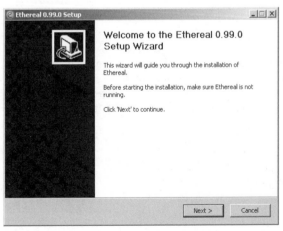

5. On the License Agreement screen, click I Agree.

6. On the Choose Components screen, leave the defaults and click Next.

GTK2 is the newest interface for Ethereal. Loading additional components is optional, but may alter the application's user interfaces or performance or cause other potentially undesirable manifestations.

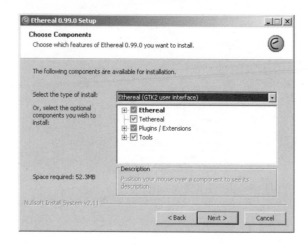

7. On the Additional Tasks screen, leave the defaults and click Next.

8. On the Choose Installation Location screen, leave the default and click Next.

9. On the Install WinPcap? screen, leave the defaults and click Next.

NFP refers to the Netgroup Packet Filter—npf.sys—a system driver that is essential for the operation of Ethereal. If you start NPF at startup, nonadministrator users can use Ethereal to capture packets. This could be a bad thing. If nonadministrator users can capture frames on a network, they could be gaining unauthorized access to sensitive information. We trust that administrators adhere to a higher standard of ethics and would not exceed their intended level of privilege and access.

Feel free to click the What Is WinPcap? button. This opens a browser on an informational web page regarding WinPcap.

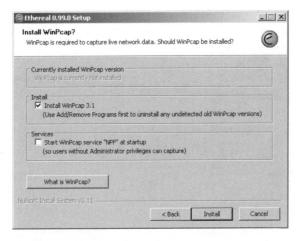

10. An installing screen is presented.

11. About halfway through the installation, WinPcap installation is triggered. Click Next to proceed.

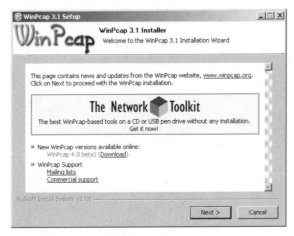

12. On the License Agreement screen, click I Agree.

13. A progress screen is displayed.

14. Upon completion, click Finish.

15. The Ethereal installation now continues. Upon completion, click Next.

16. On the Completing screen, enable the Run Ethereal 0.99.0 checkbox, and click Finish.

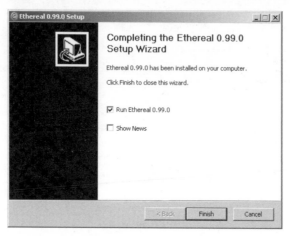

Using Ethereal to Perform a Network Capture

1. When Ethereal launches, you must specify which network interface, or network adapter, you wish to have Ethereal monitor to perform the capture. Select Capture ➤ Interfaces.

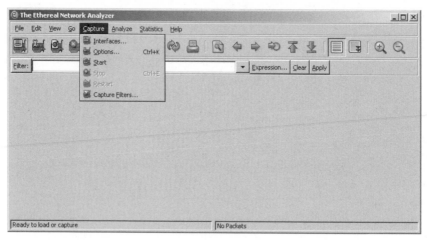

2. In the Capture Interfaces dialog box, identify each adapter. On the adapter that you are using to connect to the Internet, click the Prepare button to the right.

If you are not sure which adapter to select, click the Details button adjacent to each adapter to try to identify the correct adapter.

3. You are presented with the Capture Options dialog box. This dialog box is a busy one; spend some time reviewing its options:

-   You can limit the capture file size with buffer size.

-   You can turn off promiscuous mode of operation.

-   You can discard the trailing end of the frame by limiting the packet size. This gets more frames in the buffer limit but loses payloads.

-   You can implement a prebuilt filter. Filters are used to capture only certain types of traffic, like a specific protocol, or traffic to a specific IP or MAC address, etc., rather than all traffic.

-   You can configure the display during an active capture. This may consume some resources and cause the capture to miss some frames.

-   You can implement automatic name resolution, to more easily identify who is sending frames to whom.

-   You can preprogram the end of the capture by number of packets, by file size, or by time.

    Once you've reviewed this dialog box, click Start to begin the capture.

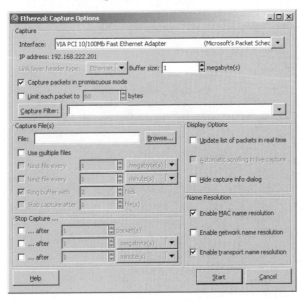

4. You will be presented with an active Capture dialog box indicating that you are currently recording frames on the selected network interface. This dialog box is where you'll stop the capture later.

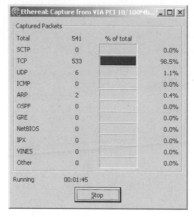

5. To generate network traffic, launch Internet Explorer and go to http://www.google.com. Do a Google search for "Ethereal."

6. From the hits list, select the hyperlink for www.ethereal.com. Browse around on the Ethereal website.

7. In the address bar of Internet Explorer type **www.sybex.com** and press Enter.

8. Browse the Internet for a minute or two.

9. In the active Capture dialog box, click Stop to end the capture.

Using Ethereal to Perform Network Analysis

1. Ethereal now populates with the frames it captured during the exercise.

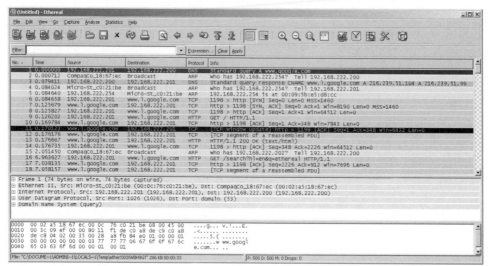

If you followed the steps properly, your capture should resemble the one in the graphic, but with the exception that your home page in Internet Explorer may be configured to something other than Google, as ours is. If you scroll down your capture you should see a Protocol/DNS (like the very first frame in the graphic) frame for www.google.com. Begin there.

2. A tremendous amount of information and learning can be done by carefully studying captures, even as innocuous as this one. You are looking at the true mechanics of the network and protocols, the nuts and bolts. You can verify of details that you have been told about how protocols work.

    In the graphic, notice frames 4 and 5, using Protocol/ARP. Frame 4 is from 192.168.222.201 and asks for the MAC address of 192.168.222.254, the default gateway. It is a broadcast. Frame 5 is the reply from 192.168.222.254. It is a Unicast back to 192.168.222.201, the requester, and supplies 192.168.222.254's MAC address.

    The ARP request is a broadcast. The ARP reply is a Unicast to the MAC address of the requester (21:be).

    Now find this similar sequence in your capture.

 You can confirm the MAC address of your system by running Ipconfig /all at a command prompt.

3. Observe frames 1 and 3 in the previous graphic: the DNS query for www.google.com, and the DNS response from the DNS server at 192.168.222.200.

    Explore these frames by expanding the lines in the center section of the display.

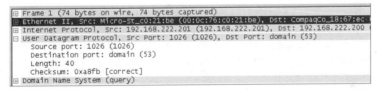

    Notice that the DNS query uses User Datagram Protocol (UDP) to the DNS server's port 53. The DNS server replies back using UDP to the randomly selected port number 1026 on the client.

    Now find this similar sequence in your capture.

 The bottom section of Ethereal displays the contents of the highlighted section of the selected frame. This is where attackers find unencrypted passwords when users log on with applications like FTP and Telnet.

4. The more you look at captures, the more you will see. Ten seconds of captured data can become hours of incredibly worthy study time. Expand one of the frames of interest to expose all lines if data and review each section. You may want to review the basics of TCP/IP online. A starting point for this review is `http://www.garykessler.net/library/rfc2151.html`.

5. When you have finished reviewing the capture, close Ethereal.

Criteria for Completion

You have completed this task when you have downloaded and installed Ethereal, the protocol analyzer, performed a capture, and reviewed the capture data.

Task 9.5: Recovering Previous Versions of Files

Very often, when a system has been compromised, or when you find unacceptable use of a system, the attacker attempts to cover his tracks by deleting the incriminating evidence, either content within a file or the file itself. It is possible to recover this deleted content using a tool that was introduced with Windows Server 2003 and XP. It is called Volume Shadow Copy (the backup portion) and Previous Versions (the recovery portion).

Volume Shadow Copy (VSC) is available only on Server 2003. Server 2003 servers and all Microsoft clients (including NT 4, 9x, ME, Windows 2000, and XP) can recover previous versions of the files. By default, at scheduled times each day, the server takes a VSC snapshot of all content on the partition configured with VSC enabled. It records the changes to each file since the last VSC. This does, of course, occupy hard drive space—300MB minimum—and can occupy as much hard drive space as you allow it to use. Server 2003 has the Shadow Copy Client (also called Previous Versions Client, or Time Warp Client) already installed and available.

After you install the Shadow Copy Client software, any Microsoft client can review up to 64 previous versions to recover any copy the server has available. The add-on Shadow Copy Client software can be downloaded from `http://www.microsoft.com/technet/downloads/winsrvr/shadowcopyclient.mspx`.

This recovery can be used by clients to recover modified or deleted files, and can be used by administrators to recover evidence that has been deleted in an attempt to cover the tracks of an attacker. This should not be used for disaster recovery, even though it may help in some disaster-recovery situations. Since the shadow copy often resides on the same disk as the content, if the disk fails both copies will be lost.

Scenario

You are the administrator of a Microsoft network. You need to configure your environment to be able to recover deleted content and files for investigative purposes as part of your CERT program.

Scope of Task

Duration

This task should take 45 minutes.

Setup

You will first configure VSC on a Server 2003 system. You will then manipulate files on a share point to create multiple previous versions. Then you will download and install the Shadow Copy Client on an XP system and perform selected content and file recovery procedures to confirm the validity of the shadow copies.

Caveat

Allowing clients to utilize the Shadow Copy Client is definitely a double-edged sword, at best. While it may allow a client to recover their own deleted content, if they recover the content incorrectly, they can easily overwrite the most recent copy of the content, resulting in lost data. Any time this type of error occurs, somehow the blame falls squarely on the shoulders of the administrator; it's going to be your fault that the client lost their new data.

If you're diligently backing up content, you may be able to recover their lost data, or you may even be able to pick their new data out of the previous versions client. But frankly, don't you have better things to do? In a real corporate environment, you might want to keep the recovery capability in the hands of the administrators, and not install or train the client on previous versions.

Procedure

First, you will configure and enable the VSC feature on a Server 2003 system. Next you will create and manipulate content, by adding and deleting content and files, to create differing previous versions.

You will then download and install the Shadow Copy Client on an XP system. Once that is accomplished, you will perform multiple recovery procedures to validate the recovery processes for future use.

Equipment Used

For this task, you need the following:

- Windows Server 2003 system
- Windows XP Professional system
- Administrator access
- Internet access

Details

Configuring and Enabling the Volume Shadow Copy Feature on Server 2003

1. Log on the Windows Server 2003 system as the Administrator.

2. Launch Windows Explorer. In the left pane, expand the view sufficiently to select the root of the C:\ drive.

3. In Explorer, in the left pane, select the root of the C:\ drive. In the right pane, right-click on white space and select New ➤ Folder. Name the folder **STUFF**.

4. Share the folder with default permissions.

 NOTE   Review Task 4.8 for instructions on sharing folders, if necessary.

5. In Explorer, in the left pane, right-click on the root of the C:\ drive and select Properties.

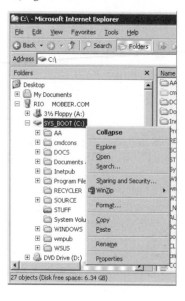

6. In the Properties dialog box for the C:\ drive, select the Shadow Copies tab.

 This is only available by default on Server 2003.

7. Notice that Shadow Copies is not enabled by default. This feature consumes system resources that you may not want to commit. For this task, accept the performance degradation. Click Settings.

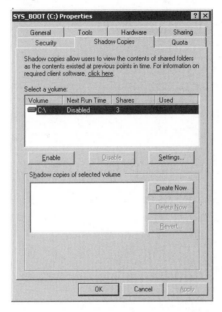

 If you click Enable first, and later wish to change where you want to store the shadow copies, all existing shadow copies will be deleted for this volume (partition). Always configure your settings first.

8. In the Settings dialog box, you can move the shadow copy content to a different volume, configure a space limit for the shadow copy content, and adjust the automatic shadow copy schedule for this volume. Click the Schedule button.

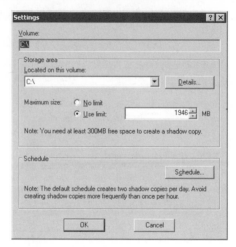

9. By default, once enabled, the VSC automatically creates copies at 7 AM and 12 PM, Monday through Friday. Select the drop-down list in the top field to view the default schedule.

10. To add one more copy event each day, click the New button in the Schedule dialog box.

11. In the Schedule dialog box, select Weekly from the Schedule Task drop-down list. Adjust the Start Time field to 3 PM. Configure the Schedule Task Weekly to every week on Monday, Tuesday, Wednesday, Thursday, and Friday.

12. Once you have the proper configuration, select the drop-down list in the top field to view the newly modified schedule of 7 AM, 12 PM and 3 PM Monday through Friday.

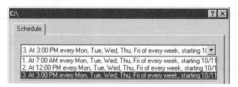

13. Click OK to close the Schedule dialog box.

14. On the Shadow Copies tab of the C:\ Drive Properties dialog box, click the Create Now button to fire off the first shadow copy manually.

15. Once the shadow copy displays in the Shadow Copies Of Selected Volume section, click the Settings button.

16. In the Settings dialog box, click the Details button to view the properties of the first shadow copy.

Notice the first shadow copy consumed 300MB of disk space.

17. Click OK to close Details dialog box. Click OK to close Settings dialog box.

18. You have now successfully configured the C:\ drive of the Server 2003 system to create Volume Shadow Copies three times daily, Monday through Friday.

19. Leave the C:\ Drive Properties dialog box open, but move it aside for the moment. You'll be using this shortly.

Manipulating Content on the C:\ Drive to Produce Previous Versions

1. On the Windows Server 2003 system, logged in as Administrator, in the Windows Explorer application, with the STUFF folder selected in the left pane, right-click in the right pane and select New ➢ Text Document. Name the document **GoodStuff1.txt**.

2. Repeat Step 1 to create the files **GoodStuff2.txt** and **GoodStuff3.txt**.

3. In the C:\ Drive Properties dialog box, on the Shadow Copies tab that you left open earlier, click the Create Now button to create another shadow copy of the C:\ drive.

4. You're going to manipulate these files and make multiple shadow copies. To keep track of the contents of each copy, fill in this table as you complete the following steps. Write the time of the shadow copies you've created in the My Time field that matches up the proper Steps and Contents.

VSC #	Step	VSC Time from Graphic	Contents of Stuff	My Time from VSC
1	14 Above	12:08 PM	Initial Volume Shadow Copy. The folder STUFF is empty.	
2	3	12:14 PM	GoodStuff1.txt, GoodStuff2.txt, GoodStuff3.txt; All files are empty.	
3	7	12:17 PM	GoodStuff1.txt has ABC content. GoodStuff2.txt and GoodStuff3.txt are empty.	
4	10	12:20 PM	GoodStuff1.txt has ABC XYZ content. GoodStuff2.txt and GoodStuff3.txt are empty.	
5	14	12:26 PM	GoodStuff1.txt has ABC 123 content. GoodStuff2.txt and GoodStuff3.txt are empty.	
6	16	12:29 PM	GoodStuff1.txt has ABC 123 content. GoodStuff2.txt has been deleted. GoodStuff3.txt is empty. This is the final state of the folder STUFF.	

Log your VSC times for #1—the Initial VSC—and #2—the VSC created in Step 3—in the table provided. Flag this page. You'll be double-checking content later using this table as a reference.

5. In Explorer, double-click on the file GoodStuff1.txt to open it in the Notepad application. Edit GoodStuff1.txt with the content ABC.

6. In Notepad, select File ➢ Save to save the new content ABC in the file GoodStuff1.txt.

Leave GoodStuff1.txt open in Notepad.

7. In the C:\ Drive Properties dialog box, on the Shadow Copies tab, click the Create Now
button to create another shadow copy of the C:\ drive.

Log your VSC time on line # 3 in the table provided.

8. Edit GoodStuff1.txt by adding XYZ to the content, resulting in the content ABC XYZ.

9. In Notepad, select File ➢ Save to save the new content ABC XYZ in the file GoodStuff1.txt.

Leave GoodStuff1.txt open in Notepad.

10. In the C:\ Drive Properties dialog box, on the Shadow Copies tab, click the Create Now
button to create another shadow copy of the C:\ drive.

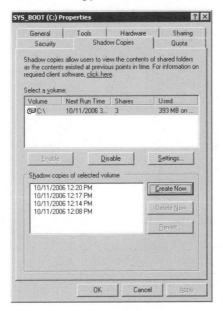

Log your VSC time on line # 4 in the table provided.

11. Edit GoodStuff1.txt by deleting XYZ and then adding 123 to the content, resulting in the content ABC 123.

12. In Notepad, select File ➤ Save to save the new content ABC 123 in the file GoodStuff1.txt.

13. You can (finally) close GoodStuff1.txt.

14. In the C:\ Drive Properties dialog box, on the Shadow Copies tab, click the Create Now button to create another shadow copy of the C:\ drive.

 Log your VSC time on line # 5 in the table provided.

15. In Windows Explorer, delete GoodStuff2.txt by right-clicking on the file and selecting Delete.

16. In the C:\ Drive Properties dialog box, on the Shadow Copies tab, click the Create Now button to create another shadow copy of the C:\ drive.

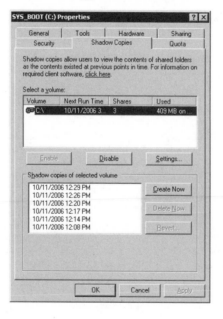

 Log your VSC time on line # 6 in the table provided.

Testing Previous Versions on Server 2003

1. While logged on to Windows Server 2003 as the Administrator, in Explorer, in the left pane, right-click on the folder STUFF and select Properties.

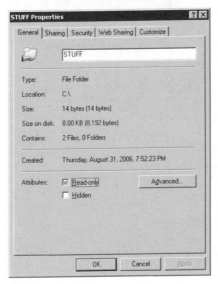

 Notice that the Previous Versions tab does not exist when you're checking Properties locally.

2. Select Start ➢ Run. In the Open field, type **\localhost\stuff** and click OK to connect to the STUFF share point.

3. An Explorer window will open and should show GoodStuff1.txt and GoodStuff3.txt.

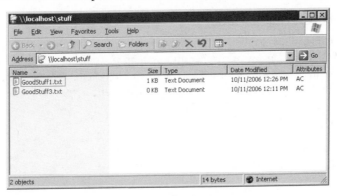

4. Right-click on GoodStuff1.txt and select Properties. Select the Previous Versions tab in the GoodStuff1.txt Properties dialog box.

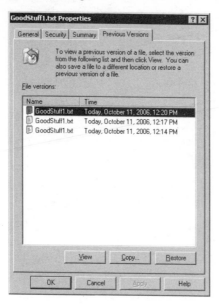

 The Previous Versions feature is only available when you're connected to content through a share point. You must connect to the share point STUFF from the network. This is not a typical way to access content locally, but is necessary if you must recover local content using Previous Versions.

5. Close the Properties dialog box for GoodStuff1.txt.

Installing Previous Versions on XP

1. Previous Versions is not installed by default on operating systems other than Server 2003. To run Previous Versions on any other operating system, you must install it on each system you need it on. See the installation instructions for down-level clients at http://www.microsoft .com/technet/downloads/winsrvr/shadowcopyclient.mspx.

2. While logged on to Windows Server 2003 as the Administrator, in Explorer, in the left pane, expand folders as necessary to select the folder `Windows\system32\clients\` `twclient\x86`. In the right pane, notice, **but do not execute** the file `twcli32.msi`. There is a newer version that you'll be installing.

Twcli32.msi stands for Time Warp Client for 32-bit OSs Microsoft Installer package. The Time Warp Client is also called Previous Versions Client and Shadow Copy Client. While this file works fine, do not use this file to install the Shadow Copy Client on XP. It is always better to download a fresh copy from the trusted source, just in case there is a newer version. You'll do this in a few moments.

3. Log on to the XP Professional system as Administrator.

4. Select Start button➣ Run. Type *****server_name***\STUFF** in the Open field, where ***server_ name*** is the name of the Windows Server 2003 that is hosting the STUFF share point. Then click OK.

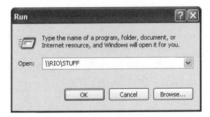

5. This should open an Explorer window that shows the two remaining files in the STUFF share point: `GoodStuff1.txt` and `GoodStuff3.txt`. Right-click on `GoodStuff1.txt` and select Properties.

6. Notice that the properties page for the content accessed through the network share point does not have a Previous Versions tab. Click OK to close the GoodStuff1.txt Properties dialog box.

7. Launch Internet Explorer. In the address bar, type this URL: **http://www.microsoft.com/ technet/downloads/winsrvr/shadowcopyclient.mspx** and click the Go button.

8. On the resulting web page, select to download the Shadow Copy Client for XP.

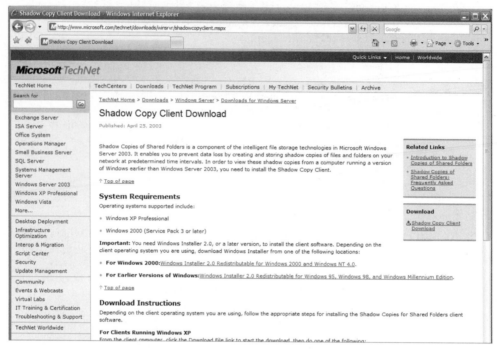

9. Save the ShadowCopyClient.msi file to your XP desktop.

10. Once the download is complete, close Internet Explorer.

 Notice the file size is different than the twcli32.msi file.

11. Double-click the file ShadowCopyClient.msi located on your desktop to begin installation of the Previous Versions Client.

12. On the Welcome screen of the wizard, click Next.

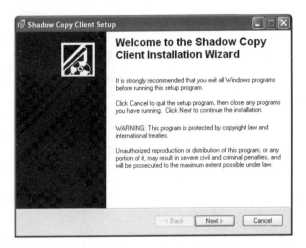

13. On the End User License screen, click I Accept, and then click Next.

14. Installation will continue by displaying a progress window.

15. When you are presented with the Successful Installation screen, click Finish to close the Shadow Copy Client Setup Wizard.

16. In the Explorer window that is connected to *server_name*\STUFF (where *server_name* is the name of the Windows Server 2003 server that is hosting the STUFF share point) right-click on GoodStuff1.txt and select Properties. Now you can select the Previous Versions tab.

17. Select the most recent previous version (VSC 4, Step 10 version from the table you filled in earlier—in the graphic, it is the 12:20 PM version) and click the View button. This should open Notepad with a copy of GoodStuff1.txt. The version from Step 10 had the content of ABC XYZ.

The current version of GoodStuff1.txt contains content of ABC 123. There is no VSC 5 or 6, Steps 14 or 16 versions in the Previous Versions list since those versions of GoodStuff1.txt are the current version. If you want the VSC 5, Step 14 (12:26) version that reads ABC 123, open the current GoodStuff1.txt file directly from the share point. View each Previous Version of GoodStuff1.txt on the list. Confirm its proper content against the table you filled in earlier.

18. After viewing deleted content in the previous version files, close Notepad with GoodStuff1.txt.

19. In the Explorer window that is connected to *server_name*\STUFF, right-click the white space and select Properties. Select the Previous Versions tab of the STUFF Properties dialog box.

20. Select the VSC 5, Step 14 (12:26 PM) version, and then click the View button.

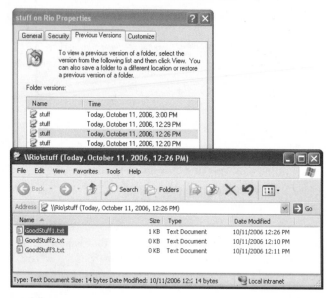

21. The VSC 5, Step 14 (12:26 PM) version was recorded prior to deleting the GoodStuff2.txt file. Observe the GoodStuff2.txt file.

22. Close the window showing the VSC 5, Step 14 (12:26 PM) version files.

23. On the Previous Versions tab of the STUFF Properties dialog box, with the VSC 5, Step 14 (12:26 PM) version highlighted, click the Copy button to recover the STUFF folder that contains the deleted GoodStuff2.txt file.

24. In the Copy Items dialog box, select the C:\AA folder. If this folder does not exist, create a new folder and name it **AA**.

25. Click the Copy button in the Copy Items dialog box.

26. Open a new instance of Explorer. In the left pane, expand folders to select C:\AA\STUFF. Observe the recovered file GoodStuff2.txt.

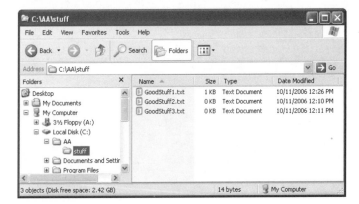

Criteria for Completion

You have completed this task when you have configured Volume Shadow Copies on Windows Server 2003; manipulated content on a share point; created multiple shadow copies; downloaded and installed the Shadow Copy Client on an XP system; and examined the previous versions to recover deleted content and deleted files.

Phase

10

Security Troubleshooting

Earlier in this book, we mentioned three main facets of your information assets that you, as the security professional, are required to protect:

- It is your job to protect the *confidentiality* of the organization's information assets—that is, to keep the company's secrets secret.

- It is your job to protect the *integrity* of the organization's information assets—that is, to protect the information from being tampered with. No one is allowed to "cook the books."

- It is your job to protect the *availability* of the organization's information assets. If users cannot access the valuable information assets when they are needed, the information has lost its value, and the users lose productivity.

Security troubleshooting has largely to do with disaster recovery, which is a subset of protecting the availability of the information assets. If the server fails due to a bad driver or Registry modification, the resources that the server provides to users are no longer available. You must quickly return the system to a stable state, and allow users to regain access to the resources that the server had been providing.

You will look at Safe mode, which loads a minimum of drivers in an attempt to provide recovery after a faulty driver has been installed. Then you will look at Last Known Good Configuration (LKGC), which replaces the current Registry with a previously "known good" Registry. And finally, you'll perform an Automated System Recovery (ASR) backup, and then an ASR restore. ASR restores the operating system, Registry, and drivers, but does not protect data. You must use a backup utility to provide disaster recovery for your data.

One final task for the security professional is related to magnetic media reuse. This task involves installing a hard drive in a system that had previously been installed in a different system.

As the security professional, you must protect the confidentiality of the data previously written on the disk. Data can be recovered from the free space on a disk after the file has been deleted and the Recycle Bin has been emptied. Data can even be recovered off a disk after re-partitioning and reformatting.

The tasks in this phase map to Domains 3 and 5 objectives for the CompTIA Security+ exam (http://certification.comptia.org/security/).

Task 10.1: Booting into Safe Mode

Have you ever replaced a device or installed new drivers, and after rebooting the system, you get nothing but a black screen, or even worse, the dreaded blue screen? Safe mode was designed to help you resolve just this type of problem.

Safe mode boots into the operating system while loading only the bare minimum of drivers—like the low-level VGA video driver—hoping to avoid initializing the bad driver that is causing the system to fail on reboot. While in Safe mode, you can (you hope!) figure out where the problem is coming from and find a resolution. Then you can reboot into Normal mode, which initializes all drivers configured.

Safe mode cannot be used to resolve all problems. Although it minimizes the number of drivers it loads, it must still load some drivers. For example, Safe mode must load drivers for mass storage devices, like controller cards, tape drives, and optical drives. These are loaded because these devices might be required to access disaster recovery media to help with the repair. If the cause of the failure involved one of these device drivers, Safe mode will also fail on boot-up.

Further, while in Safe mode, since many drivers are not loaded, many devices are unavailable. You will have limited access to system resources, since they were not initialized.

Scenario

You are an administrator in an Active Directory environment. After installing a new set of drivers for an existing device, a system that you are responsible for is blue screening on reboot.

Scope of Task

Duration

This task should take 20 minutes.

Setup

You will reboot into Safe mode and initialize a driver update, as if there had been a system failure.

Caveat

Safe mode does not initialize all system devices. Safe mode does initialize all mass storage device drivers, in case you need to perform a restore from one or more backup devices. Since there has been no actual device failure, do not complete any driver updates or other system changes.

Procedure

For this task, you will boot into Safe mode and implement a device driver update procedure, but you will not complete the update.

    Since there is no actual driver failure, do not replace any drivers.

You will cancel out of the driver update process before making any system changes.

Equipment Used

For this task, you need the following equipment:

- Windows XP Professional system
- Administrator access

Details

1.   Power up the system. Immediately after the BOIS screen clears, press the F8 function key repeatedly until you are presented with the Windows Advanced Options Menu.

```
Windows Advanced Options Menu
Please select an option:

    Safe Mode
    Safe Mode with Networking
    Safe Mode with Command Prompt

    Enable Boot Logging
    Enable VGA Mode
    Last Known Good Configuration (your most recent settings that worked)
    Directory Services Restore Mode (Windows domain controllers only)
    Debugging Mode

    Start Windows Normally
    Reboot

Use the up and down arrow keys to move the highlight to your choice.
```

    If you see the color Windows startup screen with the progress bar sliding from left to right, you've missed the timeslot for entering the Windows Advanced Options Menu. Reboot the system and try again.

2. Select Safe Mode from the Windows Advanced Options Menu.

3. Log on the Windows XP Pro system as the Administrator.

4. You will be presented with a message identifying Safe Mode operation. Review the message and click Yes to proceed into Safe mode.

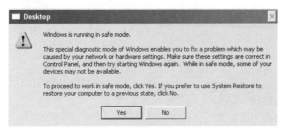

5. You will see a black desktop with Safe mode clearly labeled in the four corners of the desktop.

6. Right-click on My Computer and select Manage (or select Start ➢ Programs ➢ Administrative Tools ➢ Computer Management). In the Computer Management console, select Device Manager.

7. In the right pane, expand Network Adapters. Click on the first adapter listed.

8. Right-click on the first adapter and select Update Driver.

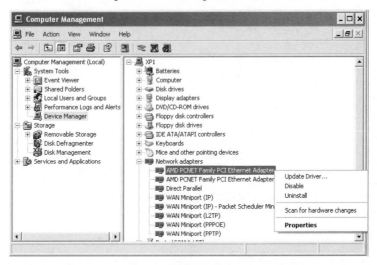

9. This should start the Hardware Update Wizard. Select Install From A List Or Specific Location (Advanced), and click Next.

10. On the next screen, select Don't Search. I Will Choose The Driver To Install and then click Next.

11. On the next screen, select Have Disk, as if you were going to restore from the earlier set of driver installation disks, or point to where the earlier drivers resided on the system.

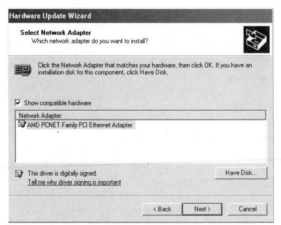

12. In the Install From Disk dialog box, you would browse to the earlier driver files and proceed with the driver update procedure.

  WARNING   Since there is no actual driver failure, do not replace any drivers.

13. Click Cancel to close the Install From Disk dialog box.
14. Click Cancel to close the Hardware Update Wizard.
15. Shut down the XP Professional system.

Criteria for Completion

You have completed this task when you have booted into Safe mode and initialized a driver replacement procedure. You should not have completed the driver update, since there really was no driver failure.

Task 10.2: Implementing Last Known Good Configuration

Last Known Good Configuration (LKGC) is a boot-up option from the Windows Advanced Options Menu. It rolls the current Registry settings back to the state of the Registry at the last successful logon. That successful logon represented a "known good" Registry. If the system booted and the logon service was functional enough to authenticate you, the configuration recorded in the Registry must have been good.

There are times when the LKGC will correct the problem, and there are times where it will not. The LKGC only restores the Registry to its earlier state. It does not make any changes to the filesystem, other than related to the Registry files. It does not restore deleted or overwritten files.

If you had been mucking about in Regedit and lost track of what you were doing, or you've just changed your mind on some changes to the Registry, simply reboot the system into LKGC to undo your changes.

Another example of where LKGC cannot help is if you have updated and overwritten driver files with the same name and path. LKGC will not correct a problem with these driver files. The Registry is calling the same driver filenames, and you've replaced those files with bad driver files.

Scenario

You are an administrator in an Active Directory environment. After making a system modification (in the Registry), you change your mind and wish to revert back to the earlier configuration.

Scope of Task

Duration

This task should take 15 minutes.

Setup

You will make changes to a system configuration, and then reboot into LKGC to restore the system to its earlier configuration.

Caveat

A configuration is declared "known good" upon successful logon. At that point, the earlier "known good" Registry is discarded, and this current configuration is copied into the last known good slot.

If you have made changes and have logged on to the system, LKGC now holds your current configuration as known good, and cannot return your system to the earlier state.

Procedure

You will configure your system with a desktop background. Then you will reboot and observe that your new background has become the current configuration. You will then change the desktop to a different background.

Then you will reboot into LKGC and observe that your desktop has reverted back to the original background.

Equipment Used

For this task, you need the following equipment:

- Windows XP Professional system
- Administrator access

Details

Setting the Desktop: A "Known Good" Configuration

1. Log on the Windows XP Professional system as the Administrator.
2. Right-click on the desktop and select Properties.

3. In the Desktop Properties dialog box, select Radiance as the desktop background. (This is also referred to as the desktop wallpaper.) Click OK to set the background.

This change of background was recorded in the Registry. This change is representative of any other configuration change that affects the Registry. This could have been a manual edit of the Registry, the installation of an application or drivers for a hardware device, or some other configuration change that gets written to the Registry.

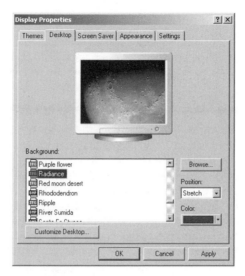

4. Reboot the computer.

Booting Into a "Known Good" Configuration

1. Log on the Windows XP Professional system as the Administrator.

> This successful logon copies this current configuration in the Registry, with Radiance as the desktop, into the LKGC in the Registry.

2. Confirm that Radiance is the desktop background.
3. Right-click on the desktop and select Properties.
4. In the Desktop Properties dialog box, select Red Moon Desert as the desktop background. Click OK to set the background.

> This modifies the current configuration (only) in the Registry.

5. Shut down the computer.

Booting into Last Known Good Configuration

1. Power up the system. Immediately after the BOIS screen clears, tap the F8 function key (repeatedly) until you are presented with the Windows Advanced Options Menu.

If you see the color Windows startup screen with the progress bar sliding from left to right, you've missed the timeslot for entering the Windows Advanced Options Menu. Reboot the system and try again.

2. Select Last Known Good Configuration from the Windows Advanced Options Menu.

3. Log on the Windows XP Professional system as the Administrator.

Your desktop should have reverted back to Radiance as the desktop background from the LKGC. When you chose Last Known Good Configuration from the Windows Advanced Options Menu, the current configuration in the Registry, which contained Red Moon Desert as the desktop background, was discarded, and the LKGC, which contained Radiance as the desktop background, was copied into the current configuration.

Criteria for Completion

You have completed this task when you have booted into Last Known Good Configuration and recovered your previous desktop settings.

Task 10.3: Using System Restore

System Restore is a great feature in Windows XP. It automatically records the state of the operating system, a restore point, just prior to the installation of drivers and patches; just prior to a restore from backup; and it also generates a daily restore point, just for good measure. If third-party applications are compliant with the restore point API, the installation of these will also trigger the automatic creation of a restore point. These restore points can also be manually triggered if you know that you're about to do something a little dangerous.

The restore point records the Registry, local profiles, COM+ database, Windows protected files, Windows Management Instrumentation (WMI) database, the Internet Information Services (IIS) metabase, and files with the following extensions: `.CAT`, `.COM`, `.DLL`, `.EXE`, `.INF`, `.MSI`, `.OLE`, and `.SYS`.

System Restore consumes a minimum of 200MB on the hard drive. The system keeps track of your restore points and allows you to roll back to an earlier system configuration.

System Restore can be added to a Windows Server 2003 system, but it is not supported by Microsoft. You can access the instructions and installation files at `http://www.msfn.org/win2k3/sysrestore.htm`. However, use this unsupported add-on at your own risk.

Scenario

You installed a new application, and later decide that you do not want the application installed. You know that the uninstall routine has some problems and you need to return the system to its previous state.

Scope of Task

Duration

This task should take 30 minutes.

Setup

You will need to download Adminpak.msi from the Microsoft website, or from a Server 2003 installation CD in the \i386 folder, or on an installed Server 2003 system in the \Windows\System32 folder.

If you have already installed Adminpak.msi on your system, you can install any other new application on the system. System Restore will remove the configuration settings for the application; however, the application files may remain on your hard drive. The application will probably not operate correctly, and would need to be reinstalled after Task 10.3 is completed to operate the application correctly after restoring the system to its previous state.

Caveat

Any time you are manipulating critical system files, risk is involved. You should always make backups of all your data and your system configuration.

System Restore does not record data files. You must implement a standard backup routine to maintain fault tolerance for your data.

Procedure

You will perform a manual system restore point and then install a new application on the system. You will then perform a system restore to roll the system back to its state prior to the application installation.

Equipment Used

For this task, you need the following equipment:

- Windows XP Professional system
- Administrator access
- Adminpak.msi (See "Setup" to learn where to locate Adminpak.msi)

Details

Confirming System Restore and Creating a Manual Restore Point

1. Log on the Windows XP Professional system as the Administrator.

2. Right-click on My Computer and select Properties. Select the System Restore tab.

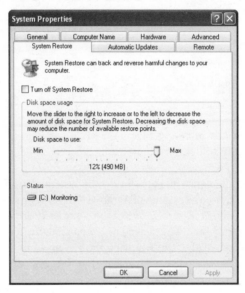

Confirm that System Restore is turned on (the checkbox Turn Off System Restore is cleared), and maximize the disk space usage.

3. Close System Properties.

4. From the Start button, select Programs ➤ Administrative Tools, and observe the collection of default, installed administrative tools.

5. From the Start button, select Programs ➤ Accessories ➤ System Tools ➤ System Restore.

6. In the System Restore Wizard, select Create A Restore Point. Click Next.

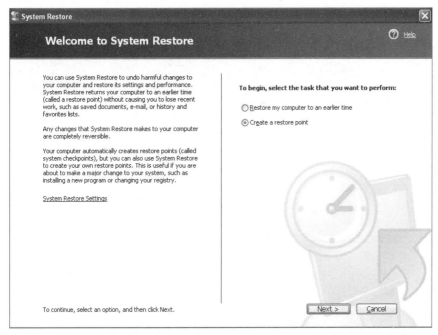

7. On the next screen, type a name for your restore point (in this example, we used **Admin Pack Install**). Click Next.

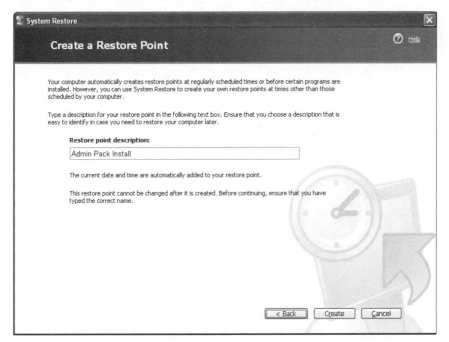

8. The system will be busy for a few moments and then should present confirmation that a restore point has been created. Click Close to close the System Restore Wizard.

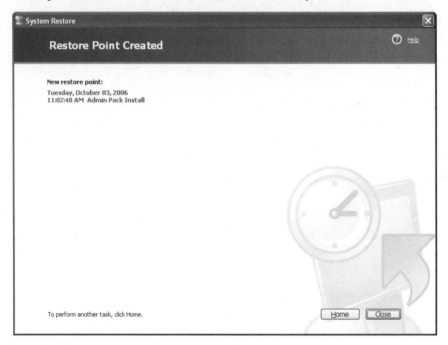

Installing a New Application

1. On the Windows XP Professional system, acquire `Adminpak.msi` from the Microsoft website, or from a Server 2003 installation CD in the `\i386` folder, or on an installed Server 2003 system in the `\Windows\System32` folder.

 If you have downloaded the `Adminpak.exe` file from the Microsoft website, it must be extracted to gain access to the `Adminpak.msi` file. Extract `Adminpak.exe` into a new folder on your desktop.

2. Double-click on `Adminpak.msi` to launch the installation application. Click Next in the Administration Tools Setup Wizard.

3. Select the I Agree button on the EULA. Click Next.

4. You should see the Installation Progress dialog box.

5. Click Finish to close the Administration Tools Setup Wizard.

6. From the Start button, select Programs ➤ Administrative Tools, and observe the collection of newly installed administrative tools.

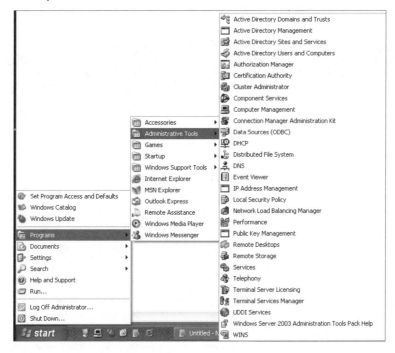

Performing a System Restore

1. From the Start button, select Programs ➤ Accessories ➤ System Tools ➤ System Restore.

2. Select the Restore My Computer To An Earlier Time option. Click Next.

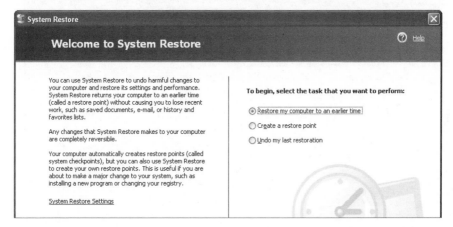

3. You should see your manually triggered restore point on the list of restore points for today. You will notice that the installation of `Adminpak.msi` triggered an automatic restore point. Select either one of these restore points, since they both contain the same system state. Click Next.

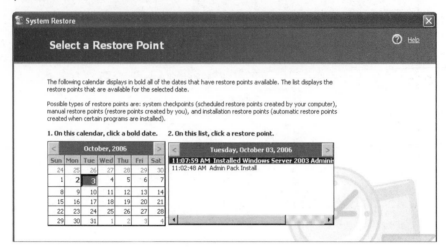

4. Review the details of the configured system restore. Once you have done so, click Next.

 WARNING The restore procedure will reboot your system. Save all of your open files and close all other applications.

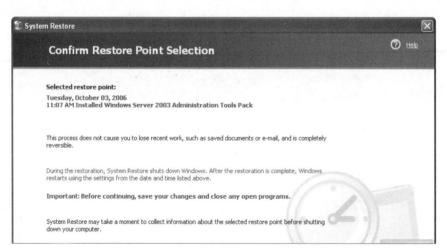

5. The system will log you off and then perform the configured restore. The system will then automatically reboot.

6. Log on the Windows XP Professional system as the Administrator. You will be presented with a notification of the successful completion of the system restore process. Click OK.

7. Confirm that the application is no longer installed. From the Start button, select Programs ➢ Administrative Tools, and observe the collection of original, default, installed administrative tools, with the supplemental Admin Pack tools removed.

 If desired, you can undo the system restore by selecting Start ➢ Programs ➢ Accessories ➢ System Tools ➢ System Restore and selecting to undo the last restoration.

Performing a System Restore from Safe Mode

System restore can be initiated while in Safe mode. This would be beneficial if your system was failing to boot up properly after the installation of some new application or driver set.

1. Power up the system. Immediately after the BOIS screen clears, tap the F8 function key repeatedly until you are presented with the Windows Advanced Options Menu.

 If you see the color Windows startup screen with the progress bar sliding from left to right, you've missed the timeslot for entering the Windows Advanced Options Menu. Reboot the system and try again.

2. Select Safe Mode from the Windows Advanced Options Menu.

3. Log on the Windows XP Professional system as the Administrator.

4. You will be presented with a message identifying Safe mode operation. Review the message and click No to proceed into System Restore.

Criteria for Completion

You have completed this task when you have restored the system to a previous system restore point.

Task 10.4: Sanitizing Media

This task deals with the discarding or reusing media, like paper documents, CDs, DVDs, old tapes from backup systems, and hard drives. Discarding or reusing this media is a potential security breach, unless the media has been successfully and completely purged of recoverable data.

There are times when you don't want to purge all data on a disk but just the deleted files. When you delete a file off your computer, the filesystem doesn't actually remove the file from the disk. In the table of contents for the partition, it simply overwrites the first character of the filename with a question mark. This tells the filesystem that the space previously occupied by the file is now free space. The actual file content remains on the disk itself and can be recovered, by a good guy, or by a bad guy with many digital forensic tools.

The National Institute of Standards and Technology's Special Publication 800-88 Guidelines for Media Sanitation (February 2006) recommends sanitizing magnetic media by physical destruction; by magnetic degaussing, which requires a special magnetic chamber; or by using a software tool called Secure Erase (`hdderase.exe`), a free download from UCSD at `http://cmrr.ucsd.edu/Hughes/subpgset.htm`.

WARNING Caution! The Secure Erase tool (`hdderase.exe`) will destroy all data on the entire disk!

Many software tools are available to protect yourself from anyone recovering your deleted files. You can also use a free tool provided by Microsoft called `Cipher.exe`, which can be used to overwrite the free space on a partition, to accomplish this task.

WARNING Using this tool on your partition will also mean you cannot recover your own files that you've, perhaps, inadvertently deleted.

Scenario

You want to ensure that all files that you've deleted are rendered unrecoverable. You do not wish to destroy all data on the disk but just protect the deleted files from being recovered.

Scope of Task

Duration

This task should take 25 minutes to initiate. The completion of the disk-wiping process may vary, depending on the amount of free space on the partition being wiped and other factors.

Setup

`Cipher.exe` is built into Microsoft Windows 2000 and later Microsoft operating systems.

Caveat

These tools are destructive and render deleted files intentionally unrecoverable. Be sure you have copies of any files you do not intend to lose.

Cipher.exe only overwrites free space (that is, the space in clusters that are marked as free in the partition's table of contents), and does not overwrite slack space. Forensic tools can recover old data from slack space.

Slack space is the unused space in the last cluster of each file.

Procedure

You will calculate the amount of free space and slack space on your drive. You will then use Cipher.exe to wipe all free space on your partition.

Equipment Used

For this task, you need the following equipment:

- Windows XP Professional system with an NTFS partition
- Administrator access

Details

Determining the Amount of Free Space and Slack Space

1. Log on the Windows XP Professional system as the Administrator.

2. Open a command window. Select Start ➢ Run, and then type **CMD** in the Open field. Click OK.

3. In the command window, at the command prompt, type **chkdsk /?** and press Enter.

4. Review the help information for CheckDisk.

5. At the command prompt type **chkdsk c: /i** and press Enter.

```
C:\>chkdsk c: /i
The type of the file system is NTFS.

WARNING!  F parameter not specified.
Running CHKDSK in read-only mode.

WARNING!  I parameter specified.
Your drive may still be corrupt even after running CHKDSK.

CHKDSK is verifying files (stage 1 of 3)...
File verification completed.
CHKDSK is verifying indexes (stage 2 of 3)...
Index verification completed.
CHKDSK is verifying security descriptors (stage 3 of 3)...
Security descriptor verification completed.

   4184900 KB total disk space.
   1613424 KB in 11053 files.
      3056 KB in 867 indexes.
         0 KB in bad sectors.
     37628 KB in use by the system.
     22976 KB occupied by the log file.
   2530792 KB available on disk.

      4096 bytes in each allocation unit.
   1046225 total allocation units on disk.
    632698 allocation units available on disk.

C:\>_
```

If you add the /f switch, the system will need to be rebooted to complete the scan. The CheckDisk scan will take several minutes to complete.

6. Notice the amount of space available on disk (approximately 2.5GB in the graphic). This is the amount of free space. You will be wiping that space using the Cipher.exe utility.

7. Notice the number of bytes in each allocation unit. An allocation unit is a cluster. In the graphic, the cluster size is 4KB.

8. Minimize the command window.

9. Launch Windows Explorer by right-clicking on the Start button and selecting Explore.

10. In the left pane, select the Local Disk (C:).

11. In the right pane, right-click on the white space and choose Select All.

12. In the right pane, right-click on the selected files and folders and select Properties.

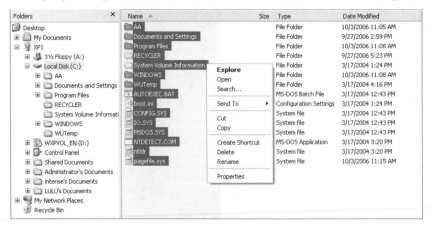

This may take a few minutes to complete.

13. Once the properties page completes, view the number of files on the C:\ drive at the top of the dialog box.

In the graphic, there are 10,510 files on the C:\ drive.

14. Statistically speaking, the amount of data in slack space is the number of files on a partition times 50 percent of the cluster size. Calculate the slack space on the C:\ drive. From the data in the graphics:

> 4KB (the cluster size) × 50% (statistical slack space/file) = 2KB (slack space/file) × 10,510 (files on C:\) = 21MB (recoverable data in slack space on C:\)

Many partitions grow to have several hundred thousand files. Each 100,000 files will typically yield 200MB of recoverable data from slack space.

The data in the slack space will remain unprotected from recovery using Cipher.exe. To protect the data in the slack space, third-party tools will be required.

15. Close the System Volume Information Properties dialog box.

Protecting Deleted Data from Recovery Using Cipher.exe

1. In the command window, at the command prompt, type **cipher /?** and press the Enter key.

2. Review the help information for Cipher.exe.

3. At the command prompt, type **cipher /W:c:** and press the Enter key.

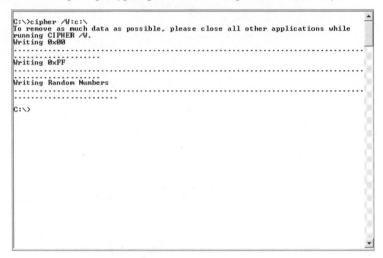

```
C:\>cipher /W:c:\
To remove as much data as possible, please close all other applications while
running CIPHER /W.
Writing 0x00
.......................................................................
............
Writing 0xFF
.......................................................................
.......................
Writing Random Numbers
.......................................................................
........................
C:\>
```

This could take several minutes to possibly longer than 1 hour. Cipher first writes all 0's in all free clusters on the partition. Then it writes all 1's in all free clusters on the partition, and then it writes a random pattern of 1's and 0's in all free clusters on the partition. This provides three overwrites of data in the free clusters.

4. After Cipher completes its series of overwrites, close the command window.

Criteria for Completion

You have completed this task when you have calculated both the amount of free space to be protected with Cipher.exe and the amount of data in slack space, which could be compromised.

Index

Note to the Reader: Throughout this index **boldfaced** page numbers indicate primary discussions of a topic. *Italicized* page numbers indicate illustrations.